William Wallace

For My Parents

William Wallace
A National Tale

Graeme Morton

EDINBURGH
University Press

© Graeme Morton, 2014

Edinburgh University Press Ltd
The Tun – Holyrood Road
12 (2f) Jackson's Entry
Edinburgh EH8 8PJ
www.euppublishing.com

Typeset in 10.5/13 Sabon by
Servis Filmsetting Ltd, Stockport, Cheshire
and printed and bound in Great Britain by
CPI Group (UK) Ltd, Croydon CR0 4YY

A CIP record for this book is available from the British Library

ISBN 978 0 7486 8539 4 (hardback)
ISBN 978 0 7486 8563 9 (paperback)
ISBN 978 0 7486 8564 6 (webready PDF)
ISBN 978 0 7486 8565 3 (epub)

The right of Graeme Morton to be identified as author of this work has been
asserted in accordance with the Copyright, Designs and Patents Act 1988 and the
Copyright and Related Rights Regulations 2003 (SI No. 2498).

Contents

Preface

It is not often that an author gets the chance to wander back through his memories. This work represents a reimagining of *William Wallace: Man and Myth* (Stroud: Sutton Publishing, 2001, 2004), a book written at a different time for a different audience. The aim then had been to capture and represent in its historical context a slice of the fast-moving retelling of the life and legacy of Wallace in the immediate post-*Braveheart* (1995) tumult. That movie was the first Scottish-themed blockbuster of the internet age. Two years after its release came the 700th anniversary of Wallace's victory at the battle of Stirling Bridge, and two years later came the referendum to re-establish a Scottish parliament. It was difficult for sober historical reflection to be made at that time, simply because so much was ongoing. In historical terms time has shifted only slightly, but it is clearer to me now, writing on the eve of a referendum on whether Scotland should be an independent nation, that the globalisation of 'Wallace's Scottish nation', carried by these coterminous events in the 1990s, was not simply the capture of Scottish history by an outsider, *pace* 'Orientalism', or a misguided reading of the historical past; although both views retain validity. Instead what marked this phase of nationalist narrative-making was its symbiosis with the personal history of those who over the last twenty years were compelled to offer analysis, comment, or political point-scoring on Wallace's legacy. Published through the Internet, but via other media too, there was what amounted to a representing of national history framed by the reader's world view of Wallace. Freed from the historian's bedrock of empiricism by a lack of corroborative sources, the biography of this short-lived late-medieval Guardian of Scotland has long been incorporated into the ideology of nationalism. It is a desire to explain this assimilation, and to deconstruct the myriad ways in which Wallace's biography has been endlessly refreshed as a national narrative, over many generations, that has motived this investigation. To operationalise the analysis, the concept of national tale is introduced; in so doing I take the concept beyond its temporal limits as literary genre to offer a historical reading. What then follows is an investigation into nationalism formed by the juxtaposition of historical events that are transmitted over time by text, image and symbol before film and digital reproduction accelerate the spread of the word on the street.

I am grateful to The History Press for all permissions to the original publication, and to John Watson of Edinburgh University Press for seeing the potential of revisiting the tale. No discussion of the national tale in Scotland can be offered without reference to Jane Porter (bap. 1776–1850) and her second romantic novel *The Scottish Chiefs* (1810). I am therefore grateful to Edinburgh University Press, the Centre for Scottish Studies at the University of Guelph, and the Research Institute for Irish and Scottish Studies at the University of Aberdeen for permission to reproduce material from, respectively: 'The Social Memory of Jane Porter and her Scottish Chiefs', *The Scottish Historical Review*, Vol. 91, 2: 232 (October 2012), pp. 311–35; 'The Scottish Nation of Jane Porter in Her International Setting', in J. A. Campbell, E. Ewan and H. Parker (eds), *Shaping Scottish Identity: Family, Nation, and the World Beyond* (Guelph: Centre for Scottish Studies, 2011), pp. 235–49; and 'Scotland's Feminine Nationalism: Some Distant Views of Jane Porter', in *Journal of Irish and Scottish Studies*, Vol. 4, issue 1 (Autumn 2010), pp. 79–98.

Figures

Chapter 1

Episodic Nationalism

Janus, ancient Greek deity, gatekeeper of the nation, harbinger of peace, signifier of a future forged from the past in communication with the present. William Wallace, medieval patriot, *Geist* of the nation, for seven centuries the guide-light to Scotland's future.

Powerfully, and moulded into a chosen historiographical trajectory, Janus heralds nationalism's hold on the nation. The concept of nationalism envelops the nation not by means of the empiricist's command of evidence firmly planted and contextualised in time, period and place, but by narrative ascendancy. The Janusian influence finds historical precision passed over for narrative terms such as 'invention' and 'manufacture', concepts that have come increasingly to dominate the historical contribution to nation making. Foregrounding discontinuous episodes, and shorn of empiricism's requirement for progressive and incremental flows over the *longue durée*, neither is the concept of nationalism readily answered by the use of biography. The span of a single human life is too short to encompass the temporal breadth upon which foundational histories are forged. A life, though, will act as a critical Janusian conduit for popular hagiography and intellectual lionising, its influence dependent on levels of accepted authenticity. Political elites, 'great men' and 'extraordinary women' make historical figures out of ordinary historical people.

It happens, of course, that individuals change the world in their own lifetimes. William Wallace (?1270–1305) achieved remarkable and impactful outcomes during his short time on this earth, yet influenced his nation's development to a significantly greater extent in the centuries long after death had come. Even when the focus falls away from charismatic leaders of Wallace's stamp, personal biography still has a role to play in forging the nation. Historians of the everyday document and recount the lives people led. Personal biographies located within norms and conventions of society are those of ordinary people expressing their personality, character and identity within the minutia and detritus of their existence. When person-centredness is foregrounded within identity formation, charismatic lives and national tales only attain recognition and acceptance when they relate to 'our world view' of the historical nation.[1] If the life, death and afterlife of Wallace are Scotland's national tale, then it is because Wallace is our national tale.

The personal reading of Janusian history sits alongside the collective construction of charismatic biography as it does the state's embodiment of national life. Problematising the deconstruction of the Wallacian national tale is nationalism's appeal to the people, for it operates at both instrumental and existential levels. The instrumental basis is identified most clearly within the modernist school of analysis, exemplified in the relationship between uneven economic development and the growth and mobilisation of nationalist resources in pursuit of recovery and enhancement. That the relationship is too imprecise to be causal, unidirectional, or periodised across regions, and is most problematic outside of Europe, does not weaken the observation that people will look to compare and contrast their respective societies. The concept of the existential nation offers a central pathway to ordering that rational appraisal, yet also stands distinct as an emotive appeal to an idealised past and historical destiny, to ethnic and symbolic nationhood realisable irrespective of instrumental decision making.

The Czech intellectual Ernest Gellner has framed scholarly analysis of uneven economic development and the spread of nationalist claims, expressed most cogently in *Nations and Nationalism* and throughout subsequent and increasingly involved debates with Anthony D. Smith and those who underline the persistence of ethnic divisions into the age of states and nations.[2] Incorporating Gellner's materialist approach into the Scottish example, Tom Nairn stressed the importance of the middle class to leading the 'ordinary folk' in responding to the British state's domination of economic and cultural resources. That this was only to qualified success – if measured in terms of nationalist gains embodied by the American and French revolutions or the European risings of 1848 – resulted from the middle classes staking their own claim to those resources, using the ideology of nationalism as the medium to mobilise action but declining to re-create the pre-Union nation-state, and by evoking Wallace to secure equality with England rather than attain separation.[3] Scotland was peripheral to England in Nairn's model, and shaped its nationalism against an English 'other', yet throughout the modern period when the ideology of nationalism took root, Scotland had access to the political and economic levers of state, and to lucrative overseas territories.[4] Besides, this kind of argument remains empirically problematic. Placing Gellner within Wallerstein's world systems approach, Michael Hechter maintains that 'the initial advantage to one cultural group or another was a historical accident caused by the uneven spread of development', yet nationalism comes too late to explain the development of nation-states.[5] Hechter's causal link is difficult to prove, and the evidence, indeed, can been interpreted the other way round, with the 'peripheral tail wagging the dog' as Scotland outperformed England in key economic benchmarks.[6] Furthermore, the long process of transition out from small-scale proto-industrial production into the industrial age militates against an idea of revolutionary change, or at least a transformation of sufficient immediacy and necessary traction to carry nationalism. Even at the height of Scotland's late Victorian dominance of the UK's steel, chemical, ship and rail production, the majority of Scots were employed in industrial units of fewer than fifteen people.[7] Still, there is consensus for identifying the political ideology of nationalism within the military, taxation and citizenship actions of modern states, and also, discontinuously, that the cultural mobilisation of the nation persisted more widely and during earlier periods.[8]

The Wallacian national tale has attained its principal place within Scotland's nationalism in the form of a narrative mastered for both instrumental and essentialist purposes. The historian will always point to imprecision in the underlying relationship between the material underpinning of modernity and the intellectual and popular conceptions of ideology; context and comparison are too great to ignore. But nationalist discourse incorporates heroic figures such as Wallace because the temporal distance of his biography offers instrumental benefits through conjuring up evidence 'out of its history' that can be exploited for contemporary purposes. This persistence of older loyalties appearing to mirror the nation even before the nation came into being questions the functionalist nature of the modernist position. It also points to freeing the national tale from modern temporal strictures, while indicating strongly the modernist's ideological debt to pieced-together historical juxtapositions. While it is not necessary to have a pre-modern past to create nations, still ethnic narratives bleed out from the periodisation recognised by the modernist. Smith, indeed, rejects those who pin the rise of nations little further back than the coming of mass democracy.[9] Since distinct ethnic building blocks sustained nationalism in the modern age, the nation, and by extension the ideology of nationalism, cannot be confined to the nineteenth century, or be the product of a cultural vacuum as some of the more brusque understandings of the modernist school would have it.[10] Building the ethnic nation comes from a combination of pre-modern myths, symbols and memories that produce a sense of common past and shared destiny that can be either state-created or sustained in opposition to the state.[11] From this standpoint scholarship is right to be wary of ignoring the persistence of national narratives from the medieval past, despite the sway of the eighteenth-century democratic revolutions and of Western secularisation.[12] Yet something very different happened to these concepts after the creation of the state-nation and the political development of democracy, when the state had to create identities, resulting in the ethnie becoming a 'cultural production of nationalism, rather than its cause'.[13] This marks something of a causative shift, but the relationships remain opaque. One of Smith's last chidings of the modernist approach focused on those who acknowledge the role of institutional nationalisms that transcend the pre-modern into the modern world, yet still the modernist is minded to draw attention away from such antecedents.[14] So when turning his attention to Scotland – and while others have prioritised the earlier kingships of Kenneth I (*d.* 858) and Macbeth (*d.* 1057) as the fount of the Scottish nation and its national history[15] – Smith cites the early fourteenth-century Declaration of Arbroath (1320) and concept of the 'community of the realm' as the basis of the hierarchical nation.[16]

With medieval origins suitably timely for placing Wallace at the heart of modern identity formation, still it must be emphasised that the carriers of Scottish nationalism have made only sporadic use of ethnic markers autonomous from the instrumental structures of state and society. Scotland is no example of a 'free-formed' cultural nationalism,[17] and Meinecke's divide between the *Staatsnation* and the *Kulturnation* is too rigid to be applied.[18] A closer representation of Scotland's balance of culture and structure is the terminology used by the nationalist movements of nineteenth-century Europe, where consciousness of the *'patria'* – the true home of the national soul exiled from heaven, bounded by the nation[19] – mobilised older narrative forms as modernity took hold. Transmission of the *patria* through the presentation of symbols and narratives transforms cultural patterns into easily understood and politicised nationalisms – including national tales – where rituals and ceremonies are mobilised by politicians and other cultural, economic and political leaders.[20]

Central to its place within nationalism is how effectively the national tale is authenticated as the embodiment of their *patria* by the common people. Within the liberal tradition of projecting the sovereign people, essentialist nationalism is not subsumed by the instrumental ideology of the state, and an authentic national tale is one that is deemed to represent the home nation.[21] In terms of the national tale maintained overseas, the perception of homeland exists irrespective of the state, whether it be maintained through personal and cognate experience, ancestral link, imagination or affinity.[22] The pull of motherlands and fatherlands, of *Heimat* and homeland, the volk, the *pulkas*, the fowk – the common people – was as much an existential ideology as it was a top-down ideology of political opportunity, where the liberal state claims to act for and in the name of the people. Irrespective of how limited was the franchise prior to 1921, the flexibilities of a constitutional monarchy in the British system (the 'king in parliament') brought the people into their state and precluded the revolutionary pathway taken by the people of France in 1789. As a concept, liberal nationalism puts the individual at the heart of society, where individual choices are equally valid – a conception, Kennedy shows, liberal nationalists apply to the nation.[23] This is suggestive that nationalism operates within a number of environments over time, and with a range of objectives, not all of which are matched between leaders and supporters, existential believers and instrumental rationalists. Nevertheless, in each version the people are fundamental, whether by their actions, or because in their name the nation is evoked. For the instrumentalist the time frame is more immediate and sensitive to proximate concerns. But each is a process of accumulated circumstances: the dark age, the golden age, the renaissance, and periods marked by banal descriptors such as 'depression' and 'prosperity', calling forth past times through Janusian comparisons with the present and with expectations of future improvement. History permeates nationalism because the very concept, and the human experience of it, is a historical one.

*   *   *

Writing from the standpoint of a political scientist and activist, Brand makes the observation that Scottish nationalism in the 1960s was coloured by feelings of historical loss rooted within the early stages of Scottish history. Analysing the period acknowledged as the birth of the nation's electoral nationalism, Brand blends contemporary politics with historical narratives that pre-date the modern age. In doing this he highlights the medieval wars of independence that overturned English claims of suzerainty – emphasising *The Bruce* and *Wallace* for shaping the narrative – alongside 'ample evidence' that the 1707 Union was unpopular among contemporaries.[24] Brand's Janusian narrative eschews a historical continuum for a series of threaded juxtapositions, forming a historiographical trajectory of a kind readily captured by the nationalist. The strongest historical contribution to the national narrative are events and heroes that carry national hagiography with acceptable and accepted authenticity relating to 'our world view' of the historical nation. Modernists are not unaware of this, and the influential 'invented tradition' and 'manufacture of history' literature is deployed to conceptualise these discontinuities.[25] Malleability not fixity is the hallmark of the essentialist nation as it is of the instrumental nation.

Yet when Scottish philosopher David Hume asked 'what would become of history, had we not a dependence on the veracity of the historian according to the experience which we have had of mankind?', his trust was placed in the empirical method.[26] With similar imperatives, the Enlightenment's sociological Whigs on either side of the Border presented competing truths as to the origins of Scotland and its ancient independence.[27] Here the empiricist's confirmation of historical reality as a past verifiable by documentation and weighted judgement leaves the national tale as a discoverable truth. Irrespective of its episodic construction, the perception that historical truth comes from objective reflection and rational observation is common in post-Enlightenment nations. When nationalist writers turned their hand to historical writing, as well as giving temporal depth to their political statements, the likes of Charles Waddie, Douglas Young and Wendy Wood offered up examples of Scotland's true and suppressed history, premised on a belief that the discoverable truth is both rational and knowable, and that the truth is that 'England's historiographers know little' of Scotland's take on shared events. Similarly, in Paton's influential polemic published in 1968, the assumption taken is that empirical objectivity will prevail once 'understanding' is reached. As well as an academic career as a philosopher, Paton held appointments in the Admiralty and Foreign Office and joined the British delegations to the 1919 Peace Conference. Written late in life, his plea for his nation accepts that historians from different nations will reflect differently on their respective countries' interrelationships, but that each should strive for the essential truth of history. Scotland's future, he proposed, cannot be separated from the grip of history: 'The troubles of Scotland have their roots deep in past history – that is, in the long series of events which have made Scotland and England what they are.'[28] His nationalist past – a 'long series of events' – foregrounds the royal regalia, symbols and titles of the nation, the removal of the Stone of Destiny to England in the fourteenth century, and the growth of administrative devolution in the twentieth century. Throughout his plea, it is not the long march of progress that attracts Paton's eye. By assigning a mix of pejorative and simplistic headlines, he instead chooses to illustrate dissimilarities in the interpretation of shared historical episodes, highlighting 'The Legend of Elizabeth', 'The Legend of Scottish Intolerance', 'The Wars with England', 'The Trial of Wallace', 'The Union of Crowns', and 'The Treaty of Union', each, in Paton's view, a historical solitude that fires nationalist oppositions:

> To Englishmen Westminster Hall in London is an ancient court of justice, where freedom has broadened down from precedent to precedent. To Scotsmen with any imagination it must appear as a place that is sinister and even dreadful. It was there – to give only one example – that Sir William Wallace, who had fought loyally for his country, was condemned a traitor by an extraordinary parody of a more sacred trial – the details may here be spared – and was sentenced to an obscene and cruel death even more horrible than crucifixion.[29]

'His' reading of history comes from his understanding of the world, rooted in contemporary politics and a career in public service. From this perspective Paton determines that the Scots possessed a dual loyalty to Scotland and Britain whereas English loyalty was only to England. It was a common refrain in the home rule and devolution periods that Scots not only cared more about Union than the English, but that the English did not even think in such terms. Paton's plea for England to develop a 'change of attitude' flows from the accusation that the 'innocence of the English in regard to their political misdeeds is almost beyond belief.'[30] Yet the duality of national identities within Union is too vague to measure in socio-economic or even in broad political terms, and indeed can only be said to be measurable at all because there was a nationalist movement in Scotland that expressed its ideology, whereas there was no equivalent in England. Nationalisms of acquisition diverge from nationalisms of persistence, but still the duality thesis is one constructed to explain why Scots and the Scottish nation have persisted for so long in constituted monarchical and political unions with England. The two nations diverge because in Scotland's national tale duality marks the relationship with England, whereas for England there is no such constraint.

*   *   *

Each historical pathway that opens itself to the national narrative can be captured and the message transformed as if endlessly malleable – that is the power of nationalist ideology. As well as by leaders and intellectuals, these representations of the past are mobilised and vocalised by public opinion. The teaching of history in the schools and scholarly surveys of the nation's historiography are, whatever their original target audience, also abstracted through public opinion and received understanding. Analysis of public opinion foregrounds the channels of power exploited by elites, but also its corollary, the opinion of 'national society', whether expressed by means of the presentation of historical episodes through the construction of monuments, or through film or digital reproduction.[31] Habermas's influential thesis on the coming of bourgeois society has demonstrated how the public sphere is the outcome of the public's use of its reason.[32] In practical terms, the coming of bourgeois society is a product of reading, writing and debating. The centrality of the printing press and literary culture in the formation of Anderson's imagined community and the hegemonic sway of the intellectual leaders in progressing Hroch's stages of nationalism make similar claims to the formation of national society from the public's reading of literature and history. With no artefacts extant, the origins of the Wallacian national tale are overwhelmingly text-based, with no invariant evidence to counter the public's reading of those texts. Significantly, and echoing the requirements of A. D. Smith, the tenets of the tale had matured prior to the age of mass print. It would change further under the strictures of Romanticism and socialism, but the Wallace tale was effectively fully formed prior to its popular appearance, with *Wallace* among the first outputs of the Chepman & Myllar Press, the nation's first printers, in 1508.[33] First appearing in manuscript form and then printed, with numerous impressions thereafter, Hary's epic poem *Wallace* is canonical. The literary canon is by definition the nation's literature: its existence a mark of the nation, its nonexistence a reflection of another's cultural imperialism. So fundamental is a literary canon, Herder asks, albeit rhetorically, whether 'a nation has anything more precious' than its literature.[34] What the canon comprises has been a debate held since its earliest entrants, and throughout its subversion by the Kailyard school in the nineteenth century, then renaissance, politicisation, and modernisation in the twentieth century.[35] Each of these characterisations is periodised and contested, with debate couched in terms of national confidence, intellectual self-worth and literary independence. The place for literature in conceptualising nationalism is to show 'it was possible' to have a literature that was identifiably Scottish. And it is of interest, surely, that a number of nationalist politicians first came to the movement in the 1970s through the arts and humanities.[36] Literary nationalists Hugh MacDiarmid and Compton Mackenzie and Imperial nationalist John Buchan were explicit in the political agenda of their writing, as Liz Lochhead and Alasdair Gray were a century later.[37] The national bard (Burns) and national author (Scott) have encapsulated the nation by their lives as they have by their writings.[38] In the phoney war prior to the referendum vote on Scottish independence in 2014, Burns' biographer claimed the poet would vote for independence if he were alive.[39] Burns was the ploughman poet, Scott the enlightened lawyer. Burns represented the nation in language; Scott represented the nation in Union. Signifying how much the symbiosis of national literature and national lives can capture wider identities, Ian Duncan has argued from the standpoint of Scott's *Waverley*, where the novel's

Jacobite sensibilities are worked out within Union, that Scotland was embedded within the British nation.[40]

As *Wallace* and *Waverley* were for Scotland, nationalism in other nations has matured out of canonical literature. *Anna Karenina* and *The Brothers Karamazov* were central to defining Russia and being Russian, for example. And despite Russian overlordship, a flourishing Finish cultural nationalism was epitomised by the poet Johan Ludvig Runeberg's commemoration of the Swedish–Russian war of 1808–9, Runeberg presenting it as the Finnish nation's liberation.[41] In Ireland, the centrality of Yeats, among others, to Irishness countered the conception of that identity as the antithesis of Britishness, resisting the imposition of British culture as the colonised would oppose the coloniser;[42] whereas in England, so often symbolised as the coloniser, Shakespeare was educed by later generations to define Britain from an English standpoint, sustaining a monarchical English nationalism through Richard III's exhortation to protect and nurture the sceptr'd isle: 'This happy breed of men, this little world, This previous stone, set in the silver sea ... This blessed plot, this earth, this Realme, this England.'[43]

The conception of the national tale has, as the novel has, foregrounded women and made them central, and its Wallacian construction is no exception (see Chapter 2). Yet women have mostly been absent from the ideology of nationalism except, that is, in the abstract, and in an essentialised form.[44] The result is that women have found difficulty in relating to texts that have 'no place for them except as symbols', which marginalise the public use of their reason, and which deny them the same access as men to the citizenship rights and resources of the nation-state.[45] Yet despite being excluded from nationalism's democratic objectives, in allegorical terms women have come to represent the nation. The 'women-as-nation' allegory, indeed, is a masculinised trope brought forward in times of international dispute.[46] 'Dame Scotia', for example, first appeared in Robert Wedderburn's *Complaynt of Scotland* published around 1550.[47] In this masculine conception, women's bodies are regarded as the preserve of the nation, where women are 'active transmitters and producers of the national culture' as well as 'symbolic signifiers of national difference'.[48] The masculine tone of nationalism rings loudest when the weaker or defeated nation is feminised, penetrated, occupied and culturally dominated.[49] Whether it is soldier rape as the epitome of power over another nation or mothers providing the new-born life to build up military or economic forces, women and the nation are coupled in the symbolism of nationalism, but only tangentially in its ideological and policy-oriented construction.[50]

Yet women's writing – and women's reading – has been in the vanguard of the national tale in the form of the novel. Roy Foster might warn that the 'idea of nationality as narrative is becoming a cliché'; nevertheless, stories have sustained collective identity in diverse societies, orally and then through the mechanical and digital reproduction of text.[51] The reason Benedict Anderson's concept of 'imagined community' has attained such influence is that it historicises with such clarity the transition from vernacular literature to widespread and common understanding. He shows nation building flowing out of a 'hypnotic confirmation of the solidity of a single community'.[52] The narrative of nationality magnifies the 'one, yet many' of national life, where the national tale is foregrounded for offering some level of permanence.[53] The push given by developing technologies from the eighteenth century created first a provincial press and then a national press which enabled 'sustained, frequent and precise communication between strangers'.[54] The national story comes from this change: it is not singular, but plural. A range of stories are manifest. Stuart Hall reminds us that the processes of globalisation and modernity go together, and have gone together for longer than many theorists who stress the novelty of these social and economic processes care to admit.[55] Importantly, also, these operations are not just about the Internet and transnational organisations: their roots go back to whenever regional identities were subsumed by national identities and when links were made across national boundaries. Of course, these processes have intensified in recent decades, and the result today is that identity has become a 'movable feast' where 'any one of a range of identities would be used ... before a new identity becomes fashionable'.[56] Such, indeed, is the Wallacian national tale, one that has evolved over time to fit new imperatives and sustain alternative political agendas.

The national narration, then, is about values, beliefs, attitudes and a 'state of mind'.[57] This narration is forever changing, yet never evades some level of capture. It is not merely coincidence that modern conceptualisations of society and culture were formed simultaneously with the great age of the novel, and the rise of the modern novel is coterminous with the rise of the modern nation. Our sense of history's diachronic properties is itself 'novelistic', as Anderson asserts: 'The idea of a sociological organism moving calendrically through homogeneous, empty space is a precise analogue of the idea of the nation, which is also conceived as a solid community moving steadily down (or up) history.'[58] So strong is the influence that, by 1850, the novel dominated the representation of national cultural identity in Britain.[59] And if we accept that novels of the eighteenth and nineteenth century feminise masculine events, then the national tale is a key component of national identity, whether it be narrowly or more broadly conceived.[60]

The conceptual discussion leads to the conclusion that identity is not made, but is a production, and that national culture is a product of discourse.[61] The concept of national tale is embedded in history for the Janusian purposes of nation building. Understood in this way, the national tale is extended beyond the literary trope into contested territories around which historical evidence is marshalled and brought to bear upon geopolitical and cognitive definitions of the nation. Sir Walter Scott, above all, fashioned the historical novel, but it was Porter's *The Scottish Chiefs*, first published in 1810, that recast this genre by fixing the Wallace narrative within the politics of Britain's Napoleonic engagements. What has given the Wallacian national tale such elasticity has been the relationship of Scotland to England, and within that bond the institutions, intellectuals, and ordinary folk who have carried the narrative for their own ends. The conceptual tools available to study nationalism offer insight into how the national tale has been deployed in nation building. Both the modernist and pre-modernist schools legitimate the use of myth in explanations of nationalism's rise. Even Gellner's materialistic foundations for the spread of nationalism as a product of modernism and industrialisation give due weight to the fabrication of the past, forming the ideology with which nationalism brings the nation into being.[62] The nuanced retort from Gellner to Smith is not to dismiss the importance of older loyalties to structuring modern (in particular) state nationalism, but rather to say it is inessential to their creation. Some nation-states are forged closely from past loyalties, some are not.[63] Nevertheless, examples abound from around the world of the use of myth-history to maintain continuity with these pre-modern attachments. The Spanish 'obsession' with the past developed in the nineteenth century around Basque, Catalan and Galician identities that internalised a concept of nation first formed in the sixteenth century.[64] Likewise looking to an exclusive past, a Serbian sense of being 'special' elect peoples is based on a mix of history, mythology and 'Serb purity' that has sustained ethnic forms of nationalism.[65] These debates mirror competing Victorian claims to be the chosen people of Israel, backed up by nationalist interpretations of archaeological discoveries.[66] England has long sought the status of 'elect nation' singled out by God as an instrument of Divine Providence. In Bede's *Ecclesiastical History of the English People* (written 731) England is linked to Jerusalem, and the English are adjudged an ancient people in communication with God.[67] Following in Bede's footsteps, the influential scholar and educationalist Ernest Barker distilled Englishness from the intellectual continuity of the Greek city state and the Glorious Revolution of 1688, allied to a remarkable optimism in the character of the English people ('the English*man*') based on the squire, the gentleman, and the long-held acceptance by the state of social and religious pluralism.[68] Each comprised a chosen historical pathway, one that best fitted national character and proposed Janusian solutions to contemporary religious and political imperatives.

*   *   *

To introduce the centrality of the historical past and the national canon to the ideology and politicisation of modern nationalism, the Greek deity Janus is summoned. With a future forged in the past, Janus binds the nation synchronically in what was, and what will be – creating a narrative ascendancy. This narrative is conceptualised as the national tale, a term taken out of its literary moorings to examine how personal biography has been reforged and presented as the nation's biography over seven centuries of time. Ascendancy comes from acceptance of the tale's authentic construction, the authenticity of the voices that dominate its expression, and the tale's recall within contemporaries' lives and within personal readings of 'our' nation. Necessarily episodic, critically feminised, this mix of history and literature falls effortlessly into the grip of nationalism. The text, not the empirical record, is the discoverable truth, just as for the nationalists the nation is a discoverable truth – an outcome of a long series of events that are both rational and knowable.

The intention of the chapters that follow is to examine how the afterlife of Sir William Wallace has elided into a narrative ascendancy – of shared myth of origin, community and history – that has supported the ideology of nationalism in the modern age. Wallace was no noble by birth; he was not part of the state that lost in battle to England. Wallace did gain a knighthood and the guardianship of the nation, for a year after the battle of Falkirk (1298), the reward for a man promoted through the ranks by his own efforts, rather than pulled up by patronage and birth.[69] Religiously 'made Protestant', with a Protestant version of Blind Hary's verse to confirm it in 1570, Wallace was a fitting role model for post-Reformation Scotland.[70] Wallace was no Highlander, although there are Highland claims to his memory and depictions of his rustic simplicity, honesty, strength and prowess on the battlefield have been likened to similar portrayals of the attributes of the noble savage in the late eighteenth century.[71] Nor was Wallace a Jacobite, although this did not stop his deeds of valour from appearing in Jacobite songs. But pre-dating the Stuart attempts to regain the crown of Britain did ensure Wallace's commemoration would focus Scottish nationhood on parliamentary rule and the wider institutions of governance, not monarchical and religious restoration. Wallace's deployment of guerrilla techniques of warfare, after failing with the set-piece approach at the battle of Falkirk, added to the sense of his own personal independence.[72] Being outlawed while remaining the leader of others fitted the sense of obligation and self-service of civil society as it developed in the Enlightenment phase of the nation's development. More acutely, the outlaw trope added romance, with Wallace living beyond the law yet sanctioned by the moral economy of the people.[73] Wallace began and ended his career 'as a forest bandit, living free and defiant in "outlaw" wise'.[74] This status added structure upon which further fabrications could be hung. Finally, of course, Wallace was a hero who pre-dated the Union of 1707. He was not sullied by early eighteenth-century politics, nor reacting to the quiet spread of Anglicisation. Not Scotland after Union, but Scotland during the Wars of Independence was his time. Not negotiation with England, but capture and execution by England. For the national tale, Wallace's biography is suitably ephemeral, distant and uncompromised.

NOTES

1. J. Hearn, 'National identity: banal, personal and embedded', *Nations and Nationalism*, 13, 4 (2007), pp. 657–74; B. Anderson, *Imagined Communities*, 2nd edn (London: Verso, 2006); M. Billig, *Banal*

Nationalism (London: Sage, 1995); J. M. MacKenzie, 'Empire and national identities: the case of Scotland', *Transactions of the Royal Historical Society*, 6th series, 8 (1998), pp. 215–32; A. P. Cohen, 'Personal nationalism: a Scottish view of some rites, rights, and wrongs', *American Ethnologist*, 23, 4 (1996), pp. 802–15; A. P. Cohen, 'Peripheral vision: nationalism, national identity and the objective correlative in Scotland', in A. P. Cohen (ed.), *Signifying Identities: Anthropological Perspectives on Boundaries and Contest Values* (London: Routledge, 2000); A. Ichijo, *Scottish Nationalism and the Idea of Europe* (London: Routledge, 2004).

2. Ernest Gellner introduced his theory of nationalism in *Thought and Change* (London: Weidenfeld & Nicolson, 1964), and developed it in *Nations and Nationalism* (Oxford: Blackwell, 1983); E. Gellner, 'Reply: do nations have navels?', part of the 'Warwick Debate' with A. D. Smith, published in *Nations and Nationalism*, Vol. 2, No. 3 (1996), pp. 357–70.

3. G. Morton, *Unionist Nationalism: Governing Urban Scotland, 1830–1860* (East Linton: Tuckwell Press, 1999); J. Kennedy, *Liberal Nationalism: Empire, State and Civil Society in Scotland and Quebec* (Montreal and Kingston: McGill-Queen's University Press, 2013), p. 19.

4. T. M. Devine, *Scotland's Empire: 1600–1815* (London: Allen Lane, 2003), pp. xxiv–xxxvi.

5. M. Mann, 'A Political Theory of Nationalism and Its Excesses', in S. Periwal (ed.), *Notions of Nationalism* (Budapest: Central European Press, 1995), p. 47.

6. T. C. Smout, 'The core and periphery in history', *Journal of Common Market Studies*, 18, 3 (1980), and, in reply, M. Hechter, 'Internal colonialism revisited', *Cencrastus*, 10 (1982).

7. G. Morton, *Ourselves and Others: Scotland, 1832–1914* (Edinburgh: Edinburgh University Press, 2012), pp. 141–6.

8. Kennedy, *Liberal Nationalisms*, pp. 20–1, D. McCrone, *The Sociology of Nationalism: Tomorrow's Ancestors* (London: Routledge, 1998), p. 11; J. Breuilly, *Nationalism and the State* (Manchester: Manchester University Press, 1982), pp. 1–16, 54–5; J. Breuilly, 'Dating the nation: how old is an old nation?', in I. Atsuko and U. Gordana (eds), *When Is the Nation? Towards an Understanding of Theories of Nationalism* (London: Routledge 2003), pp. 15–39.

9. A. D. Smith, *The Cultural Foundations of Nations: Hierarchy, Covenant, and Republic* (Oxford: Blackwell, 2008), p. 2.

10. E. Gellner, *Nations and Nationalism* (Oxford: Basil Blackwell, 1983); Gellner, 'Reply: do nations have navels?'; B. Anderson, *Imagined Communities: Reflections on the Origin and Spread of Nationalism*,

rev. edn (London: Verso, 1996); M. Billig, *Banal Nationalism* (London: Sage, 1995).

11. McCrone, *The Sociology of Nationalism*, p. 12.
12. Smith, *Cultural Foundations of Nations*, p. 8.
13. McCrone, *Sociology of Nationalism*, p. 14.
14. Smith, *Cultural Foundations of Nations*, pp. 6–7.
15. This is discussed in M. Lynch, *Scotland: A New History* (London: Century, 1991), pp. 39–50.
16. Smith, *Cultural Foundations of Nations*, pp. 102–4.
17. D. McCrone, *Understanding Scotland: The Sociology of a Stateless Nation* (London: Routledge, 1990), pp. 174–96.
18. The divide is based on an analysis of Germany prior to unification in 1871 as a nation sustained through its culture. For a critique, see S. Brockmann, *Literature and German Reunification* (Cambridge: Cambridge University Press, 1999), pp. 6–10.
19. S. Woolf, 'Introduction', in *Nationalism in Europe: 1815 to the Present*, ed. S. Woolf (London and New York: Routledge, 1996), p. 5.
20. M. E. Geisler, 'National symbols', in G. H. Herb and D. H. Kaplan (eds), *Nations and Nationalism: A Global Historical Overview, Vol. 1, 1770 to 1880* (Santa Barbara and Oxford: ABC Clio, 2008), pp. 111–15; H. J. Gans, 'Symbolic ethnicity: the future of ethnic groups and cultures in America', *Ethnic and Racial Studies*, 2, 1 (January 1979), pp. 9, 14.
21. J. Brand, *The National Movement in Scotland* (London: Routledge & Kegan Paul, 1978), p. 10.
22. T. Bueltmann, A. Hinson and G. Morton, *The Scottish Diaspora* (Edinburgh: Edinburgh University Press, 2013), pp. 16–31.
23. Kennedy, *Liberal Nationalisms*, pp. 29–31.
24. Brand, *The National Movement in Scotland*, pp. 12–13.
25. E. J. Hobsbawm and T. Ranger (eds), *The Invention of Tradition* (Cambridge: Cambridge University Press, [1983] 1994); I. Donachie and C. Whatley (eds), *The Manufacture of Scottish History* (Edinburgh: Polygon, 1992).
26. D. Hume, *An Enquiry Concerning Human Understanding* (New York: Harvard Classics, 1910 [1748]), p. 178.
27. C. Kidd, *Subverting Scotland's Past. Scottish Whig Historians and the Creation of an Anglo-British Identity, 1689–c.1830* (Cambridge: Cambridge University Press, 1993).
28. H. J. Paton, *The Claim of Scotland* (London: Allen & Unwin, 1968), p. 33.
29. Ibid., p. 42.
30. Ibid., pp. 24, 42–3.
31. Studies of the civic mobilisation of a historically specific reading of

the democratic nation are found in: A. Henderson, *Hierarchies of Belonging: National Identity and Political Culture in Scotland and Quebec* (Montreal and Kingston, 2007); G. Morton, 'The moral foundations of constitutional change in Canada and Scotland at the end of the twentieth century', *International Review of Scottish Studies*, 33 (2008), pp. 87–122.

32. J. Habermas, *The Structural Transformation of the Public Sphere. An Inquiry into a Category of Bourgeois Society*, trans. Thomas Burger (Cambridge: Polity Press, 1989).

33. The slow but steady spread of printing establishments in Scotland, numbering 38 printers between 1508 and 1801, can be explored at http://www.500yearsofprinting.org/printing.php (accessed 25 January 2014). And the geographical spread of these printers, which predominate in the costal Lowlands and Borders, is collated at: http://digital.nls.uk/printing/texts-titles.cfm; http://digital.nls.uk/printing/towns.cfm (both accessed 28 January 2014).

34. Cited in A. D. Smith, *The Nation in History: Historiographical Debates about Ethnicity and Nationalism* (Cambridge: Polity Press, 2000), p. 23.

35. M. Palmer McCulloch, *Scottish Modernism and Its Contexts 1918–1959: Literature, National Identity and Cultural Exchange* (Edinburgh: Edinburgh University Press, 2009); I. Brown, T. O. Clancy, S. Manning and M. G. H. Pittock (eds), *The Edinburgh History of Scottish Literature. Volume Two: Enlightenment, Britain and Empire (1707–1918)* (Edinburgh: Edinburgh University Press 2007).

36. M. Macdonald, 'Scottish literature and visual art: a Caledonian synergy', *International Review of Scottish Studies*, 38 (2013), pp. 80–3, 90–4.

37. Liz Lochhead was appointed to be the nation's poet, the Scots Maker, in 2011; A. Gray, *Independence: An Argument for Home Rule* (Edinburgh: Canongate Books, 2014); Buchan, in particular, was quick to bracket Scots and indigenes in his observations of the Imperial parliament, both in his fiction and his role as Governor General in Canada. See K. Hutchings, '"Teller of Tales": John Buchan, First Baron Tweedsmuir of Elsfield, and Canada's Aboriginal Peoples', in G. Morton and D. A. Wilson (eds), *Irish and Scottish Encounters with Indigenous Peoples: Canada, the United States, Australia and New Zealand* (Montreal and Kingston: McGill-Queen's University Press, 2013).

38. R. Crawford, *The Bard: Burns, A Biography* (Princeton: Princeton University Press, 2009), pp. 7–9.

39. 'Academic says Robert Burns would have voted for independence', *The Courier*, 10 January 2014.

40. I. Duncan, *Modern Romance and the Transformations of the Novel: The Gothic, Scott, Dickens* (Cambridge: Cambridge University, 1992), p. 55.
41. Paterson, *The Autonomy of Modern Scotland*, p. 94.
42. T. Tracy., *Irishness and Womanhood in Nineteenth-Century British Writing* (Aldershot: Ashgate, 2009), p. 10.
43. Brand, *The National Movement in Scotland*, p. 89.
44. M. G. H. Pittock, 'The Complaint of Caledonia: Scotland and the Female Voice', in P. Schwyzer and S. Mealor (eds), *Archipelagic Identities: Literature and Identity in the Atlantic Archipelago, 1550–1800* (Aldershot: Ashgate, 2004), pp. 141–52.
45. K. Stirling, *Bella Caledonia: Women, Nation, Text* (Amsterdam: Rodopi, 2008), p. 110 (quotation); A. McClintock, 'Family feuds: gender, nationalism and the family', *Feminist Review*, 44 (Summer 1993), p. 61 (quotation); M. Molloy, 'Imagining (the) difference: gender, ethnicity and metaphors of nation', *Feminist Review*, 51 (Autumn 1995), p. 105.
46. J. Edmunds, 'Generations, women and national consciousness', in J. Edmunds and B. S. Turner (eds), *Generational Consciousness, Narrative and Politics* (Boston: Rowman & Littlefield, 2002), p. 46; A. Rauser, 'Death or liberty: British political prints and the struggle for symbols in the American Revolution', *Oxford Art Journal*, 21, 2 (1998), pp. 151–2, charts the American challenge to Britannia's claim on liberty.
47. Quhou The Affligit Lady Dame Scotia/Reprochit Hyr Thre Sonnis Callit/The Thre Estaitis Of/Scotland.
48. N. Yuval-Davis and F. Anthias (eds), *Women–Nation–State* (London: Sage, 1989), p. 7, quoted in McLintock, 'Family feuds', pp. 62–3.
49. R. S. Herr, 'The possibility of nationalist feminism', *Hypatia*, 18 (2003), p. 137.
50. Ibid.; S. Pryke, 'Nationalism and sexuality: what are the issues?', *Nations and Nationalism*, 4, 4 (October, 1998), pp. 538–40; T. Mayer, 'Gender ironies of nationalism', in T. Mayer (ed.), *Gender Ironies of Nationalisms: Sexing the Nation* (London: Routledge, 2000), pp. 10–11.
51. R. Foster, 'Storylines: narratives and nationality in nineteenth-century Ireland', in G. Cubitt (ed.), *Imagining Nations* (Manchester: Manchester University Press, 1998), p. 38.
52. B. Anderson, *Imagined Communities: Reflections on the Origin and Spread of Nationalism*, rev. edn (London: Verso, 1996), p. 33.
53. Timothy Brennan, quoted in H. K. Bhabha, *Nation and Narration* (London: Routledge, 1990).
54. Gellner, *Nations and Nationalism*, pp. 33–4. The best historical

study of the rise of the regional newspaper press remains D. Read, *The English Provinces, c.1760–1960: A Study in Influence* (London: Arnold, 1964).

55. S. Hall, 'The question of cultural identity', in S. Hall, D. Held and A. McGrew (eds), *Modernity and Its Futures* (Cambridge: Polity Press, 1992), p. 299.

56. Ibid., pp. 273–5.

57. J. Giles and T. Middleton 'Introduction', in J. Giles and T. Middleton (eds), *Writing Englishness 1900–1950* (London and New York: Routledge, 1995), pp. 1–12. The type of politics which is shaped by a 'state of mind' has been superbly studied for Ireland: O. Macdonagh, *States of Mind: A Study of Anglo-Irish Conflict, 1780–1980* (London: Allen & Unwin, 1983).

58. Tracy, *Irishness and Womanhood in Nineteenth-Century British Writing*, p. 12; Anderson, *Imagined Communities*, p. 26.

59. I. Duncan, *Modern Romance and the Transformation of the Novel, The Gothic, Scott, Dickens* (Cambridge: Cambridge University Press, 1992), p. 2.

60. Tracy, *Irishness and Womanhood*, p. 13.

61. McCrone, *Sociology of Nationalism*, pp. 30–1.

62. Gellner, *Nations and Nationalism*; E. Gellner, *Nationalism* (London: Weidenfeld & Nicolson, 1997); McCrone, *The Sociology of Nationalism*, pp. 67–72, 83; D. Conversi, 'Ernest Gellner as critic of social thought: nationalism, closed systems and the Central European tradition', *Nations and Nationalism*, 5, 4 (1999), p. 565; M. Guibernau, *Nationalisms: The Nation-State and Nationalism in the Twentieth Century* (Cambridge: Polity Press, 1996), p. 141.

63. Gellner restated his position just before he died in 'Reply: do nations have navels?' part of the 'Warwick Debate' with A. D. Smith, published in *Nations and Nationalism*, 2, 3 (1996), pp. 357–70; A. D. Smith, 'Memory and modernity: reflections on Ernest Gellner's theory of nationalism', *Nations and Nationalism*, 2, 3 (1996), pp. 371–88. The ethnic/civic conceptions of nationalism are worked out in many case studies, but one of the best early studies is L. Greenfeld, *Nationalism: Five Roads to Modernity* (Cambridge, MA: Harvard University Press, 1992), Ch. 1. Accessible summaries of the debate, including attempts, most explicitly by McCrone, to reject the division, are found in McCrone, *Sociology of Nationalism*, pp. 8–10; A. Morris and G. Morton, *Locality, Community and Nation* (London: Hodder & Stoughton, 1998), pp. 77–81; Hearn, *Claiming Scotland*, pp. 3–8.

64. M. Díaz-Andreu, 'The past in the present: the search for roots in cultural nationalism. The Spanish case', in J. G. Beramendi, R. Máiz

and X.M. Núñez (eds), *Nationalism in Europe: Past and Present, Volume I* (Santiago de Compostela: University Press of Santiago de Compostela, 1994), pp. 199, 203–4.

65. A. Hastings, 'Special peoples', *Nations and Nationalism*, 5, 3 (1999), pp. 381–2.

66. S. Grosby, 'The chosen people of ancient Israel and the Occident: why does nationality exist and survive?', *Nations and Nationalism*, 5, 3 (1999), pp. 357–80; P. L. Kohl and C. Fawcett, 'Archaeology in the service of the state: theoretical considerations', in P. L. Kohl and C. Fawcett (eds), *Nationalism, Politics and the Practice of Archaeology* (Cambridge: Cambridge University Press, 1995), pp. 10–14.

67. H. Kearney, *The British Isles: A History of Four Nations* (Cambridge: Cambridge University Press), pp. 37–8; N. Evans, 'Introduction: Identity and Integration in the British Isles', in N. Evans (ed.), *National Identity in the British Isles* (Harlech: Coleg Harlech Occasional Papers in Welsh Studies, No. 3, 1989), pp. 15–16; A. Grant and K. Stringer, 'Introduction: The Enigma of British History', in A. Grant and K. Stringer (eds), *Uniting the Kingdom? The Making of British History* (London and New York: Routledge, 1995), pp. 3–11.

68. J. Stapleton, *Englishness and the Study of Politics: The Social and Political Thought of Ernest Barker* (Cambridge: Cambridge University Press, 1994).

69. G. W. S. Barrow, *Robert Bruce and the Community of the Realm of Scotland*, 2nd edn (Edinburgh: Edinburgh University Press, 1976), p. 130.

70. M. Lindsay, *History of Scottish Literature* (London: Hale, 1977), pp. 22–3; the 'Protestant' edition was published in Stirling by Robert Lekprevik.

71. J. Rendall, 'Tacitus Engendered: "Gothic Feminism" and British Histories, c.1750–1800', in G. Cubitt (ed.), *Imagining Nations* (Manchester: Manchester University Press, 1998), p. 60; C. W. J. Withers, 'The Historical Creation of the Scottish Highlands', in I. Donnachie and C. Whatley (eds), *The Manufacture of Scottish History* (Edinburgh: Polygon, 1992), p. 145.

72. Barrow, *Robert Bruce*, p. 130.

73. G. Seal, *The Outlaw Legend: A Cultural Tradition in Britain, America and Australia* (Cambridge: Cambridge University Press, 1996), p. 2.

74. M. Keen, *The Outlaws of Medieval Legend* (London: Routledge & Kegan Paul, 1961), p. 74.

Chapter 2

A National Tale

The Lübeck letter forms one of the few documents associated with Wallace's hand. There is no proof the patriot ever wrote or saw the communication, though it was compiled and sent in his name and closed with his and Murray's seal. When, in 1998, the Museum of Scotland opened in Edinburgh, the textual basis of the Wallacian national tale become a matter of public indignation. The new museum, later renamed the National Museum of Scotland, presented a history of the nation from its geological beginnings to the near present, but did so without reference to Wallace. There is, after all, no extant artefact to illustrate his life.

The letter first came to the attention of the historical community in a collection of sources on the history of the Hanseatic League collated by Georg Friedrich Christoph, Baron Sartorius von Waltershausen, which he published between 1802 and 1808, and later reinterpreted in 1830. It was reproduced both in Carrick's *Life of Wallace* and Stevenson's collection of sources illustrative of Wallace produced for the Maitland Club in 1841. Of greater visibility still, the letter was loaned to the Scottish National Exhibition held in Glasgow in 1911, seen up close by any of the 9.4 million people who attended the spectacle.[1] The belief persisted that the Lübeck letter was destroyed during the 1939–45 war when German bombs fell upon the archives in London, despite it having been returned to Lübeck in 1912 where it safely saw out both World Wars.[2] The Scottish historical community in 1998 were aware of its survival, but found their voices drowned out in the outcry.[3] When allowed to borrow and display the letter in 1999, only then did Scotland's national museum mark Wallace within its national tale.[4] Contrast this with the rediscovery in 2010 of a letter of safe passage for Wallace, written by the king of France, where the Scottish

Government has without fanfare involved the Scottish historical community in determining its provenance before seeking its repatriation from the National Archives in England.[5] This, then, was a process that gained democratic impetus when a petition was lodged with the Scottish Parliament in 2010 to consider requesting its permanent return, backed by 2,577 signatures.[6] As those discussions continued, it was agreed that the Safe Conduct would be exhibited in the main hall of the Scottish Parliament in 2012, and then sent on long-term loan to the National Archives in Scotland where it was displayed alongside the Lübeck letter.[7]

The ongoing debate that surrounds the final resting place of both these documents is illustrative of the enduring hold of text over the Wallacian national tale. The artefacts have passed away into history, but these letters, along with a smattering of others, have survived, and give credence to the authenticity of Wallace and credibility to the significance of his life and actions. The paucity of alternative contemporary evidence is an important part of the moves to repatriate the letters, but so too is the nationalist act of repatriation itself. For the nationalist, the nation should possess its historical canon as it should its literary canon. The wider point is that these records are textual and offer too little substantive detail to sustain a national tale without further inventiveness. Attention, therefore, turns to such creativity, and to the literary national tale.

*   *   *

Just as identity is reimagined by each generation, so the concept of national tale remains malleable and open to textual reinterpretation. In literary criticism, the concept sheds some of its breadth to become more precise in form and temporality. Specifically, the literary national tale reflects relations between nations. Its origins associated most commonly with Maria Edgeworth and Sydney Owenson, the genre developed within Irish female writing in the 1790s and in response to the politics of the Anglo-Irish Union.[8] Within Great Britain, the national tale is geographically oppositional between Scotland and England and demanding of an aesthetically coherent recovery of the past, tending towards conservative romanticism.[9] Studying the influence of women novelists on the national tale in the period from 1790 to 1815, a selection guided by Sarah Green's *Scotch Novel Reading* (1824), Shields presents a literary and historical dialectic premised solely on connections to eighteenth-century Highland clearances and the romanticism of Jacobitism. Her description of Jacobitism is one that is singularly Highland and coherently Scottish.[10] In this interpretation, the Gael is accorded a universality within Britain and Empire that sits uncomfortably with post-1707 constitutional realities and the historical conclusion that Jacobitism was no movement of opposition between England and Scotland, either before or after the Union of 1707. What is more, historians confirm there was no place of any consequence for Jacobitism within political nationalism after 1760.[11] In other words, Shields presents us with a national ethos that lies outside the intellectual structures of either Anglo-British or unionist-nationalist structure and identity.[12]

The literary concept of national tale has greatest validity when framed within the historical reality of its authorship, and the complexities of post-Union Britain. Of the female writers contributing to this genre in the 1790–1815 period, Jane Porter penned the most successful and influential narrative of Scotland within Britain, *The Scottish Chiefs*. The aesthetics and locale of Porter's novel contrast Highland and Lowland life – including geographical variation in spoken English, Scots and Gaelic – with a level of granularity not found among her female contemporaries. Tellingly, Porter produced a text that offered cultural self-reflection within the political pragmatism of the British core, where the Scottish–English elegiac is only recalled when fully resolved in modern British unity.[13]

Significantly, placing Porter's historical romance within the genre of the historical novel is not universally accepted. Both Thomas Carlyle and George Lukács demand that such works account for the transformative power of change over time.[14] Within the parameters defined by those two critics, it was Walter Scott who founded that genre upon the foundational works of a range of primarily female authors, including over 200 'pseudo historical' novels – *The Scottish Chiefs* among them – produced between 1800 and the publication of *Waverley* in 1814.[15] To raise Porter above the status of a 'pesudo-historical' novelist, Fiona Price argues one would have to emphasise her ability to connect to ordinary people by the repetition of key historical narratives, an approach that encouraged identification with the nation through an inheritance of the past.[16] In other words, one would have to redefine the historical novel. At no time was Porter herself shaken from a belief in her own literary role, and she emphasised this claim (as discussed in more depth below) by association with Scott.[17] At best, Porter – with her overt moralising on the present – offers a didactic rather than a defining contribution to the historical novel, one, indeed, that is more powerful as a national tale.

What this observation suggests is that Porter undermined her place as a historical novelist to produce a national tale in period, topic and construction that fitted Britain's contemporary constitutional, political and military anxieties. To emphasise this point she locates the epic geography of *The Scottish Chiefs* within Western cultural traditions, where any opposition between Scotland and England portrayed in the novel is resolved not by Scotland's victory but in British unity. And again showing her distance from the historical novel, Porter uses both national and supranational heroic devices to foreground Wallace's domesticity, not the nation's political loss: her hero's motivation flows directly from a desire to avenge matrimonial honour, not national defeat. Porter then uses the outcome of Wallace's martyrdom not to eulogise past cross-border conflict, but to strengthen Britain's military endeavours against a foreign foe.[18] It is for these reasons that the national tale represented by *The Scottish Chiefs* is not motivated by a 'diminished past' but a 'diminished present'.[19] Unlike others in these years, Porter eschews the romance of Jacobitism in favour of the struggles being faced on the battlefields of Europe.[20]

Ill fitting the historical novel for her temporal indiscretions, Porter's deployment of the national tale's domestic trope is of greater significance. In Owenson's *The Wild Irish Girl: A National Tale* (1806), an early exemplar of the genre, Glorvina seduces the Englishman Horatio into marital bond. Here the allegorical marriage is indicative of a transformation of the colonial relationship 'from one largely characterized by absenteeism and mutual ignorance and hostility, to a relationship of reciprocal responsibility and equal rights shared by settler and native, with the blessing of the "parent" society of the colonist'.[21] Horatio is led to accept Roman Catholicism as an earlier stage of British Protestantism where the latter's extension would help reduce prejudice between the two nations.[22] He is also persuaded that Irishness could be maintained along with the unity of the UK.[23] Accepting Fielding's caution that neither Owenson's *Wild Irish Girls* nor any other single novel, in plot or structure, came to define the national tale, the deployment of domestic harmony in order to attain political union is characteristic of the genre, a path towards an idealised British national culture also trod by William Makepeace Thackeray.[24] The success of *Waverley* was to chart the development of the nation temporally rather than topographically, whereas the national tale has made no such transition. The Scottish writers of the romantic period possessed a historicised geography of their nation, and the picturesque engravings within *Waverley* gave impetus to the use of geographic illustrations in the novel.[25] Yet their non-sequential plotting placed the national tale firmly within contemporary politics, narrating nationalism with a powerful – albeit false – pathway the historical novel could not match. As Renan famously reminds us, getting our history wrong is an essential precept of nationalism.[26]

Still, Porter's command over Scotland's national tale from 1810 was secured through the façade of her having written a credible historical novel. She was never hesitant in projecting her biography in order to secure authenticity for her voice. Porter's connection to Walter Scott was central here – to her if not to him – with the pair having known each other since childhood. As Porter reflected on this relationship, following the death of her mother, her personal reading of history is outlined:

> And as her [Mrs Porter's] faculties near failed her one moment to the hour of her death, even to the age of eighty five, she enjoyed conversing with him [Sir Walter] in his books; and talking of his boy days, with those about her who appreciated the safe gratification but who had near seen the author. This memorable parent and friend was born in the memorable year 1745, on the day of the Duke of Cumberland's march through her native city of Durham, to the eventful field of Culloden! And, on the 18th June 1831, the anniversary of the important day of Waterloo, she was taken from this world of still awful expectancy! Having always been impressed with a foreboding that as 'she came into the world in so troubled a public time, she would be called to quit it in some season of similar circumstances!'. But thanks be to God, that whatever has been the stir in Europe, nay all over the Globe, as well as in this little land, she laid down her [. . .] head in Peace. And with prayers for her country, and for her children near and distant, gently resigned her meek soul into the saviour's promised safe keeping.[27]

As well as being brought together at their mother's home-based soirées, Porter and Scott would later share Longman & Co. as their publisher and compete to claim the genesis of the first historical novel. Porter, though, was sufficiently gracious to suggest, in following her lead, that Scott bettered and mastered the approach. She conspired to create her own *Waverley*-like mystery with the unknown location and authorship of *Sir Edward Seaward's Narrative* (1831), and mirrored Scott's interest in the material culture of history, acquiring mementos passed between Queens Margaret and Mary.[28] Jane also came across unpublished letters of the tragic Scottish queen when visiting her brother in St Petersburg in 1841, which she later transcribed from the original French and delivered to Agnes and Elizabeth Strickland for their *Letters of Mary, Queen of Scots* (1842–3).[29] Sir Walter's intense antiquarianism was well-known, his renowned collection at Abbotsford the result of his searches as well as many gifts, although he can be found complaining at the request he start a hunt for the real Wallace sword.[30] Porter herself was to receive gifts carved from Wallace's great oak, cut down to its roots in 1790, and other relics sent by those whom she had inspired.[31] Scott, indeed, owned a chair carved from the wood of the house at Robroyston where Sir John Stewart of Menteith betrayed Wallace in 1305, presented by the storyteller and antiquarian Joseph Train.[32] Nurturing her association with the most renowned Scotsman of the age, Jane Porter relied upon her formative friendship to broker visits to Abbotsford:

> But to see Sir Walter Scott would be a rich satisfaction to them both! Captain Montgomery has seen much foreign service; and is now returning to the West Indies, by the way of Scotland, to his native country, Ireland. A brave man, suffering under service, is worthy indeed a candid grasp of the hand from the Chivalry poet of Dear Old Caledonia.[33]

It tended to be returnees to Scotland from abroad for whom she wrote, saying her guests were '[i]nterested in the magical pen, before which all the world has bowed';[34] and in another case, a likely contact of her brother Sir Robert Ker Porter, she described 'The present pilgrim to bonnie Scotland' as an officer of the Prussian Imperial Guard.[35]

Born of mixed English and Irish parentage, Jane Porter lived her youth in Scotland, but her adulthood in England. There is no evidence that she ever returned back across the border, although she always maintained a fond attachment for the country that set her imagination towards a literary path. It was after living in England that she began publishing, first for the journal *The Quiz* in 1797 – and after sixteen years in the south she produced *The*

Scottish Chiefs. In its first preface, dated 1809, she takes care to assign Scotland as the identifier of William Wallace, and to stress the importance of lineage to the nation. Yet she also does this for both England and Britain:

> It is now too common to condemn as nonsense even an honest pride in ancestry. But where is the Englishman who is not proud of being the countryman of Nelson? Where is the British sailor that does not thirst to emulate his fame?

She pleads that this sentiment must be right, and if so then 'respect for noble progenitors cannot be wrong, for it proceeds from the same source – the principle of kindred, of inheritance, and of virtue'.[36] It was a personal virtue, but also a national one, not for Scotland, or for England, but for Britain:

> Happy is for this realm that the destiny which now unites the once contending arms of those brave families has also consolidated their rival nations into one, and by planting the heir of Plantagenet and of Bruce upon the throne hath redeemed the peace of Britain, and fixed it on lasting foundations.[37]

In a revised preface written in 1828 she reflected on how this message of British nationhood had been accepted by her readership, expressing 'her grateful sense of the candour with which so adventurous a work from a female pen has been generally received'. It was a source of pride to her that the text had been translated into the European languages, as were the endorsements she had received from those countries and from those even further distant, including India and Australia. In preparing the retrospective preface to the illustrated edition of 1840, Porter still felt the need to explain what had 'impelled her to choose a theme so unusual to a female pen – a theme of war and bloodshed!'. The reason, she surmised, was that the time of Wallace was a time when 'men [were] true to themselves, to the laws and rightful independence of their country', a contrast made with her fears for contemporary Europe.

As national narrative, *The Scottish Chiefs* is teleological. Porter identifies a clear pathway from the past to the present, and it remains primarily ahistorical because of her chosen juxtaposition of past events. 'Such subjects', she argues, 'are consecrated to a purpose beyond the time of their action' – and here she links the battles of Falkirk (Scottish elegiac defeat – 1298) and Runnymede (English constitutional memory – 1215) with 'our own glorious field of Waterloo' (British victory – 1815).[38] This was Janusian nationalism in the making, piecing together past events in order to construct a suitable historical future.

* * *

The narrative construction is, of course, only one half of the national tale, its corollary being the nation, and how the national tale relates to the territorial nation. The land mass of Scotland has been remarkably unchanging, with the early modern annexation of the Orkney and Shetland islands being the sole significant acquisition. The nation's single land border is with England, and Scotland comprises around 30 per cent of that British island. The relationship of each is framed in the map as in text.[39] It is not just the nation's flags that are part of banal national identity; the predominantly feminine silhouetting of the country's outline is also important, seen in the many ways that national maps have been reproduced in the form of tea towels, clothing and pottery. In increasingly accurate, prescriptive but also ornate forms, the maps contextualised in Enlightenment social science were part of the nation's historical identity. David MacPherson's *Geographical Illustrations of Scottish History* from 1796 claimed 'Geography is one of the eyes of history'.[40] And when Samuel Johnson chose to write 'of our own island', he was using geography to place Scotland in the modern world, and to place Scotland within a national narrative formed in British history.[41]

Also important to the ongoing negotiation of Scotland within Britain was the timing of Union, this having taken place within debates carried over from the seventeenth century, with negotiators from the post-1688 discussions again involved in the treating of 1706–7.[42] This constitutional removal of the Scottish and English states into the new structure of Great Britain was formed well before the politicisation of the people of Europe and America into modern nationalism. The Scots were left to debate the franchise and parliamentary democracy within a Union state, not against it. This meant that the genre of national tale, formed in the decades prior to electoral reform in 1832 and more than a century before the parliamentary franchise was extended to women, adds further doubt to the causality of its narrative production alongside state formation. Indeed, Scotland's national identity has been nurtured in areas separate from the formal political process, maintaining a coherence irrespective of the British state. In the constitutional and administrative arrangements established in the Union between England and Scotland, in the cultural accommodation these two nations reached from the second half of the eighteenth century, and the non-interference of the Westminster state during the age of laissez-faire, the Scottish nation was sustained 'state-free' in narratives, institutions and imaginings.[43]

This conclusion impacts on how the national tale is contextualised alongside national identity, an identity that has – from the eighteenth century most clearly – been located in civil society.[44] The sociologist Tom Nairn analysed the rift between the Westminster state and Scottish civil society in order to explain how mistaken we are to regard the UK as a coherent nation-state.[45] Better to call it a state-nation or, in James Mitchell's analysis, a union not a unitary state, because of the agreements, bargains and compromises which hold its component nations together.[46] The gap is where Scottish national identity has flourished coterminous with the governance of the nation.[47] This governance was enacted through political managers, municipal councils, and the institutions and organisations of civil society. Fixing the national tale to this sociological construction of nationalism also ties it to further strictures. These include the constant interplay – and continued coexistence – of Scottish and British identities since 1707; the strong identification of the Scottish people with the Scottish nation despite monarchical and parliamentary union; the institutional independence of the nation rarely manifest in the demand for a law-making parliament; and the disconnection between national identity and political parties. There have been a number of political organisations since the 1850s which have mobilised some version of national identity (Chapter 11). At times their focus has been on securing a 'local national' parliament – a case made by the Scottish Home Rule Association in the 1880s – and the call for a federal or a devolved structure has been stronger than the call for an independent parliament in the century that followed.[48] These have been organisations to join, where membership is akin to a declaration of intent. And yet national identity has been more expansive than that. The Wallacian national tale is fed by a wide evidential base, some of it contemporary to its construction, much of it fitting later

ideological and political aims. The national tale comprises the
written word of nationalists, organisations in civil society, expatri-
ate groups, and disenfranchised peoples, as well as finding expression in poems and songs by those who lack any formal organising
principle. Of all in the modern period, *The Scottish Chiefs*, and
the personal biography of its author, have contrived to shape the
narrative outwards from the parameters of state mobilisation.
Remaining defined by its ahistorical juxtapositions of the past and
the present, the concept of national tale goes beyond the literary
genre. A vessel with no lid nor base, incessantly refilled with new
content over time, the national tale works to shape the ideology of
nationalism because the narrative lacks appropriate and sequential
transformation from one age to the next. Where Jane Porter fails
as a historical novelist she succeeds as a nationalist. Yet her claim
to be a historical novelist akin to Scott gave credibility to her narrative. The national tale may be contradictory, superficial or even
facile; expediency and social crisis will insist on elements antitheti-
cal to the Wallace narrative; but the national tale has accompanied
nation building, based on an interpretation of the past authenticated by contemporary reading of the present.

NOTES

1. A. A. M. Duncan, 'William, Son of Alan Wallace: The Documents',
   in E. J. Cowan (ed.), *The Wallace Book* (Edinburgh; John Donald,
   2007), pp. 46–7; J. D. Carrick, *Life of Sir William Wallace of
   Elderslie* (London: Whittaker & Co., 1840); J. Stevenson (ed.),
   Documents Illustrative of Sir William Wallace, his life and times,
   Maitland Club 54 (Edinburgh: Maitland Club, 1841). The exhibited
   Lübeck letter is noted in the annual index of *The Times* for 1911,
   p. 1,505.
2. Duncan, 'William, Son of Alan Wallace', p. 46.
3. Barrow, *Robert Bruce*, p. 128, fn. 2. The 1976 edition states that the
   letter was destroyed during the Second World War, but notes that it
   had been displayed at the Glasgow Exhibition of 1911, p. 129, fn.
   3. That the Scottish historical community was aware of the letter's
   survival was confirmed by Michael Lynch, then the Sir William Fraser
   Chair of Scottish History at Edinburgh University.
4. *Scotland on Sunday*, 21 February 1999 reports on the Museum of
   Scotland's new display on Wallace, one including the Lübeck letter.

5. The terms of reference for the working group established by the National Archives of Scotland in 2010 was to 'Establish the providence and original intent of the "Wallace document" (SC 1/30/81)'; http://www.nas.gov.uk/documents/WilliamWallaceWorkingGroupT NAmeeting5August2010.pdf (accessed 6 January 2014).

6. *Scottish parliament PE 1350*. Petition 1350, SPICe Briefing: 'Petition by Nick Brand calling on the Scottish Parliament to urge the Scottish Government to make a formal loan request to the National Archive at Kew to return the Wallace Safe Conduct to Scotland under a permanent loan agreement' (lodged 24 April 2010); http://www.scottish.parliament.uk/parliamentarybusiness/ CurrentCommittees/40047.aspx (accessed 31 January 2014).

7. http://www.nationalarchives.gov.uk/news/661.htm; http://www.fife today.co.uk/news/local-headlines/snp-looks-to-bring-last-william-wa llace-possession-home-1-812887 (accessed 31 January 2014). A facsimile of the Latin document can be downloaded at: http://discovery. nationalarchives.gov.uk/SearchUI/details/C10518923 (accessed 31 January 2014).

8. K. Trumpener, *Bardic Nationalism: The Romantic Novel and the British Empire* (Princeton: Princeton University Press, 1997), pp. 131–2; F. Price, 'Introduction', *The Scottish Chiefs: A Romance* (Plymouth: Broadview Press, 2007), p. 17.

9. A. Monnickendam, 'The Scottish national tale', in M. G. H. Pittock (ed.), *The Edinburgh Companion to Scottish Romanticism* (Edinburgh: Edinburgh University Press, 2011), p. 100.

10. J. Shields, 'Family roots to the routes of Empire: national tales and the domestication of the Scottish Highlands', *English Literary History*, 72 (2005), pp. 919–40. Shields offers a more nuanced periodisation of the Anglo-Scottish argument in her *Sentimental Literature and Anglo-Scottish Identity, 1745–1820* (Cambridge: Cambridge University Press, 2010), pp. 1–7, 136–8, 169. This is, however, still premised on Jacobitism as both singularly 'Highland' and universally 'Scottish', and again excludes Porter.

11. M. G. H. Pittock, *The Myth of the Jacobite Clans* (Edinburgh: Edinburgh Univeristy Press, 1995); D. Szechi, *The Jacobites: Britain and Europe, 1699–1788* (Manchester: Manchester University Press, 1994).

12. C. Kidd, *Subverting Scotland's Past: Scottish Whig Historians and the Creation of an Anglo-British Identity, 1689–c.1830* (Cambridge: Cambridge University Press, 1998); G. Morton, *Unionist Nationalism: Governing Urban Scotland, 1830–1860* (East Linton: Tuckwell Press, 1999).

13. Monnickendam, 'Scottish national tale', pp. 101–3, 111; Price, 'Introduction', pp. 19–20.

14. T. Carlyle, 'The amoral Scott', *London and Westminster Review*, January (1838); G. Lukács, *The Historical Novel* (London: Merlin Press, 1963).
15. P. Garside, 'The English novel in the Romantic Era', in Peter Garside and Rainer Schöwerling, *The English Novel 1770–1829. A Bibliographical Survey of Prose Fiction Published in the British Isles, II, 1800–1829* (Oxford: Oxford University Press, 2000), p. 60; D. Looser, *Women Writers and Old Age in Great Britain, 1750–1850* (Baltimore: Johns Hopkins University Press, 2008), pp. 146–7; I. Ferris, *The Achievement of Literary Authority* (Ithaca: Cornell University Press 1991), pp. 105–8, 137–44.
16. F. Price, 'Resisting "the spirit of innovation": the other historical novel and Jane Porter', *Modern Language Review*, 101 (2006), pp. 638–51.
17. Price, 'Introduction', pp. 25–33; Price, 'Resisting "the spirit of innovation"'; Thomas McLean, 'Nobody's argument: Jane Porter and the historical novel', *The Journal for Early Modern Cultural Studies*, 7 (2007), pp. 88–103; I. Dennis, *Nationalism and Desire in Early Historical Fiction* (Basingstoke: Palgrave Macmillan, 1997), p. 15.
18. Monnickendam, 'Scottish national tale', pp. 101–3, 111.
19. I. Ferris, 'Melancholy, memory, and the "narrative situation" of history in post-Enlightenment Scotland', in L. Davis, I. Duncan and J. Sorenson (eds), *Scotland and the Borders of Romanticism* (Cambridge: Cambridge University Press, 2004), p. 79.
20. Price, 'Introduction', pp. 18–20.
21. Tracy, *Irishness and Womanhood*, p. 15; A. Clayton, 'Enunciating difference: Sydney Owenson's (extra-) national tale', *The Journal of Irish and Scottish Studies*, 1, 2 (March 2008), p. 89.
22. Tracy, *Irishness and Womanhood*, p. 17.
23. Clayton, 'Enunciating difference', p. 93.
24. P. Fielding, 'Genre, geography and the question of the national tale: D. P. Campbell's Harley Radington', *European Romantic Review*, 23, 5 (2012), p. 596; Tracy, *Irishness and Womanhood*, p. 108.
25. Tracy, *Irishness and Womanhood*, p. 18; Trumpener, *Bardic Nationalism*, p 141; Fielding, *Scotland and the Fictions of Geography*, p. 4; R. J. Hill, *Picturing Scotland through the Waverley Novels. Walter Scott and the Origins of the Illustrated Novel* (Aldershot: Ashgate, 2010), chs 3 and 4.
26. E. Renan, 'What Is a Nation?', in G. Eley and R. G. Suny (eds), *Becoming National: A Reader* (Oxford: Oxford University Press, 1996), pp. 41–55.
27. Jane Porter to Walter Scott, 5 October 1831. NLS: MS 5317 fo. 185–6.

28. Katherine Grimston, Countess Clarendon, Letter: 1843 July 1, Grosvenor Crescent [London] to Agnes Strickland. A request originating from Miss Jane Porter and expressed through Lady Clarendon relating to a 'small wooden casket' once the property of Margaret, Queen of Scotland, then Mary Queen of Scots. Edinburgh University Library, Gen. 1070 fos 278–9. Letters from Miss Porter during this trip to her friends back in England were transcribed by *The Public Ledger*, 19 April 1842, p. 4.

29. Brown, Clements and Grundy, 'Jane Porter'; U. Pope-Hennessy, *Agnes Strickland: Biographer of the Queens of England* (London, 1940), pp. 112–13. Agnes Strickland, *Letters of Mary, Queen of Scots, and documents connected with her personal history. Now first published with an introd.* (London: Henry Colburn, 1842), XX [note].

30. 'Letter to Alexr. Young from Sir Walter Scott [November 1821]', in H. J. C. Grierson *et al.* (eds), *The Letters of Sir Walter Scott*, Vol. 7 (London, 1932–7). One 'rogue', having written to Sir Walter to compliment him on *Heart of Midlothian*, except for its fourth volume, then demands in a postscript for the novelist to recover Wallace's sword from England, *The Journal of Sir Walter Scott. From the Original manuscript at Abbotsford*, Vol. 1 (New York, 1970 [1890]), 10 December 1825.

31. 'Miss Jane Porter', in *National Portrait Gallery of Illustrious and Eminent Personages of the Nineteenth Century; with Memoirs*, Vol. V (London, 1834), p. 5; J. D. Carrick, *Life of Sir William Wallace of Elderslie* (London: Whittaker & Co., 1840), p. 96.

32. J. G. Lockhart, *Memoirs of the Life of Sir Walter Scott, Bart* (Edinburgh, 1844), 516; J. Patterson, *Memoir of Joseph Train, F.S.A. Scot., the antiquarian correspondent of Sir Walter Scott* (Glasgow, 1857); A description of Charles Dickens' encounter with Train is reported in *Household Words*, No. 173, 16 July 1853, pp. 475–6.

33. Jane Porter to Walter Scott, 31 May 1823, National Library of Scotland [NLS]: MS 3896 fo. 183–4.

34. Jane Porter to Walter Scott, 8 April 1828. NLS: MS 3906 fo. 196–7.

35. Jane Porter to Walter Scott, 10 September 1825. NLS: MS 3901 fo. 118–19.

36. J. Porter, *The Scottish Chiefs* (1840) 'Preface to the First Edition' [1809], p. vi.

37. Ibid.

38. J. Porter, 'Preface to the Second Edition', *The Scottish Chiefs* (1840), p. xii.

39. S. Daniels, 'Mapping National Identities: The Culture of Cartography

with Particular Reference to the Ordnance Survey', in G. Cubitt (ed.), *Imagining Nations* (Manchester: Manchester University Press, 1998).

40. C. W. J. Withers, 'The social nature of map making in the Scottish Enlightenment, c. 1682–c. 1832', *Imago Mundi*, 54 (2002), p. 52.
41. P. Fielding, *Scotland and the Fictions of Geography: North Britain, 1760–1830* (Cambridge: Cambridge University Press, 2008), p. 1.
42. C. Whatley, *The Scots and the Union* (Edinburgh: Edinburgh University Press, 2006).
43. D. McCrone, *Understanding Scotland: the Sociology of a Stateless Nation* (London: Routledge, 1992); McCrone, *Sociology of Nationalism*; R. J. Morris, 'Scotland, 1830–1914: The Making of a Nation within a Nation', in W. H. Fraser and R. J. Morris (eds), *People and Society in Scotland, Volume II, 1830–1914* (Edinburgh: John Donald, 1990); L. Paterson, *The Autonomy of Modern Scotland* (Edinburgh: Edinburgh University Press, 1994); L. Paterson, 'Civil Society and Democratic Renewal', in S. Baron, J. Field and T. Schüller (eds), *Social Capital: Social Theory and the Third Way* (Oxford: Oxford University Press, 2001); J. Hearn, *Claiming Scotland: National Identity and Liberal Culture* (Edinburgh: Polygon, 2000), pp. 19–21, 59–65, 117–19; Morton, *Unionist-Nationalism*; Morton and R. J. Morris, 'Civil Society, Governance and Nation: Scotland, 1832–1914', in W. Knox and R. A. Houston (eds), *The Penguin History of Scotland* (Harmondsworth: Penguin, 2001).
44. J. Keane (ed.), *Civil Society and the State: New European Perspectives* (London: Verso, 1988); K. Kumar, 'Civil society: an inquiry into the usefulness of a historical term', *British Journal of Sociology*, 44, 3, September 1993, p. 383.
45. T. Nairn, *The Break-Up of Britain*, 2nd edn (London: Verso, 1981), pp. 126–95.
46. T. Nairn, 'Internationalism and the second coming', *Daedalus*, 122, 3 (1993); T. Nairn, *Faces of Nationalism: Janus Revisited* (London: Verso, 1997), pp. 73–88; J. Mitchell, 'Conservatism in Twentieth Century Scotland: Society, Ideology and the Union', in M. Lynch (ed.), *Scotland, 1850–1979: Society, Politics and the Union* (London: Historical Association for Scotland, 1993), 26–34; J. Mitchell, *Strategies for Self-government: The Campaigns for a Scottish Parliament* (Edinburgh: Polygon, 1996), pp. 38–9.
47. G. Morton, 'What If? The Significance of Scotland's "Missing nationalism" in the Nineteenth Century', in D. Broun, R. Finlay and M. Lynch (eds), *Image and Identity: The Making and Re-making of Scotland through the Ages* (Edinburgh: John Donald, 1998).
48. Histories of the modern Scottish national movement can be found in: M. G. H. Pittock, *The Road to Independence: Scotland since*

the 1960s, 2nd edn (Edinburgh: Edinburgh University Press, 2014); Mitchell, *Strategies for Self-government*; R. J. Finlay, *Independent and Free: Scottish Politics and the Origins of the Scottish National Party, 1918–1945* (Edinburgh: John Donald, 1994); R. J. Finlay, *A Partnership for Good?: Scottish Politics and the Union since 1800* (Edinburgh: John Donald, 1997).

Chapter 3

Chronicles of Wallace

The historical record of William Wallace is not an extensive one, but what little survives is sufficiently robust to meet von Rankean stress on 'history as it was'. The most coherent set of documentation relates to Wallace's trial at Westminster Hall, a litany of accusations that can be set alongside summaries of his actions, capture and demise recorded within the *Lanercost Chronicle* (1272–1346). When taken along with a handful of evidential fragments, the mix of state records and contemporary testimony confirms a national tale built on historical not allegorical foundations. Wallace was a documented person, his biography recorded by contemporaries and by England's and Scotland's earliest historians. There is an empirical record that provides the kernel of fact to restrict parabolic seduction of the tale.

The most prominent historical record associated with Wallace, which survives in its original form, is the trading letter dispatched on 11 October 1297 to the merchants of Lübeck and Hamburg, sent in the name of Wallace and Andrew Murray when the two were stationed in Haddington.[1] A second letter, issued in their name in November of that year, marks a statement of protection 'under life and limb' to the Canons of Hexham Abbey, and is preserved within *The Chronicle of Walter Guisborough*. Recently discovered, a letter dated 7 November 1300 records King Philip IV of France urging Pope Boniface to grant Wallace support, although its exact context is uncertain.[2] Closer to home, a charter made out to Alexander Scrymgeour, dated 29 March 1298, grants him rights to the constabulary of Dundee castle and heritable entitlements to lands nearby. The charter is made in the name of William Wallace, knight, Guardian of the kingdom and leader of the army in the name of King John by consent of the kingdom's community.[3]

With little else contemporaneous with Wallace, it is with delicate foundations that the allegorical imagination of his life has developed. Given this empirical paucity, what is remarkable still is that the heroic tropes that formed have remained coherent over the long term, served by successful management of internal contradictions. Variously emphasised over time, the binaries that valorise Wallace are those of the single-handed hero, yet someone who is deeply communitarian in his motives; metaphorically a small man without a kingdom, but physically of a tall frame; a leader of weak Scotland, yet personally strong; the head of a group of lawbreakers, yet leader of the folk; an outlaw, yet knighted; an outsider, yet Guardian; a man of the people, yet a scion of the aristocracy.

Born around 1270, William Wallace was the second son of Alan Wallace, not, as was thought until recently, of Sir Malcolm Wallace.[4] The records suggest Alan famed land in Ayrshire, and members of his extended family can be traced to the lands in and around Renfrewshire. As a son of a minor noble William received few favours in securing a position, and he started to make his way in the world as an archer.[5] In the *Lanercost Chronicle* he is introduced as 'a certain bloody man' who 'had formerly between a chief of brigands in Scotland'. The earliest narratives set the tone, determining Wallace as a traitor to both Scotland and the English crown, with no support for his actions being freely offered by those he commanded.[6] His revenge upon Sir William Heselrig, Sheriff of Lanark, enacted for the death of his wife or mistress in 1297, is cited and condemned.[7] Wallace's victory over a larger-sized English army under the auspices of Warrene at the battle of Stirling Bridge in the same year is widely found, but usually set along with the accusation that Wallace skinned a strip of skin, from head to foot, of the English Treasurer Hugh de Cressingham.[8] The accusations here, and at the battle of Falkirk, over the actions of the Scottish nobility are much harder to pin down, yet these claims are made in subsequent accounts.[9] Wallace's knighthood is confirmed from a number of different directions, although this is still not without doubt – it appears to be 'community appointed' but accepted and commonly used.[10] Wallace's appointment as Guardian of Scotland in 1297, however, is not in question, evidenced by the trading letter to Lübeck and other administrative matters, and also by the chronicles recording his resignation (or removal) from this position after defeat at Falkirk in 1298.[11]

With each of the chronicles being written within powerful spheres of political intrigue and patronage networks, what is absent from them is also of interest. The *Lanercost Chronicle* passes over the betrayal by Menteith that led to Wallace's capture, offering no summary of the trial or reflection upon the weight of evidence against him. Nor is there any comment on the implications of his death: the source simply records the verdict that he was to 'die three times', to be drawn and hanged, disembowelled and dismembered, and his entrails burnt, after which his body was to be distributed to different parts of the land: his head upon London bridge, one arm to the bridge of Newcastle upon Tyne, the other to Berwick, his right foot to Perth, and his left to Aberdeen.[12] The trial document offers a slightly different dismemberment, determining one quarter of the body to be destined for Newcastle upon Tyne, one quarter for Berwick, one quarter for Stirling and one quarter for Perth; detail that comes from an eighteenth-century translation of the contemporary Latin record of the proceedings, contained with the Sir Robert Cotton collection.[13] In this translation, Wallace's crimes were listed as 'sedition, homicides, plunderings, fire-raisings, and diverse other felonies', and that 'he feloniously and seditiously slaughtered religious men and monks dedicated to God'. Couched in the rhetoric of peaceful overlordship, these charges were listed in order to restate Edward's control over Scotland and to remind the Scots that he appointed those who governed their nation. Edward warned the Scots 'to maintain his peace and give justice to all whomsoever according to the laws and customs of that land'. Yet while there are indications contained within other English sources, there is no corroboration for these indiscretions against the church-men, nor specifics on when they might have happened.[14] Moreover, their effect on later narrative accounts was to strengthen the heroic trope, enhancing Wallace's superhuman actions in order to face down the repetition of such impossibly abominable crimes.

The Lanercost and trial account of Wallace's life is backed up by the records of the English royal court showing the organisational effort made to support the campaign being waged in Scotland.[15] Little, though, is heard of the patriot after 1298, with conflicting evidence on his visit to France in 1299 or 1300, although the letter written on his behalf by Philip IV, dated 7 November 1300, is suggestive of a personal audience with the French king.[16] By 1302 or 1303 Wallace had returned to Scotland and into hiding, with the English records reporting Edward's rejection of a negotiated peace settlement.[17] A series of short, sharp interventions, harrying the English soldiers and stretching their resources, then followed, but Wallace's power base was weakened. By 1304, when Comyn looked to begin peace negotiations with Edward, the process was predicated on the capture of Wallace. By Edward's order, the Scots were to

> make an effort between now and the twentieth day of Christmas to take Sir William Wallace and hand him over to the king so that he can see how each one bears himself whereby he can have better regard towards the one who takes him, with regard to exile or ransom or amend of trespass or anything else in which they are obliged to the king.[18]

Individual and cross-border corroboration of Wallace's biography is of course undermined by the propaganda aim of these records. The historian, indeed, must remain cognisant of the contemporary agendas as well as the danger of projecting current political understandings onto the machinations of the Wars of Independence.[19] Nor are there personal artefacts to confer contemporaneity onto the national tale. Wallace left no self-reflective diary or letters in order that insight might be gleaned as to his character.[20] The chronicles give some account of speeches and battle-cries, but these sources are not directly of Wallace's time and their authenticity in this respect – despite replication – is doubtful. The Scottish chroniclers, though, offer an interpretation at odds with the English sources, one that 'reflect[s] differently on their respective countries' (pp. 6–7), yet the narrative sway is not straightforward. John of Fordun's *Chronica Gentis Scotorum* (c.1370), incorporating the *Gesta Annalia*, is the first of the Scottish narratives to mention Wallace.[21] Fordun's five books are described as the basis of every history prior to the death of James I, 'the indispensable groundwork of our annals' for the twelfth and thirteenth century.[22] The *Chronica Gentis Scotorum* was produced as a response to the compilation made primarily from the English chronicles.[23] Yet it is at this point that the origins of the myth begin to form, as the work of Edward Cowan has demonstrated.[24] In Fordun's tale Wallace rose from his 'den' and later resigned his guardianship to fight with the plebeians. It was determined that his defeat at the battle of Falkirk was due to the perfidiousness of the established aristocracy who resented this parvenu, with Fordun blaming Bruce for hastening the defeat by attacking the Scottish army with his own troops.[25] The event was undoubtedly decisive, as within one week Edward I had journeyed to Stirling and within two more weeks he had control of Stirling Castle.[26] Yet whereas Fordun was much less enthusiastic for Bruce than Barbour's renowned epic verse *The Bruce* (1375), the aristocratic betrayal of Wallace was less than complete.[27] MacDuff of Fife sent his two sons to fight with Wallace at Falkirk and for this earned the tag 'principled patriot',[28] yet this acts as no more than a footnote to the greater narrative of betrayal.

Fordun's use of source material from the thirteenth century is a mark of empirical integrity, but his choice of examples was deliberately presented to demonstrate the international credibility of an independent Scottish nation and of the Scottish monarchy.[29] This principal patriotic narrative was given further strength by the two chroniclers in the first half of the fifteenth century: the prior of Lochleven, Andrew of Wyntoun, who completed the *Oryginale Cronykil of Scotland* in the 1420s, and the Abbot of Inchcolm Abbey, Walter Bower, whose *Scotichronicon* was a continuation of Fordun and a product of the 1440s.[30] Each author relied on patronage to produce his chronicle. Wyntoun was supported by Sir John Wemyss of Leuchars and Kincaldrum (1372–1428), and Bower's patron was Sir David Stewart of Rosyth (d. 1444).[31] In Bower's account it is Wallace who brought the Scots to fight, done on the pretext of freeing Scots held captive.[32] In the Scottish propaganda, the English, who were defeated in 1297 'at a bridge on the river Forth beyond Stirling', were described as 'savage' and Wallace's victory was offered as a 'celestial gift to the faithful Scots'. Continuing the patriotic tone, the Scots were celebrated for the destruction they caused to the English lands as far as Stainmore in Northumbria,[33] complemented by Wallace's order that 'all Englishmen (both regular and secular clergy and laymen) [be expelled] from the kingdom of Scotland'.[34] Of all these accounts, it is Walter Bower who produced the earliest and most complete description of Wallace's family background, including an outline of his physical appearance that was later copied by Hary:

> He was a tall man with the body of a giant, cheerful in appearance with agreeable features, broad-shouldered and big-boned, with belly in proportion and lengthy flanks, pleasing in appearance but with a wild look, broad in the hips, with strong arms and legs, a most spirited fighting-man, with all his limbs very strong and firm.[35]

As a counter to the extraordinary barbarism foregrounded in the English chronicles, here Wallace's virtues were extolled as those of a conventional hero: he was claimed to be a handsome man who won the 'grace and favour of the hearts of all loyal Scots', and a generous helper of the poor and of widows. Wallace was recorded as a distinguished speaker who abhorred treachery and meted out his own (fair) justice upon thieves and robbers.[36] The extraordinary aspects of his personal chronicle came in his military exploits, including the story of Wallace having slain the English sheriff of Lanark, and his success as Guardian in marshalling all the local magnates under his authority, giving him the confidence to attack the English-controlled fortified towns and castles.[37] Other events are detailed, but it is the description of Wallace's betrayal by the aristocracy in the years 1297–8 where the most emotive language is used: phrases such as 'seditiously entered a secret plot', and 'What stubborn foll[y] of fools this was', lay down interpretative chords recalled regularly by later generations.[38] Simply because Wallace was not a man of their rank, Bower ascribes jealousy to the Scottish nobility, projecting their meagre support to his readership in the strongest of tones. And while there is no repeat of Fordun's claim that Bruce attacked the Scottish lines, the future king's desertion of the field is highlighted, as is a chastened Bruce spurred into rejecting the English side on the accusation of 'womanish cowardice' by Wallace.[39] Thereafter, Bower was keen to present Bruce as the key patriot-king, a path first trod by Fordun and then enhanced by Wyntoun.[40]

Wyntoun likely compiled his work in 1420, sixty years in advance of Hary, and his accounts of Wallace's early biographical detail, including his fights in Lanark, Stirling Bridge, and Falkirk, mark the patriot's first appearance in a chronicle produced in the Scots vernacular.[41] The use of the people's language, as Chapter 1 highlighted, is key to widening the story, creating the 'one, yet many' of national life.[42] But whereas the Scots vernacular was acceptable north of the border, this was not the case to the south. In order to reach an English audience with his history, the Scot John Mair (or Major) chose Latin in which to construct a Wallacian heroic trope in his influential *History of Greater Britain* (1521). Specifically in his interpretation, Mair defends the patriot's reputation from his characterisation in Caxton's Chronicle before countering those chroniclers who doubted Wallace would make the

upward journey from purgatory to Heaven. Claiming excesses are
an unfortunate consequence of warfare, and that Wallace was fighting for the higher principle of his country's freedom, Mair defends
the blood spilling as just, part of the patriot's efforts to reclaim the
boundaries of Scotland as established under Alexander.[43]

The connection Mair draws between Wallace and the heroes of
antiquity placed the patriot in classical terms: 'Like Hannibal or
Ulysses he understood to draw up an army in order of battle, while
like another Telamonian Ajax he could carry out the fight in open
field'.[44] In interpreting both the battle at Falkirk and the death of
Wallace as the betrayal of the magnates, Mair chose equanimity
over outrage, arguing 'it is a feature of nobles generally . . . to prefer
the yoke of a superior to that of an inferior', before adding a con-
spiratorial twist that the aristocracy wished to weaken the power of
both Wallace and Edward in order to facilitate their own return to
power.[45] The empiricism behind this analysis is based on little but
the repetition of others: Mair's proof on the execution of Wallace,
for example – placing it at Tyburn on 24 August 1305 – is based on a
simple reference to 'the English chroniclers',[46] evidence he would not
otherwise rely on to determine if Wallace did visit France, finding no
corroboration in the Latin chronicles or in the French accounts.[47]
Yet Mair was a historian whose admiration for Wallace was sufficiently influential to balance the otherwise damning verdict that had
been fixed by the English state records and by the English chroniclers. Of longest-lasting influence was his emboldening of Wallace
as a hero who embodied 'the people', a superhuman ordinary man
who fought in the interest of the folk; whereas, contrastingly, 'the
Scottish nobles pursued him with a deadly hatred, inasmuch as his
conspicuous valour threw their own deeds into the shade'.[48]

*   *   *

The conflicting early modern interpretations of the limited evidence
served to create a Wallacian national tale that remained mutable.
While being one of the best English accounts of Scottish affairs,
the *Lanercost Chronicle* contains much on Scottish depredations
in England.[49] The Prior's description of the battle of Stirling Bridge
highlights atrocities that came after the Scots' victory: Hugh de
Cressingham being skinned on the orders of Wallace; Wallace
and his supporters chasing the survivors as far as Berwick before
'putting to death the few English that they found therein'; Wallace's

soldiers moving to Northumberland where they 'wast[ed] all the land, committing arson, pillage and murder'; the same happening in Carlisle before the soldiers returned to Northumberland 'to lay waste more completely what they had left at first'.[50] Wallace is accused of besieging the English-held fortresses in April, achieving victory through 'famine in the castles' which was followed up by behaviour decidedly lacking in chivalry: 'when they had promised to the English conditions of life and limb and safe conduct to their own land on surrendering the castles, William Wallace did not keep faith with them'.[51] Such language has been labelled xenophobic, but is contextualised by fears that Edward was underestimating Wallace's threat in the north of England.[52] The priory of Lanercost is eight miles from Carlisle, and the consternation of the writers – if that was where it was complied, and there is some debate – is understandable.[53] Unlike the gloss of Fordun or Wyntoun, Wallace's exploits are not justified within the 'outlaw tradition', where legitimacy and morality are ascribed to the underdog when faced by unbending and cruel authority.[54] Wallace's morality, then, is the first heroic myth to be undermined:

The vilest doom is fittest for thy crimes
Justice demands that thou shoudst die three times
Thou pillager of many a sacred shrine
Butcher of thousands, threefold death be thine!
So shall the English from thee gain relief,
Scotland! be wise, and choose a nobler chief.[55]

Yet the chronicle blames many of Scotland's future ills on Alexander III's wife Yolande, unfairly castigating her for Alexander's desire to be home to celebrate her birthday on the stormy night which cost his life.[56] Edward I took up the position of feudal superior in Scotland, ordering the necessary historical proof to be uncovered to back up his claim.[57] It involved consummate manipulation of the evidence, in a highly complex and confusing way that adds little security to our historical understanding.[58] Corroborating evidence does exist, though, which fleshes out aspects of the military engagement between the two nations. The army assembled by Edward on his return from fighting in France in 1298, and in anger at the defeat at Stirling Bridge, was estimated to be one of the largest of his reign.[59] The valuation rolls show the number of horses invested by the English in the campaign at over 1,350.[60] English sources were often sceptical of Edward's gains after Falkirk. The Scots' reluctance to engage them in battle wasted the time of the armies put together at great logistical expense, with siege machinery and prefabricated bridges readied for deployment.[61] Financial help came from the archbishop of York, with military supplies for Edward's army coming from throughout Yorkshire, but Scotland remained a distraction to England's military objectives in Europe.[62] Of all aspects of Wallace's biography, the sources are richest at the death. After his crimes were listed, Wallace, having been accused of issuing writs in the name of King John against the sovereignty of Edward, was made to wear a crown of thorns to represent English contempt for his rulership of the northern kingdom.[63] The means of his death, hanging, disembowelling, and execution, with his intestines burned and his body quartered, were punishments to reflect each one of his crimes – robbery, murder, treason and sacrilege.[64]

From Wallace's death at Smithfield in London, martyrdom primed a heroic narrative. What transformed this raw material into Scotland's national tale was the transformation of the chronicles by means of historical imagination allied to the use of vernacular language and the printing press. The most influential teller of the tale was Blind Hary, or Henry the Minstrel, creator of *Wallace*. He is a man of whom even less is known than his biographical subject, yet in the transformation from recitation, to manuscript, to vernacular and modernised prose, over five centuries, his epic verse on the life of Wallace has at various times been regarded as the most common book to be found in Scottish households, save the Bible.[65]

NOTES

1. F. Watson, 'Sir William Wallace: What We Do – and Don't – Know', in E. J. Cowan (ed.), *The Wallace Book* (Edinburgh: John Donald, 2007), p. 33; E. Cowan, 'The Wallace Factor in Scottish History', in R. Jackson and S. Wood (eds), *Images of Scotland*, in *The Journal of Scottish Education*, Occasional Paper, No. 1 (Dundee: The Northern College, 1997), p. 7; R. Nicholson, *Scotland: The Later Middle Ages* (Edinburgh: Oliver & Boyd, 1974), p. 55; Barrow, *Robert Bruce*, p. 128.
2. The reason the document was found in Tower of London in the 1830s is also unclear, http://www.nationalarchives.gov.uk/news/661. htm (accessed 31 January 2014).
3. A. A. M. Duncan, 'William, Son of Alan Wallace: The Documents',

in E. J. Cowan (ed.), *The Wallace Book* (Edinburgh: John Donald, 2007), pp. 42–3; Barrow, *Bruce*, p. 129; Nicholson, *Scotland: The Later Middle Ages*, p. 52.

4. Duncan, 'William, Son of Alan Wallace', pp. 50–2; Watson, 'Sir William Wallace', p. 26; whereas Nicholson, *Scotland: The Later Middle Ages*, p. 52, recorded Sir Malcolm Wallace as being the patriot's father.
5. Watson, 'Sir William Wallace', p. 27.
6. *The Chronicle of Lanercost, 1272–1346*, trans. H. E. Maxwell (Glasgow: MacLehose, 1913), p. 426.
7. Ibid.
8. Ibid., p. 428.
9. A careful exploration of how the relationship of Wallace to the Scottish nobility is recorded in the chronicles and by later scholars is found in: A. Grant, 'Bravehearts and Coronets: Images of William Wallace and the Scottish Nobility', in E. J. Cowan (ed.), *The Wallace Book* (Edinburgh: John Donald, 2007), pp. 86–106.
10. E. J. Cowan, 'Identity. Freedom and the Declaration of Arbroath', in D. Broun, R. J. Finlay and M. Lynch (eds), *Image and Identity: The Making and Re-making of Scotland through the Ages* (Edinburgh: John Donald, 1998), p. 60; Barrow, *Robert Bruce*, p. 116. Verse contained in the Lanercost Chronicle focuses on Wallace's knighthood, although the chronicle's editor, Herbert Maxwell, can find no record of this, *Chronicle of Lanercost*, p. 168; Duncan, 'William, Son of Alan Wallace', pp. 46–7.
11. Recounted by Bower, quoted in Nicholson, *Scotland: The Later Middle Ages*, p. 58; F. Watson, 'Sir William Wallace', pp. 33–5.
12. *Chronicle of Lanercost*, pp. 484–5
13. An accessible translation of the trial is found in Duncan, 'William, Son of Alan Wallace', pp. 60–3, with the intentions for displaying the patriot's body parts noted under point 9 (p. 63); see also: http://www. educationscotland.gov.uk/scotlandshistory/warsofindependence/exec utionofwallace/index.asp. (accessed 1 February 2014).
14. Duncan, 'William, Son of Alan Wallace', p. 56.
15. M. Prestwich, *War, Politics and Finance under Edward I* (London: Faber & Faber, 1972), p. 35; M. Prestwich, 'The Battle of Stirling Bridge: An English Perspective', in E. J. Cowan (ed.), *The Wallace Book* (Edinburgh: John Donald, 2007), pp. 64–6.
16. *Documents Illustrative of Sir William Wallace, his life and times*, ed. J. Stevenson (Edinburgh, Maitland Club No. 54, 1841), p. xv; Watson, 'Sir William Wallace', p. 36.
17. See J. G. Bellamy, *The Law of Treason in England in the Later Middle Ages* (Cambridge, Cambridge University Press, 1970), pp. 30–9.

18. Cited in Watson, 'Sir William Wallace', p. 39.
19. F. Watson, 'The Enigmatic Lion: Scotland, Kinship and National Identity in the Wars of Independence', in D. Broun, R. Finlay and M. Lynch (eds), *Image and Identity: The Making and Re-making of Scotland through the Ages* (Edinburgh: John Donald, 1998), pp. 23–4.
20. Cowan, 'Declaration of Arbroath', p. 58; E. J. Cowan, 'William Wallace: "The Choice of the Estates"', in E. J. Cowan (ed.), *The Wallace Book* (Edinburgh: John Donald, 2007), p. 9.
21. My thanks to Steve Boardman for advice on the early Scottish chronicles.
22. The work was added to by Walter Bower in the 1440s, with 11 additional books, known as the *Scotichronicon, Johannis de Fordun Chronica gentis Scotorum*, ed., W. F. Skene (Edinburgh: Edmonston & Douglas), Vol. I, p. xii–xiii. ix.
23. Ibid., p. 234.
24. Cowan confirms that almost all the contemporary sources on Wallace derive from 'enemy sources', E. J. Cowan, 'William Wallace', p. 9.
25. Cowan, 'The Wallace Factor in Scottish History', p. 7; Cowan, 'Declaration of Arbroath', p. 59.
26. Watson, 'Sir William Wallace', p. 35.
27. Maxwell, *Early Chronicles*, p. 247.
28. J. Bannerman, 'MacDuff of Fife', in A. Grant and K.J. Stringer (eds), *Medieval Scotland: Crown, Lordship and Community. Essays presented to G. W. S. Barrow* (Edinburgh: Edinburgh University Press, 1993), pp. 35, 38. The MacDuff family suffered great losses, which are recorded in the chronicles, *Scotichronicon by Walter Bower*, ed. N. F. Shead, W. B. Stevenson and D. E. R. Watt, with A. Borthwick, R. E. Latham, J. R. S. Phillips and M. S. Smith, Vol. 6, p. 97, lines 46–7; *The Orygynale Cronykil of Scotland by Andrew of Wyntoun*, Volume II, ed. David Laing (Edinburgh: Edmonston & Douglas, 1872), pp. 347; *A History of Greater Britain as well England as Scotland compiled from the ancient authorities by John Major* (1521), ed. and trans. A. Constable (Edinburgh: Publications of the Scottish History Society, Vol. X, 1892), p. 200.
29. A. Young, *Robert the Bruce's Rivals: The Comyns, 1212–1314* (East Linton: Tuckwell Press, 1997), pp. 1–2.
30. Ibid.
31. J. MacQueen, 'The Literature of Fifteenth-Century Scotland', in J. M. Brown (ed.), *Scottish Society in the Fifteenth Century* (London: Edward Arnold, 1977), p. 196.
32. *Scotichronicon by Walter Bower*, ed. D. E. R. Watt (Aberdeen: Aberdeen University Press, 1998), Vol. 9, p. 83, lines 313–15.

33. Ibid., p. 83, lines 321–5, 330–3.
34. *Scotichronicon by Walter Bower*, ed. N. F. Shead, W. B. Stevenson and D. E. R. Watt, with A. Borthwick, R. E. Latham, J. R. S. Phillips and M. S. Smith (Aberdeen: Aberdeen University Press, 1991), Vol. 6, p. 63, lines 50–4, p. 73, line 63.
35. Ibid., p. 83, lines 3–8.
36. Ibid., p. 83, lines 11–23.
37. Ibid., p. 83, line 24, pp. 83–5, lines 35–45.
38. Ibid., p. 93, lines 1–7, 16–19.
39. Ibid., pp. 95, 97, lines 9–42.
40. Young, *Robert the Bruce's Rivals*, p. 3; N. H. Reid, 'Alexander III: The Historiography of a Myth', in N. H. Reid (ed.), *Scotland in the Reign of Alexander III 1249–1286* (Edinburgh: John Donald, 1990), pp. 191, 193.
41. Cowan, 'The Wallace Factor', p. 7; *The Orygynale Cronykil of Scotland by Andrew of Wyntoun*, ed. D. Laing (Edinburgh: Edmonston & Douglas, 1872), Vol. II, pp. 339–45, 358.
42. Timothy Brennan, quoted in H. K. Bhabha, *Nation and Narration* (London: Routledge, 1990).
43. J. Mair, *A History of Greater Britain, As Well as England and Scotland* (Edinburgh: T. & A. Constable, 1892), pp. 204, 208.
44. Mair, *Greater Britain*, p. 197. Placing Wallace and other medieval heroes alongside the greats of antiquity is examined in F. Riddy, 'Unmapping the Territory: Blind Hary's *Wallace*', in E. J. Cowan (ed.), *The Wallace Book* (Edinburgh: John Donald, 2007).
45. Mair, *Greater Britain*, p. 199. Although Mair would otherwise support the nobility as the mainstays of the constitution, argues E. J. Cowan, 'The Political Ideas of a Covenanting Leader: Archibald Campbell, Marquis of Argyll 1607–1661', in R. A. Mason (ed.), *Scots and Britons: Scottish Political Thought and the Union of 1603* (Cambridge: Cambridge University Press, 1994), pp. 244–5.
46. Mair, *Greater Britain*, p. 203.
47. Ibid., pp. 204–6. It was the kind of argument to be later dismissed by J. D. Carrick, '. . . we do not see that a great lie told in the classical language of ancient Rome should be entitled to a larger portion of public faith than a lesser one told in the modern patois of Scotland', *Life of Sir William Wallace, Knight of Ellerslie and Guardian of Scotland*, 2nd edn (Glasgow: Griffen & Co., 1827), preface.
48. Cited in Grant, 'Bravehearts and Coronets', pp. 95–6.
49. A point made in A. King, 'Englishmen, Scots and Marchers: national and local identities in Thomas Gray's *Scalacronica*, *Northern History*, 36, 2 (2000), p. 231.
50. *Chronicle of Lanercost*, p. 164. Fergusson has pointed out that the

story of the skin being turned into horse-girths is likely to originate from the *Scalacronica*, which states: 'It was said that the Scots caused him to be flayed, and in token of hatred made thongs of his skin.' Fergusson gives greater weight to Hemingsburgh: '. . . the Scots flayed him, and divided his skin among themselves in moderate-sized pieces, certainly not as relics, but for hatred of him', J. Fergusson, *William Wallace: Guardian of Scotland* (London: Alexander MacLehose & Co., 1938), pp. 68–9.

51. *Chronicle of Lanercost*, p. 165.
52. F. J. Watson, *Under the Hammer: Edward I and Scotland, 1286–1306* (East Linton: Tuckwell Press, 1998), p. 51.
53. Reid is doubtful that the chronicle was actually completed at the priory, but is convinced that it is of northern English origin, 'Alexander III', in Reid (ed.), *Scotland in the Reign of Alexander III*, p. 183.
54. G. Seal, *The Outlaw Legend: A Cultural Tradition in Britain, America and Australia* (Cambridge: Cambridge University Press, 1996), pp. 1–18.
55. *Chronicle of Lanercost*, p. 176.
56. Reid, 'Alexander III', pp. 183–4.
57. A. A. M. Duncan, 'The Process of Norham, 1291', in P Cross and S. Lloyd (eds), *Thirteenth Century England*, No. 5 (Woodbridge: Boydell, 1995), pp. 207–8; M. Prestwich, *The Three Edwards: War and State in England 1272–1377* (London: Weidenfeld & Nicolson, 1980), p. 44.
58. Watson, *Under the Hammer*, pp. 11–20, untangles the web well.
59. Prestwich, *War, Politics and Finance under Edward I*, p. 35.
60. Ibid., p. 52.
61. Prestwich, *The Three Edwards*, pp. 49–50.
62. Watson, *Under the Hammer*, pp. 52–4, who argues that Yorkshire was an area suffering because of the Scottish threat, but not yet devastated in comparison with the English counties on the border.
63. Ibid., p. 50.
64. Prestwich, *The Three Edwards*, p. 50.
65. Cowan, 'William Wallace', p. 12.

Chapter 4

Hary's Tale

The first great, and the greatest, narration of Wallace's biography is found in Blind Hary's *Wallace*, an epic poem of 11,861 lines within eleven books that dates from the final quarter of the fifteenth century.[1] *Wallace* is written in decasyllabic couplets, for what is the first known time in any lengthy Scottish verse, and its structure alone emphasises its literary merit and place in the national canon.[2] What evidence there is of Hary's biography comes from the accounts of the Lord High Treasurer in 1490 which record payments made to 'Blind Hary' for what appears to be the reciting of poetry and song;[3] and from John Mair, who recalls: 'There was one Henry, blind from his birth who, in the time of my childhood, fabricated a whole book about William Wallace, and therein he wrote down in our native rhymes – and this was a kind of composition in which he had much skill – all that passed current among the people of his day'.[4] Whether or not Hary could perform with skill and panache, the metre deployed is not easily given to recitation, and doubt remains as to whether the poetry was truly representative of what might have been presented.[5] There is no extant manuscript which is traced to Hary's hand, and the earliest known manuscript was for a long time bound with Barbour's *The Bruce* in the Advocates Library in Edinburgh, having been transcribed by John Ramsay in 1488 (the year following his transcription of *The Bruce*).[6] Of the attempts to date *Wallace*, the most convincing work comes from Mathew McDiarmid. Comparing the known whereabouts of individuals for whom the sources are greater, McDiarmid concludes that the years 1474 to 1479 were the most likely time of its composition.[7] Hary first appeared as the named author of *Wallace* in the 1645 edition printed by Robert Bryson, which noted it was 'Written in Latine by Master Iohn Blair . . .

and tuned in Scots meeter by one called Blind Hary'. Authorship is credited to Henry the Minstrel in Robert Sanders' edition of 1665 and the author is confirmed as Henry, commonly called Blind Hary, in Morrison's 1790 edition. The popularity of the designation 'Henry the Minstrel' is settled in John Jamieson's 1820 edition and preferred throughout the Victorian period when Wallace's chivalric reputation and domestic motivations were better fitted by a biographer with such a sobriquet.[8]

The anti-Englishness that features prominently in Hary's verse has been deciphered as reflecting late fifteenth-century opposition to the pro-Englishness of James III.[9] There is certainly evidence that *Wallace* was used as propaganda by the Duke of Albany to oppose the treaty between Scotland and England in 1474 and, indeed, that the life of the duke's steward, James Liddale, was used as a model for the epic verse.[10] Macdougall notes that along with Liddale, Hary received the patronage of Sir William Wallace of Craigie.[11] But in other respects the evidence remains weak. An impression of *Wallace* published in 1709 claimed that it had been 'turned from Latin into Scots metre by one called Blind Hary', but no records are cited.[12] John Blair's Latin book is claimed as Hary's source, but again there is nothing but Hary's words to substantiate this: 'Eftir the pruiff geyffin fra the Latin buk/Quilk master Blayr in his tym vndertuk'.[13]

There are many reasons, then, to cast doubt upon attempts to verify the authenticity of Hary, or his knowledge of Wallace. It should never be downplayed that the verse set down its biographical detail over a century and a half after Wallace had been executed, and that the claim to a Latin book contemporary with Wallace is nothing more than a common rhetorical device of the period. Some have suggested that the author of *Wallace* might have benefited from Ramsay as a collaborator, although this has been dismissed by others.[14] Writing in 1803, Sibbald discarded the possibility of a co-author by arguing that Hary must be the sole author because the poem was in a universally understood (that is, simplistic) form which required no tinkering from Ramsay or anyone else. In Sibbald's characterisation Hary was a wandering mendicant and the quality of the text was appropriate for someone of that status[15] – a thin argument, yet not untypical of the analytical proof put forward when corroboration was missing. Similarly, too, the argument that 'Blind Hary' was a pseudonym for some unknown author, used as a means to deflect from the poem's anti-Englishness, although few have been prepared to project the likelihood of such empathy back to the time of Hary.[16] With the work of Dunbar being the most notable, the earliest publications by the printers Chepman & Myllar tended to be in the vernacular style.[17] A product of those printing presses, and dated around 1508, the first printed edition of *Wallace* exists only as fragments, with no new edition known until 1570. In between there is evidence of the tale entering Scottish folklore among the peasantry, passed down through recitation. The *Complaynt of Scotland*, complied in 1548 and published the next year, records shepherds telling tales of Wallace and Bruce.[18] Much more accessible than the language of the Latin chronicles of Fordun, Bower and Lanercost, the vernacular language of the *Complaynt* and *Wallace* furthered the transition from the interior world of text to the exterior thought-world of the nation's identity (p. 11).[19] The strongest evidence of the popularity of *Wallace* comes from the number of editions published by Scotland's printing houses:[20]

1	Manuscript in Advocates Library	1488
2	'A Fragment', Edinburgh, Chepman & Myllar	?1508
3	The Actis and Deidis – Robert Lekprevik	1570
4	The Life and Acts – Henry Charteris	1594
5	Robert Charteris	1601
6	Adro Hart	1611
7	Adro Hart	1618
8	Andro Hart	1620
9	Edward Raban for David Melvill	1630
10	Iames Bryson	1640
11	R. Bryson	1645
12	George Lithgow (Gideon Lithgovv)	1648
13	Society of Stationers	1661
14	Gideon Lithgow	1661
15	Robert Sanders	1665
16	Andro Anderson	1666
17	Andrew Anderson	1673/5
18	Published in Glasgow by Robert Sanders	1684
19	Published in Glasgow by Robert Sanders	1685
20	Published in Glasgow by Robert Sanders	1690
21	Published in Glasgow by Robert Sanders	1699

22	Printed in the Year	1701
23	Heirs and Successor of A. Anderson	1709
24	Heirs and Successor of A. Anderson	1711
25	Heirs and Successor of A. Anderson	1713
26	Robert Sanders	1713
27	Published in Belfast by James Blow	1728
28	Alex Carmichael & Alex Miller	1736/7
29	John Robertson & Mrs McLean	1747
30	Published in Glasgow by Archibald McLean	1756
31	Printed in the Year 1715 but suppressed until 1758	1758
32	Three Volumes by R. Morrison jnr	1790
33	James Ballantyne & Co.	1820
34	Published in Glasgow by Ogle & Co.	1869
35	Scottish Text Society	1889
36	Scottish Text Society	1938
37	Scottish Text Society	1968

This publishing history is very similar to that of Barbour's epic, although the geographical spread of *Wallace*'s printings is greater.[21] McKinlay lists twelve popular editions of *The Bruce* between 1571 and 1914, seven critical editions from 1790 to 1909, three editions of 'Gordon's *Bruce*' in 1615, 1718 and 1753, and seven editions of 'Harvey's *Bruce*' in the eighteenth century, with a further ten editions by 1859.[22] Exactly how many printings of *Wallace* were published is debatable, although they are generally assumed to have outnumbered those of *The Bruce*: there were an estimated 23 editions of *Wallace* published before 1707 and 47 editions by the eve of the First World War; a Gaelic edition, though, was not printed until the 1920s despite claims that this was the language spoken by the patriot.[23] A monopoly for twenty years on publishing *Wallace* had been granted by the Privy Council to the Edinburgh printer Thomas Finlayson (1611–31), which held firm except for Andro Hart's editions.[24] Brunsden has cast some doubt on the existence of all these different impressions, but verifies that the majority were valid and extant, and can be set alongside the undoubted sales success of Hamilton of Gilbertfield's abridgement in 1722. That shortened account was read widely across Scotland, with a new edition published every decade and ten editions issued between 1802 and 1857.[25] In its absence from Scotland's printing presses thereafter, the Wallace narrative was dominated by

Porter and numerous synopses in chapbook form, although in 1998 Hamilton's prose was once again reissued, containing a new introduction.[26]

Unlike his father with his edition of 1685, Robert Sanders (junior), upon inheriting the business, produced an edition of *Wallace* in 1713 that dispensed with a number of the Scoticisms present in Hart's editions.[27] Linguistically, the reprints of Hary had changed most with Hart's edition of 1618, but in the century that followed the idiom altered little and only limited variation is found.[28] There was, though, distinction from the 'Catholic' manuscript of 1488 in the Protestant version published by Robert Lekprevik in 1570. Here the publisher paid homage to the Protestant party in the 1560s and 1570s by producing a text that claimed to be God's word set against superstitions and blindness.[29] This modification was designed to catch the mood of patriotic Protestantism,[30] just as nearly two centuries later Hamilton of Gilbertfield appealed directly to Presbyterian Scots of his generation by introducing Dame Fortune in the place of the Virgin Mary in the dream sequences of the narrative poem.[31]

Once the eighteenth century begins, the language of *Wallace* remains fairly consistent and the narrative sustains the tropes fixed by Hary. The evidence of sales alone is suggestive that Hary was more popular that Barbour throughout the eighteenth century, a balance confirmed by the success of the modernising text by Hamilton. This conclusion can be strengthened by examining how the Wallace tale held sway over Robert Burns's thoughts, in turn confirming the book's place in the national consciousness.[32] In writing to Mrs Frances Anna Dunlop, who claimed descent from Wallace herself, Burns maintained 'The first books I met with in my early years, which I perused with pleasure, were the lives of Hannibal and Sir William Wallace' (15 November 1786).[33] Burns' oft-quoted lines to Dr John Moore are stronger still regarding the narrative's influence on his formative self: '. . . the story of Wallace poured a Scottish prejudice in my veins which will boil along there till the flood-gates of life shut in eternal rest' (2 August 1787).[34] There is evidence that Burns owned at least one edition of *Wallace*, with a 'Mr Robert Burns, Ellisland' named as a subscriber of Robert Morrison's edition in three volumes published in Perth in 1790. This impression was sponsored by the Republican and antiquarian David Steuart Erskine, 11th Earl of Buchan,[35] although

Burns claimed to have taken the last stanza of 'Scots Wha Hae'
(first published as *Robert Bruce's March to Bannockburn* in 1793)
from the 'common stall' edition of *Wallace*.[36] Whichever impression he did consult, Burns labelled the stanza a couplet worthy of
Homer:

> *Scots Wha Hae*
> Lay the proud usurpers low!
> Tyrants fall in every foe!
> Liberty's in every blow!
>
> *Wallace*
> A false usurper sinks in every foe;
> And liberty returns with every blow

As part of Scotland's cultural impression in Ireland, that would
include the poetry of Burns, James Blow published a Belfast impression of *Wallace* in 1728.[37] The connection with Burns confirmed
Hary's verse as the foundation to Scotland's national tale in the
modern period, its ubiquity leading to wide internationalisation
of the narrative's tropes. While James Hogg recalled that it was
not until his eighteenth year that he read Hary's verse, and wished
it was in narrative form, still he acknowledged its influence upon
him.[38] Thomas Babington Macaulay also recalled the biography
of Wallace from his teenage years, revelling in the stories he heard
from his father, favouring the superiority of 'Scotch blood' and of
Scottish missionary work.[39] The industrialist and philanthropist
from Dunfermline, Andrew Carnegie, who later helped fund the
'crown' added atop the National Wallace Monument, and the hall
of heroes therein, told of *Wallace* being read to him by his uncle:
'Wallace, of course, was our hero. Everything heroic centred in
him.'[40] In these examples at least, *Wallace* had a profound effect
because, in its recall, the narrative fulfilled the expectations of
personal nationalisms, sustaining a reading of history that fitted
contemporary lives.

*   *   *

Hary's reputation developed from his characterisation as a free
spirit and outsider, someone uninhibited by authority. To the
romantics, the greatness of *Wallace* comes from the appeal of its
author, despite the lack of evidence to substantiate any conclu-
sions. Only a forename is commonly accepted: Hary, or Harry

in the English usage, or Henry. Victorians preferred Henry the Minstrel.[41] Schofield, writing in 1920, sums up the transition:

> And, now, to give him more dignity, scholars write his name on the title page of editions, and elsewhere, in the form 'Henry the Minstrel', as if the 'blind' were too doubtful, the 'Harry' too familiar, and only 'the Minstrel' worthy to stand as the poet's memorable designation.[42]

The image being satirised is one which came to dominate in the nineteenth century by means of a love of chivalry, romanticism, and narrative strength in the face of earnest record compilation by Scotland's bibliographical and historical clubs. The free-spirited characterisation of Hary is typified by two patriotic historians of this period. In his analysis of Scottish poetry, John Veitch described Hary as 'truly a wandering minstrel – blind, aged and poor',[43] whereas John Hill Burton a decade later eulogised that 'Hary was a blind wandering minstrel, but he belonged to the days when his craft might be that of a gentleman . . .'[44] Veitch stated confidently that Hary's only means of subsistence came from 'the voluntary gifts of his patrons';[45] Burton affirms that 'while he addressed the commonality to rouse their patriotic ardour, he was received at great men's tables'.[46] Others tied Hary's simpleton image to the ignoble birth of Wallace.[47] Henderson's *Scottish Vernacular Literature* used the lowly origins of Hary as an excuse for the historical deficiencies and stylistic gaffes in the poem.[48] Robertson's summation in the *Lives of the Scottish Poets* (1821) is that while *Wallace* is not great poetry, if it were indeed produced by someone who was blind, that person should be ranked with Barbour or Chaucer.[49] W. T. Fyfe stated that because Hary was blind he employed others to read for him;[50] Robertson likened Hary to Homer, and therefore considered him, like Homer, blind from birth;[51] while Watson accepted Mair's statement affirming the poet's blindness without question.[52] Henderson surmised that whoever wrote *Wallace* was clearly educated and well-travelled – from the author's use of Latin and French – and that the verse could not be the product of someone who was either lowly born or who had led a sheltered and narrow life handicapped by blindness.[53] Added to this line of verification is the poet's remarkably detailed and vivid use of Scotland's scenery and regional differences in telling of Wallace's progress during the few short years of his activity, and the longer years of his exile, which would not be possible by imagination alone.[54] Schofield, meanwhile, argues against Hary's blindness on the grounds that he cites so much contemporary and near-contemporary literature (Chaucer, Barbour and Eglintoun), indicating that the poet was both sighted and educated (although acknowledging that we have no access to Hary's library or letters to allow us to know with any certainty).[55] And after surveying the analysis produced in the nineteenth century, McDiarmid comes down on the side that the evidence suggests 'it was Hary, not Blind Hary who constructed the poem'.[56]

The alternative explanation offered by the nation's historiographers was that Hary's blindness came later in life. Neilson, for balance, summoned the writings of John Mair and William Dunbar to insist that Hary was blind, but argued that the infirmity did not commence until his later years.[57] John Veitch agreed with Tytler that Hary could not have been blind from birth, but again the evidence is no more than circumstantial, based on the likely activities of a wandering minstrel needing to travel to meet the market for his work: 'carrying his rhymes in his memory as his stock-in-trade, reciting them by lowly hearth and in lordly hall, and touching with his own patriotic flame the hearts of all ranks of his countrymen'.[58] For James Moir to believe Hary could not be blind from birth, the reasoning comes from the content of the text, not historical corroboration.[59] Others looked to define 'blindness', such as W. A. Craigie, who suggested that Hary could have been blind at some time during his life or merely called blind because he suffered from less than perfect sight.[60] He was unable to offer a definitive answer, and concluded that whether Hary was blind or not, this should not impinge on judgement of the poem as a piece of literature, irrespective of whoever it was compiled the verse (there is no name on the early editions). In McDiarmid's analysis, the conclusion arrived at was that Hary wrote the text as an old man (dying three years after receiving payments recorded in the Treasurer's Accounts), who lost his sight late in life.[61] It was a more conservative view, but offered a safer yield in a field of partial evidence. Without the state of Hary's blindness (if he was blind at all), nor even who the author really was, being known, speculation had overtaken analysis – but it kept the national tale in the forefront of academic discourse.

Sobriety, again, should also be called for when the accusations of Hary's plagiarism are listed. For a blind and lowly-born man, he had a very apparent tendency of borrow the work of others. A close comparison of Hary with Wyntoun finds a level of textual similarity beyond the justification that the sources were common to each, with Wallace's speech-making at key events lifted from Wyntoun's Chronicle.[62] George Neilson has shown Hary's debt to *The Bruce*, with incidents ascribed to Wallace which happened after the patriot's death and in fact concerned King Robert.[63] A French knight who praised the prowess and integrity of Bruce is transmuted into one who praised Wallace; and a key stratagem used to win the only historical battle of Lowdonhill is taken by Hary away from Bruce and the triumph ascribed to Wallace.[64] It is little wonder that when compiling the *Calendar of Documents Illustrative of William Wallace*, Joseph Bain was compelled to castigate the integrity of Hary, citing his plagiarism from Barbour:

> Bruce has been fortunate in his historian. While the real fame of his pre-cursor Wallace has been obscured by the legendary exploits chronicled by the Blind Minstrel, Barbour's great work is a worthy tribute to his hero, and in all essential points stands the test of historical criticism. [65]

The comparisons with Barbour were another central feature of the analysis that sustained interest in the poem. *The Bruce* was close to being a chronicle, the *Wallace* best described as an imagined epic. John Barbour was a contemporary of Chaucer, the respective poets appearing in the public record at the same time, in 1356–7. Barbour was then likely to have been in his forties when he compiled his verse, which indicates that his boyhood years overlapped with Bruce's reign, and evidence suggests that he knew some of Bruce's contemporaries.[66] Andrew of Wyntoun confirms that John Barbour (?1316–96) was the author of *The Bruce*, a confirmation we do not have for Hary and *Wallace*, and we gain a number of pieces of detail from the poem in contrast to the misleading stories of Hary.[67] Few other than John Jamieson regarded Hary as the greater poet over Barbour, yet most – but not all – found some literary merit in *Wallace*'s rude fire.[68] Perhaps Agnes Mure Mackenzie is closest when she likened the *Wallace* to the forerunner of the Waverlies: 'for Hary was neither historian or romancer'.[69]

*   *   *

Hary misidentifies Wallace's father as Sir Malcolm Wallace, and there are reference to the Three Estates, to horse archers and the use of gunpowder that lie outside Wallace's time frame.[70]

The critique of Hary's historical veracity started in earnest when *Wallace* was placed in comparison with Hailes' chronicle in the 1770s.[71] Moir stated that a third-class Masters student in scientific research would point out that it is not possible to completely dismiss Hary's account, yet it is the historian who has greatest difficulty with Hary's slipshod use of chronology.[72] Modern research into Wallace was part of the mania for all things bibliographical which took such inspiration from the historical writings of Walter Scott and his patronage of the Bannatyne Club.[73] Given intellectual support by Thomas Thomson and David Laing, societies such as the Bannatyne Club and the Maitland Club took research into the annals of Scotland to an impressive level of documented scholarship. The Maitland Club's *Documents Illustrative of Sir William Wallace, his life and times* was compiled in the firm belief of the heroic quality of the man and his centrality to Scotland's well-being in a time of war:[74]

> Extraordinary circumstances give birth of extraordinary characters. The same exciting causes which produced a Tell in Switzerland, a Cromwell in England, and a Bonaparte in France, raised up a Wallace and a Bruce in Scotland.[75]

The collection contains a wide miscellany of documents in Latin, including a facsimile of the letter from Murray and Wallace to the merchants of Lübeck and Hamburg, declaring the Scottish ports open for trade with Germany and resurrecting previous shipments of hinds and wool.[76] The letter, like nearly all records of Wallace, was mistakenly thought lost in the post-*Braveheart* years (pp. 21–2). And while the letter shows Wallace's administrative activity as Guardian, historians will emphasise how relatively minor Wallace's impact was during his short life and even shorter mastery of Scotland's national affairs. His story since has been the greater legacy, having breathed life into Scotland's national tale. Belief in the honesty of Hary and the truth of Wallace is typical of much of the nineteenth-century Wallaciana, where patriotism, not historical corroboration, replenished popular knowledge. Scholars who accept Hary as having made a significant contribution to literature – not one as stylistically accomplished as Barbour, but an important one nevertheless – find the poem's historical context intractably problematic. Lord Hailes, the most vociferous critic of Hary's verse from the eighteenth century, whose text was still

current into the 1820s, directed his ire upon those who used Hary
as a historical account: 'It would be lost labour to search for the
age, name and condition of an author who either knew not history,
or who meant to falsify it.'[77] The modern equivalent of such indignation comes with the accusation of plagiarism against Mackay for
his unwarranted use of Sir James Fergusson of Kilkerran's *William
Wallace: Guardian of Scotland* (London, 1938).[78] In Cowan's
conclusion, Mackay's futile use of Hary as a historical source is an
effort more than wasteful of good paper.[79] Mackay's narrative was
a *Braveheart*-inspired account that remained on the bookshelves
in Scotland despite these claims against him, and despite Mackay
having also been accused of plagiarism with three other biographies.[80] No other rendition of the Wallace tale can be discredited in
such forceful terms as that of Mackay, although Randall Wallace's
fiction, comprising the screenplay for *Braveheart*, was dismissed
as 'a mélange of authorial hubris; mystical, quasi-blood-and-soil
ideology; and a sensibility of staggering vulgarity and sentimentality',[81] whereas the majority of the popular versions produced in the
twentieth century embrace the unverifiable as simply a feature of the
national tale. In *A Wee Guide to William Wallace* (1997), Duncan
Jones is aware that Hary should be treated as historical fiction, but
this concise account, 'based as far as possible on firm evidence',
lacks discussion of the chronicles until the very end, and no other
sources are cited to attest to any firmness in fact.[82] In a similar vein,
Alan McNie's compilation of *Clan Wallace* (1986) offers a con-
densed text of James Taylor's *Pictorial History of Scotland* (1859)
with no source criticism presented.[83] So does Carruth for his *Heroic
Wallace and Bruce* (1986),[84] which is in stark contrast to Elspeth
King's similarly pictorial production, which does keep the sources
firmly in view.[85] Only Gray and Fisher, who have written the longer
popular accounts in the late twentieth century, made a serious
attempt to engage with the mythmaking up front, with the latter's
short bibliographical essay particularly worthy of note.[86]

* * *

As the reprints of Hary waned, this new phase took little cogni-
sance of the criticism of Hailes or historians of their own time.
It was stated by John Finlay in 1804 that patriotic fervour keeps
Hary's *Wallace* at the forefront of patriotic myth-making.[87] And
in the judgement of Tytler, although the marvels of Hary must be

questioned, and often condemned by calm judgement, still the verse should be 'trod by the patriotic pilgrim rather [than] investigated by the careful antiquary'.[88] Tytler's conclusion anticipates that of Renan, but a completely falsified narrative is no basis from which a nation can forge an identity or go forward with confidence. For any one story to prevail as the national tale, it must be based on some level of fact. Hary provided enough certitude, alongside even greater fabrication and romantic embellishment, to sustain a verse that spread into the modern period, fixing the key tropes of the national tale before the age of nationalism. The balance tipped in favour of Hary's authority because of personal belief. This meant than when the authors of chapbooks and romantic novels and verse took hold of the narrative, and nationalists mobilised their product, the tale had a lineage of established authenticity.

NOTES

1. M. P. McDiarmid, 'The date of the *Wallace*', *Scottish Historical Review*, 24 (1955), p. 29, with 1478 as the most likely date of publication; M. P. McDiarmid, *Hary's Wallace (Vita Nobilissimi Defensoris Scotie Wilelmi Wallace Milits)* (Edinburgh: Scottish Text Society, 1968), Vol. I, p. xvi. Sir Archibald Dunbar's guess was 'about 1460', A. H. Dunbar, *Scottish Kings: A Revised Chronology of Scottish History, 1000–1625*, 2nd edn (Edinburgh: David Douglas, 1906), p. 215. The manuscript version is in eleven books, the printed versions tend to contain twelve, *The Acts and Deeds of Stir William Wallace, 1570*, ed. W. Craig (Edinburgh: Scottish Text Society, 3rd series, 1938), p. iii.
2. M. Lindsay, *History of Scottish Literature* (London: Robert Hale, 1977), p. 20.
3. J. T. T. Brown, 'The Wallace and The Bruce Restudied', in *Bonner Beiträge zur Anglistik* (Bonn: P. Hanstein's Verlag, 1900), pp. 7–8; MacQueen, 'The literature of fifteenth-century Scotland', p. 195.
4. Mair, *A History of Greater Britain*, p. 205. Cowan extends this quotation to include Mair's doubts on the veracity of Hary was still used to promote the greatness of Wallace, Cowan, 'The Wallace Factor', p. 11; Lindsay, *History of Scottish Literature*, p. 19.
5. J. Balaban, 'Blind Harry and *The Wallace*', *The Chaucer Review*, 8 (1974), p. 243.
6. Brunsden, 'Scotland's Social, Political and Cultural Scene', pp. 77, 107; MacQueen, 'The literature of fifteenth-century Scotland', p. 202.

7. McDiarmid, 'The Date of the *Wallace*', pp. 29–31.
8. McDiarmid, *Hary's Wallace*, Vol. I, p. xxvi; K. Stevenson, *Chivalry and Knighthood in Scotland, 1424–1513* (Woodbridge: Boydell Press, 2006), pp. 15, 150–1, 167; W. H. Schofield, *Mythical Bards and the Life of Sir William Wallace* (Cambridge, MA: Harvard University Press, 1920), pp. 6–7; McDiarmid, *Hary's Wallace*, Vol. I, p. xxvi.
9. H. E. Maxwell, *The Early Chronicles Relating to Scotland* (Glasgow: MacLehose, 1912), p. 247; Young, *Robert the Bruce's Rivals*, pp. 1–2
10. N. A. T. Macdougall, 'The Sources: A Reappraisal of the Legend', in J. M. Brown (ed.), *Scottish Society in the Fifteenth Century* (London: Edward Arnold, 1977), p. 18.
11. Macdougall, 'The sources', p. 111, fn. 106. The parish of Craigie in Ayrshire is the site of the Barnweil monument to Wallace.
12. The title page, among many, is listed in Geddie (ed.), *Middle Scots Poetry*, p. 142.
13. Quoted in Henderson, *Scottish Vernacular Literature*, p. 66.
14. Brown, 'The Wallace and The Bruce Restudied', pp. 80–1. Refutation comes from G. Neilson, 'On Blind Harry's "Wallace"', *Essays and Studies*, Vol. I (Oxford: Clarendon Press, 1910), p. 86. Almost a century earlier, Sibbald had declared there was no ground for suspecting this, J. Sibbald, *Chronicle of Scottish Poetry from the thirteenth century to the Union of the Crowns, to which is added a glossary* (Edinburgh, 1802), Vol. I, p. 82.
15. Sibbald, *Chronicle of Scottish Poetry*.
16. Ibid., pp. 7, 99; see also McDiarmid, *Hary's Wallace*, Vol. I, pp. xxvi–xxvii.
17. MacQueen, 'The literature of fifteenth-century Scotland', p. 200.
18. *The Complaynt of Scotland (1549), With an appendix of contemporary English tracts*, ed. J. A. Murray (London: Early English Text Society, 1872), p. 63, lines 16–17. My thanks go to Adam Fox for passing on a copy of this text.
19. Anderson, *Imagined Communities*, pp. 33–4. This was discussed in Ch. 1, pp. 8–12.
20. J. Smith, 'Textual Afterlives: Barbour's Bruce and Hary's Wallace', in *Scots: Studies in its Literature and Language*, ed. John M. Kirk and Iseabail Macleod (Amsterdam/New York: Rodopi, 2013), pp. 51–3; J. P. Miller, *Editions of Blind Harry's 'The Wallace' (1912, read 13 December 1913), Prepared for the Glasgow Bibliographical Society*; J. F. Miller, 'Some additions to the Bibliography of Blind Harry's Wallace' (read 19 March 1917), *Records of the Glasgow Bibliographical Society*, Vol. VI (Glasgow, 1920), p. 19; W. Geddie (ed.), *A Bibliography of Middle Scots Poets: with an introduction*

on the history of their reputations, Scottish Text Society Vol. 61 (Edinburgh: Blackwood & Sons, 1912), pp. 133–45; *The Actis and Deidis of Schir William Wallace, 1570*, ed. W. Craigie (Edinburgh: Scottish Text Society, 1938), McDiarmid, *Hary's Wallace*, 2 Vols.

21. Smith, 'Textual Afterlives: Barbour's Bruce and Hary's Wallace', p. 51.
22. R. McKinlay, 'Barbour's *Bruce*', *Records of the Glasgow Bibliographical Society*, Vol. VI (Glasgow, 1920), pp. 35–6.
23. Lindsay, *History of Scottish Literature*, p. 23; Smith, 'Textual Afterlives: Barbour's Bruce and Hary's Wallace', p. 52; Cowan, William Wallace', p. 13; Miller, 'Editions of Blind Harry's "The Wallace"'; Miller, 'Some additions to the Bibliography of Blind Harry's Wallace'.
24. Miller, 'Some additions', *Records of the Glasgow Bibliographical Society*, pp. 14–15.
25. Miller, 'Editions of Blind Harry's 'Wallace''.
26. E. King, 'Introduction', *Blind Harry's Wallace, William Hamilton of Gilbertfield* (Edinburgh: Luath Press, 1998), p. xi. Crawford, *The Bard*, p. 48; G. M. Brunsden, 'Aspects of Scotland's Social, Political and Cultural Scene in the Late 17th and Early 18th Centuries, as Mirrored in the Wallace and Bruce Traditions', in E. J. Cowan and D. Gifford (eds), *The Polar Twins* (Edinburgh: John Donald, 1999), p. 106, fn. 5. The number of copies of *Wallace* can be gauged from the estates of a number of Scottish publishers in the seventeenth century compiled in *The Bannatyne Miscellany, Containing Papers and Tracts Chiefly Relating to the History and Literature of Scotland*, ed. T. Thomson, Bannatyne Club No. 19, 1823(?) (reprinted from the 1855 edn, New York: Ams Press, 1973), p. 163.
27. Smith, 'Textual Afterlives: Barbour's Bruce and Hary's Wallace', pp. 59–60.
28. Brunsden, 'Social, Political and Cultural Scene', pp. 78–9.
29. Smith, 'Textual Afterlives: Barbour's Bruce and Hary's Wallace', pp. 56–7
30. *The Actis and Deidis of the Illustere And Vailzeand Campioun Schir William Wallace, Knight of Ellerslie by Henry the Minstrel, commonly known as Blind Harry*, ed. J. Moir (Edinburgh: Scottish Text Society, 1889, p. xix; Lindsay, *History of Scottish Literature*, pp. 22–3; Brunsden again downplays the differences in the respective texts, in 'Social, Political and Cultural Scene', p. 78. The copy of this ms. held in the British museum is said to be unique and to have been once the property of Queen Elizabeth, see: Geddie (ed.), *A Bibliography of Middle Scots Poets*, p. 134. This period of patriotic Protestantism is discussed in M. Lynch, 'A Nation Born Again?

Scottish Identity in the Sixteenth and Seventeenth Centuries', in D. Broun, R. Finlay and M. Lynch (eds), *Image and Identity: The Making and Re-making of Scotland through the Ages* (Edinburgh: John Donald, 1998), pp. 87, 94.

31. Smith, 'Textual Afterlives: Barbour's Bruce and Hary's Wallace', p. 53.

32. W. A. Criagie 'Barbour and Blind Harry as Literature', *The Scottish Review*, Vol. XXII, July (1893), p. 175; Brundsen highlights the subtitle of Hamilton's *Wallace*, which makes great claims for its easy language, 'Social, Political and Cultural Scene', pp. 76, 106, fn. 10, see: Hamilton of Gilberfield, *A New Edition of the Life and Heroick Actions of the Renoun'd Sir William Wallace, General and Governour of Scotland. Wherein the Old obsolete Words are rendered more Intelligible; and adapted to the understanding of such who have not the leisure to study the Meaning, and Import of such, Phrases without the help of a Glossary* (Glasgow: William Duncan, 1722). It was still argued a century later that Hamilton's Glossary was very incomplete, 'and without Jamieson's dictionary we can make little progress in it; even with it to aid, there are many words and some lines the sense of which is obscure to us . . . and we are inclined to think it is only the modernising *Life of Wallace* written by William Hamilton of Gilbertfield, early in the last century, which has been read by the peasantry, in recent times at least . . .', Yule, *Traditions, etc.,* , p. 22; P. F. Tytler gave credit to Jamieson's text as the basis for his *Lives of the Scottish Worthies* (London: John Murray, 1831), Vol. I, pp. 282–3.

33. Lindsay, *History of Scottish Literature*, p. 23.

34. Ibid., p. 23.

35. Smith, 'Textual Afterlives: Barbour's Bruce and Hary's Wallace', pp. 53, 64.

36. *Actis and Deidis*, ed. Moir, pp. xx–xxi; Smith, 'Textual Afterlives: Barbour's Bruce and Hary's Wallace', p. 53.

37. Ibid.

38. Lindsay, *History of Scottish Literature*, p. 23.

39. O. D. Edwards, *Macaulay* (London: Weidenfeld & Nicolson, 1988), p. 7.

40. *Autobiography of Andrew Carnegie* (Boston and New York: The Riverside Press, 1920), p. 16. The story is repeated, and accompanied with a description of the wider influence of his Uncle Lauder on Carnegie's understanding of Scotland, in B. J. Hendrick, *The Life of Andrew Carnegie* (New York: Doubleday, Doran & Co., 1932), Vol. 1, pp. 22–8.

41. Brown, 'The Wallace and The Bruce Restudied', p. 3.

42. Schofield, *Mythical Bards*, pp. 6–7.

43. J. Veitch, *The Feeling for Nature in Scottish Poetry*, Vol. I (Edinburgh: William Blackwood, 1887), p. 174.
44. J. Hill Burton, *The History of Scotland*, new edn (Edinburgh: William Blackwood, 1897), Vol. II, p. 183.
45. Veitch, *The Feeling for Nature in Scottish Poetry*, Vol. I, p. 174.
46. Burton, *History of Scotland*, Vol. II, p. 183.
47. Grant, 'Bravehearts and Coronets', pp. 87–9.
48. T. F. Henderson, *Scottish Vernacular Literature: a succinct history* (London: David Nutt, 1898).
49. *Lives of the Scottish Poets in Three Volumes*, ed. J. Robertson (Edinburgh: The Society of Ancient Scots, 1821), Vol. I, pp. 55–7.
50. W. T. Fyfe, *Wallace, the Hero of Scotland* (Edinburgh: Anderson, 1920), pp. 10–11, 157.
51. *Lives of Scottish Poets*, ed. Robertson, p. 58.
52. J. S. Watson, *Sir William Wallace, the Scottish Hero: A narrative of his Life and Actions, chiefly as recorded in the Metrical History of Henry the Minstrel on the authority of John Blair, Wallace's Chaplain, and Thomas Gray, Priest of Liberton* (London: Saunders, Otley & Co., 1861), p. iii.
53. Henderson, *Scottish Vernacular Literature*, p. 64; Neilson, 'Blind Harry's *Wallace*', p. 85; Moir provides a glossary of Harry's language, which is derived from Latin and French languages, *Actis and Deidis*, ed. Moir, while Brown, 'The Wallace and The Bruce Restudied', pp. 13–14 provides a shorter list.
54. G. L. Craik, *A Compendious History of English Literature and the English Language from the Norman Conquest* (London: Griffen, Bohn & Co., 1861), Vol. 1, p. 387; Brown, 'The Wallace and The Bruce Restudied', p. 18.
55. Schofield, *Mythical Bards*, p. 127.
56. McDiarmid, *Hary's Wallace*, i, p. xxxvii.
57. Neilson, 'Blind Harry's "Wallace"', p. 85.
58. Veitch, *Feeling for Nature*, Vol. I, pp. 173, 177; Tytler, *Lives of Scottish Worthies*, Vol. I, pp. 132–3.
59. *Actis and Deidis*, ed. Moir, pp. ix–x; J. Moir, *Sir William Wallace: a critical study of his biographer Blind Harry* (Aberdeen, 1888), p. 18. It is of passing interest to note that the copy of the latter text, now in the possession of the Special Collections Department of Edinburgh University Library, was once part of the library of Lewis Grassic Gibbon (James Leslie Mitchell).
60. Craigie, 'Barbour and Harry as Literature', pp. 200–1.
61. McDiarmid, *Hary's Wallace*, Vol. I, pp. xxvii, lviii.
62. Brown, 'The Wallace and The Bruce Restudied', pp. 20–1. See, for example, in his comparisons with Wyntoun, Book VIII, Ch. 13.

63. Neilson, 'Blind Harry's "Wallace"', pp. 93–8; G. Neilson, *John Barbour: Poet and Translator* (London: Kegan Paul, 1900), p. 1.
64. Neilson, 'Blind Harry's "Wallace"', pp. 95–6.
65. *Calendar of Documents*, ed. Bain, Vol. iii, pp. xxxvi, xxxvi–xxxvii.
66. Maxwell, *Early Chronicles Relating to Scotland*, pp. 235–6.
67. Lindsay, *History of Scottish Literature*, p. 12.
68. Craik, *A Compendious History of English Literature*, p. 387.
69. A. M. Mackenzie (ed.), *Scottish Pageant*, 2nd edn (Edinburgh: Oliver & Boyd for the Saltire Society, 1952), p. 146.
70. Neilson, 'On Blind Harry's "Wallace"', p. 92; C. Watson, 'How useful is Blind Hary's 'The Wallace' as a source for the study of chivalry in late medieval Scotland?', unpublished MSc. dissertation (University of Edinburgh, 2010), p. 2.
71. F. Watson, 'Sir William Wallace: What We Do – and Don't – Know', in E. J. Cowan (ed.), *The Wallace Book* (Edinburgh: John Donald, 2007), p. 26.
72. Moir, *Sir William Wallace*, pp. v–vi, 11.
73. C. S. Terry, *A Catalogue of the Publications of Scottish Historical and Kindred Clubs and Societies, 1780–1908* (Glasgow: MacLehose,1909).
74. *Documents Illustrative of Sir William Wallace, his life and times*, ed. J. Stevenson (Edinburgh: Maitland Club No. 54, 1841).
75. Ibid., pp. x–xi.
76. Barrow, *Robert Bruce*, pp. 15, 107.
77. D. Dalrymple of Hailes, *Annals of Scotland: From the accession of Malcome III to the Accession of the House of Stewart* 3rd edn (1776–9) (Edinburgh: A. Constable, 1819), pp. 298–9, 312.
78. G. Morton, 'Review: Sir William Wallace and other tall stories (unlikely mostly)', *Scottish Affairs*, 14, Spring 1996, pp. 103–15.
79. Cowan, 'The Wallace Factor in Scottish History', p. 17; J. Mackay, *William Wallace: Brave Heart* (Edinburgh: Mainstream, 1995), pp. 9–15.
80. Mackay's publisher Mainstream paid an estimated £22,000 in compensation on his behalf to the US publisher of historian David Armitage, author of a biography of John Paul Jones, and was forced to destroy copies of Mackay's biography of Alexander Graham Bell that mirrored the work of historian Robert V. Bruce; *The Scotsman*, 5 October 1999, back page, p. 22; *New York Times*, 25 September 1999.
81. C. McArthur, 'Braveheart and the Scottish Aesthetic Dementia', in T. Barta (ed.), *Screening the Past: Film and Representation of History* (Westport: Praeger, 1998), pp. 176–7.

82. D. Jones, *A Wee Guide to William Wallace* (Edinburgh: Goblinshead, 1997), pp. iv, 5, 80.
83. A. McNie, *Clan Wallace* (Jedburgh: Cascade Publishing, 1986).
84. J. A. Carruth's *Heroic Wallace and Bruce* (Norwich: Jarrold Colour Publications, 1986).
85. E. King, *Introducing William Wallace: The Life and Legacy of Scotland's Liberator* (Fort William: Firtree, 1997).
86. D. J. Gray, *William Wallace: The King's Enemy* (London: Robert Hale, 1991); A. Fisher, *William Wallace* (Edinburgh: John Donald, 1986), p. 139.
87. J. Finlay, *Wallace, or the Vale of Ellerslie, with other poems*, 2nd edn (Glasgow: R. Chapman, 1804), p. xi.
88. Tytler, *Lives of Scottish Worthies*, Vol. I, p. 132.

Chapter 5

Fixing the Type

Natural leaders, argues Weber, in times of psychic, physical, economic, ethical, religious or political distress, have been neither office holders nor incumbents, nor men who have acquired expert knowledge or who serve for remuneration. In periods of distress, natural leaders have instead been holders of specific gifts of the body and spirit; talents that are 'supernatural' and not accessible to everybody.[1] Weber's notion of charismatic leadership – of those people who do for others what they cannot do for themselves – determines the 'hero': he or she who is able to create and enact power and influence outwith the parameters of the state. What is more, this claim to power is made through the performance of a 'series of masks' in order that the claim be accepted as authentic.

This chapter builds out from the heroic masks of Wallace constructed by the early modern chroniclers, Hary and the historians who followed in the eighteenth century, to examine the typology that fixed the Wallacian tale as the national tale in the nineteenth century. There was one major revision of Hary's *Wallace*, with William Hamilton of Gilbertfield's abridgement in 1722. Otherwise, the numerous editions which appeared from the presses of a range of publishers were remarkably consistent with what had gone before. The conclusion reached in the last chapter emphasised the role of patriotic belief to sustain unwarranted and dangerous conjectures. Even the best of the historians, such as Patrick Fraser Tytler and John Hill Burton, were caught in this patriotic/corroboration nexus. It was a will to believe it true, despite acknowledgement of its historical inaccuracies, which sustained *Wallace* as 'the most treasured of cottage classics'.[2] Writing in 1821, Robertson claimed that many could still be found who could repeat 'the greater part' of the verse, and that it was 'rare indeed' not to be able to find someone who is ignorant of the more interesting and remarkable scenes from the tale. Yet the poem's reputation lost currency in the Victorian age, with its 'rude embodiment of popular feeling' viewed as barbarous in taste and filled with 'ludicrous prejudice and fierce vulgarity'.[3] Rather than dismiss the narrative out of hand, and block Wallace's superhuman exploits from the modern age of nationalism, a new generation of authors took to recrafting the tale into tropes better fitted to Victorian sensibilities: projecting the tale by means of the chapbook, the play and the narrative form.

This enduring relevance of Wallace's biography was the theme of Lord Rosebery's valediction to the patriot on the 600th anniversary of the battle of Stirling Bridge in 1897. Promoter of the Bill that created the Scottish Office in 1885, prime minister in 1894–5 upon Gladstone's death, Rosebery has occupied a curious position in the debates on Scottish nationalism. He was no great supporter of Home Rule, and opted instead to lead reform of Westminster structures.[4] Accepting an invitation to mark the anniversary of Wallace's greatest victory at a public banquet for 300 gentlemen, he refused to discuss the historical facts on 'so thorny a subject as Sir William Wallace', dismissing the debate on the patriot's Welsh origins, or worries over the veracity of the many legends which have grown along with the history.[5] Rosebery was convinced that Wallace must have been the greatest of heroes because his imprint on Scottish national consciousness had been so profound, when so few actual facts are known. Taking Fordun's line that Wallace 'lifted his head up from his den', Rosebery foregrounded the events that established patriotic charisma: the battle of Stirling Bridge, the defeat at Falkirk, Wallace's flight to France, then his capture and execution.[6] Rosebery's approach has been taken by others as the medium for the story to be retold.[7] Six stories have, albeit not by conscious repetition, formed the basis from which all other analysis then flows in these portrayals: the physical size of Wallace; the events at Lanark; the battles of Stirling Bridge and Falkirk; and Wallace's betrayal and his execution. By the highlighting of these superhuman masks from Wallace's biography, the dominance of charismatic leadership was underscored.

*   *   *

English culture was formed around the oak-like identity of its heroes.[8] Wallace, too, was by repute a massive man. The incongruity of a diminutive five-foot-ten Mel Gibson playing a possibly six-foot-nine William Wallace is not lost on some observers of the *Braveheart* phenomenon.[9] That Wallace was physically imposing comes directly from Hary:

> Nyne quartaris large he was in lenth indeid,
> Thryd part lenth in schuldrys braid was he,
> Rycht sembly, strang, and lusty for to se;
> Hys lymmys gret, with stalwart paiss and sound,
> Hys browys hard, his armes gret and round;
> Hys handis maid rycht lik till a prawmer,
> Off manlik mak, with nales gret and cler;
> Proportionyt lang and fayr was his wessage;
> Rycht sad off spech, and abil in curage;
> Braid breyst and heych, with sturdy crag and gret,
> Hys lyppys round, his noyss was squar and tret,
> Bowand bron haryt, on browis and breis lycht,
> Cler aspre eyn lik dyamond's brycht.
> Wynder the chyn, on the left syd, was seyn,
> Be hurt, a wain; his colour was sangweyn.
> Woundis he had in many diuerss place,
> Bot fayer and weill kepyt was his face.[10]

In *The Tragedy of the Valiant Knight* (c.1815) Wallace was 'endowed with gigantic strength of body, with heroic courage of mind, with disinterested magnanimity, with incredible patience and ability to bear hunger, fatigue, and all the inclemencies of the season ...'[11] In Alexander Keith's *Several Incidents in the Life of Sir William Wallace* (1844), locating the story within the 'romantic scenery' of Lanark, Wallace's success was distinctly superhuman, he being 'possessed of irresistible bodily strength, and endowed with the virtues of piety, generosity and patriotism in the most eminent degree'.[12] This 'gigantic strength of body' made Wallace a champion in the defence of justice,[13] as it did in the conclusion of Tytler, claiming 'Wallace's make, as he grew to manhood, approached almost to the gigantic; and his personal strength was superior to the common run of even the strongest men'. Yet for Murison this was a view of the romancers, not the serious student, although even this critic could not but be swayed from the belief that Wallace was a big man: '... in an age when warlike renown depended so essentially on personal deeds of derring-do, the astonishing thing – the incredible thing – would be if Wallace was not a man of pre-eminent physical strength and resourcefulness in the use of arms.'[14] Nor did he stop there:

> ... Ajax was taller than Agamemnon; and Jop may have stood a head taller than Wallace. But the substantial fact of his impressive physique is not to be denied. The romancers exaggerate, of course; but on this point even Hary scarcely outdoes Major or Bower.[15]

The trope of Wallace's superhuman powers helps explain the charismatic hold of his biography over the national tale, its repetition down the centuries a mark of each generation heightening the analogy: in 1921 Barr depicted his hero as 'A man of rock, fixed as the strong mountains of his native land, firm as the Stirling Rock at Abbey Craig . . .';[16] Wallace was celebrated for the 'highest heroism' in 1933;[17] the 700th anniversary of Stirling Bridge was marked by the slogan 'Big man, Big Sword, Big FUN';[18] and in 2000 Simon Schama informed the sizeable audience for the BBC *History of Britain* series that 'Wallace had hamstrings from Hell!'.[19]

*   *   *

Clear contemporary evidence of Wallace's actions are found for the first time with the attack on Heselrig (Hezelrigg) at Lanark.[20] It is one of his most notorious confrontations according to the indictment at his trial, taking place just months before the set-piece battle at Stirling Bridge. The event gains its significance because of its being presented as a revenge attack for the murder of Wallace's mistress, although Watson suggests the event was less a hot-blooded reaction than part of a pattern of action against Edward's Scottish administrators.[21] But it was not just personal retribution which was achieved: the event becomes a narrative device to explain how love for a woman was replicated with love of his nation, sealed with the ultimate sacrifice. Analysed in Chapter 2 as a central component of the literary national tale, the domestic trope has reoccurred in popular historical accounts of the nineteenth century. Many of these productions made the murder of Marion the single most important motivation for Wallace's actions against the English, usually as justification for the excessive brutality of his revenge.[22] It is 'for the sake of her that's murdered, ten thousand shall die!'.[23] According to one anonymous publication in 1840, 'Whilst brooding in secret over his country's wrongs, an event occurred which stimulated the powers of his mind and body into active existence

... the death of his sweetheart by the English Sheriff',[24] a motivation confirmed by Gabriel Alexander.[25] And when this story is
turned into a drama, then there is greater opportunity to develop
the characteristics of the dramatis personae around the key events.
In *Hodgeson's Theatrical Characters* for children, produced in
1822, Wallace's mistress, Lady Marion, fights for her man's affections against a love rival Lady Helen. Marion finally secures a ring
for her finger just as Wallace has been betrayed by Menteith.[26]
Ignoring the evidence, which is consistent in fixing Marion's death
at the hands of Heselrig in Lanark in 1297, well before the act of
betrayal in 1305, and the suggestion (from Donaldson, although
false) that Lady Helen was Wallace's second wife, this play creates
depth of characters over historical chronology or accuracy.[27]
Writing eighty years later, Scottish nationalist leader David Macrae
told his readers that Wallace and Marion secretly married 'so as
not to expose her to insult and danger from the soldiers of the gar-
rison',[28] whereas this patriarchal concern was turned on its head in
the twentieth century when, as part of the celebrations to mark the
700th anniversary of the battle of Stirling Bridge, a two-act play
Wallace's Women, by Margaret McSeveney and Elizabeth Roberts,
took as its theme 'Wallace's mother, lovers, wife and daughter; the
woman who dressed his wounds and her daughter who saved his
life'. It was 'for those who want to see a different history to the Big
Man with the Big Sword'.[29]

To add to the already heroic nature of the victory at Stirling
Bridge and the betrayal of his right to leadership at the battle of
Falkirk, Victorian historians focused on the clever stratagems of
the patriot. Peter Donaldson's *Life*, produced 'from authentic
materials of Scottish History', identified the work of the carpen-
ters in weakening the supports which held the bridge at Stirling
together.[30] P. R. Sawers is another who concentrated on the battle
when following in Wallace's footsteps in 1856 (and then turning
his attention to Bruce's stratagem at Bannockburn).[31] Alexander
Brunton wanted both to 'disprove the absurd story of the skin-
ning of Cressingham' and to determine the whereabouts of the
old Stirling Bridge. Brunton indicates that the correct bridge,
rather than being at Cambuskenneth, was at Kildean.[32] Patriotic
honour was at stake, and he was at pains to resurrect Wallace's
tactical ability in response to the criticisms by Lord Hailes.[33] Sir
James Fergusson (1938) pointed out the impracticability of Abbey

Craig being the exact spot where the Scots waited for the English to cross the bridge. The ground there was too steep and slippery to allow a safe and quick descent.[34] More likely they were on the gentler slopes to the north-west, he surmises. Both it and the bridge have proved hard to track down. The most thorough search has been carried out by the Stirling Bridge Archaeology Project led by Stirling University's Ron Page.[35] Whatever its correct siting, it was not the bridge filmed in Schama's *History of Britain*, nor that chosen by the producers of *Braveheart*, which was flat landscape in Ireland, with no river to cross.[36]

Habitually found within the national tale was the assertion that Wallace was no inferior to Bruce when it came to military engagements. The Scots Secretariat's publication of 1955 made plain that 'Despite what has been stated by modern critics, Wallace, apparently taken by surprise, had chosen his position well in view of the enemy's preponderance of heavily-armoured cavalry'.[37] The capitulation to the English army that led to Wallace's retreat from Falkirk 'has been justly considered as a masterpiece of generalship',[38] although the more common argument was that Comyn's withdrawal of his cavalry caused the defeat, as presented in the nationalist David Macrae's history.[39] When not focusing on betrayal, however, and when searching for a new voice, there can be found a heady mix of glamour and the elegiac in the stories of Wallace's military engagements. In *The Life of Sir William Wallace, the Scots Patriot* (1810), the military achievements of Wallace had a modern relevance. Referring to the 'present mighty struggle in which Britain is engaged', what more could be done, it asked, than 'to publish the history of an unequalled warrior, whose example must animate the brave youth, to whose exertions the eye of the public is directed for the defence of its native shores'?[40] Despite some curious geography, where Stirling Bridge is placed over the River Tay, the book ends with Menteith as the traitor and some of the gory details of Wallace's execution.[41]

If the lukewarm support of the nobility can be blamed for Wallace's defeat at Falkirk, no more hated a noble in these stories is that of Menteith. It was he who led Wallace's pursuers to their man. Menteith made two attempts at deceiving Wallace, with the second involving a young relative disarming the patriot while he slept before leading the captors to his bedside.[42] 'Fause Menteith' was given £150 for his part in the deception, a point emphasised in the Scots Secretariat's publication.[43] But it is the wider sentiment and wider accusations carried by the words of Thomas Carlyle that are the most indelible:

> It is noteworthy that the nobles of the country [Scotland] have maintained a quite despicable behaviour since the days of Wallace downwards – a selfish, ferocious, famishing, unprincipled set of hyenas, from whom at no time, and in no way, has the country derived any benefit.[44]

Except for those narratives that move straight to Bruce's victory at Bannockburn, the stories end with Wallace's execution. The betrayal merely added to his elevation to martyr while his speech, denying the charge of treason on the grounds of never having given fealty to Edward, has kept his name clear of corruption. Sibbald's chronicle of Scottish poetry since the thirteenth century, published in 1802, concludes his analysis of Hary with an account of Wallace's execution in London.[45] The Morison edition (1790) carries an engraving of the execution scene in its frontispiece, with Wallace depicted below the gallows and about to lose his head, while the priest holds up a Psalter before the patriot's eyes. Hary's verse (book VI, line 1,400) is quoted: 'He got a priest the book before him hauld/While they to him had done all that they would do.'[46]

This elegiac inspired Jane Porter, who in 1810 penned the kind of melodrama that was a feature of nineteenth-century romantic fiction. All mention of disembowelling while alive, the drawing or the quartering of the body, is ignored, and the story then shifts to the heroics of Bruce.[47] The emotion of betrayal and execution is so vital to the story. Sir James Fergusson ended his description of the trial with one of the most evocative juxtapositions of its momentousness and horror:

> The dead eyes stared down upon the ships in the Thames, the tall wooden houses, the hurrying, many coloured crowds, and the sea gulls wheeling about the piers of the great bridge. Seven years before, sea gulls had wheeled with the same grace, the same indifference to the bloody deeds of men, about the bridge of Stirling. Seven months later, Robert Bruce, Earl of Carrick, was crowned King of Scots at Scone.[48]

With execution following betrayal confirming his superhuman capabilities as well as his elevation into the company of saints, political martyrdom comprised higher claims to Wallace's soul. The parable of Saint Andrew gifting his sword to Scotland – the nation and patron saint linked through the Saltire, the cross upon which Andrew was crucified – was transmuted by Hary into Wallace receiving the vision.[49] And for others this vision came to the patriot when he was still a child, fixing his leadership as both innate and predestined.[50]

*   *   *

Carrick, who produced some of the most balanced work on Wallace, pointed out that since Hamilton of Gilbertfield's text has lost its place in popular reading, it has been taken by *The Scottish Chiefs*, 'a romance which, under the circumstances, may be said to have assumed the position once occupied by the Minstrel'.[51] Walter Scott had claimed he would have written his own version of Wallace's life had it not been for Porter's work, although this does not mean that he approved of her depoliticisation of the national hero.[52] Others, though, did find Porter's account inspirational. According to the American folklorist J. F. Dobie, when he received a copy of *The Scottish Chiefs* one Christmas, 'I read it to myself, and at night as we sat by the fireplace my father read it aloud by the flickering light of a kerosene lamp. What heroes to emulate Bruce and Wallace were! My blood still stirs at mention of the mere title.'[53] To be subjected by Romanticism to 'a life of tragic heroism' may not be good history, but it has conspired to make good nationalism.[54] The transition was not indiscernible to contemporaries, but few allowed themselves the time to observe:

> To try to write a biography of William Wallace from historical sources only as distinct from traditional ones is like trying to restore a very old family portrait which several painters have tried to improve. It hangs in the place of honour in the dining-room, and all strangers are taken to see it as a matter of course. Most of them are suitably impressed by it. A few, franker than the rest, comment that it is not a very lifelike portrait, and this we are inclined to admit. The truth is that the original portrait, which family tradition tells us was a very fine piece of work, has been invisible for generations, and none of us has ever seen it.[55]

The 'traditional sources' offer little beyond certain narrative episodes, and offer limited or no background information on Wallace's rise to a position of influence, 'plant[ing] Wallace at Stirling Bridge almost as if he had just started from the ground, or come down from the clouds, ready to command an army in the field'.[56] Contemporary historians struggled to get beyond the facts at their disposal and dismissed the prospect of sketching any biography of empirical merit. From the caustic rejection of Hary's literary as well as his historical worth by Lord Hailes, the modernisation of the tale by historians working within the Romanticism of the tale remained hamstrung by its pre-modern collation. The mid-nineteenth-century entry for the *Encyclopaedia Britannica* looked to distance the historical record away from Hary, declaring that *Wallace* 'possesses no poetical merit except a certain rude fire and energy, and as a literary production its place must be reckoned a very humble one'.[57] Perhaps despairingly, Craigie offered the opinion that '[o]f the fighting and slaying, which makes up by far the greater part of the poem, it is difficult to find a sample that is short enough for our purpose'.[58] Yet while the inconsistencies and the bloodthirsty language in Hary made a 'pantomime' of Wallace, still 'there are facts there not to be found in Wyntoun or Bower'.[59] Hary's 'faults' were compensated for and justified by new facts in Stevenson's work for the Maitland Club in 1841,[60] and Joseph Bain used the discovery of new documents to both criticise and support Hailes' counterpoint to Hary.[61] Indicative of the continued sway of the pre-modern version of the tale within the age of modern nationalism, even a historian of the calibre of Historiographer Royal John Hill Burton was prepared to accept the mixture of fact and legend simply because 'morsels turn up to confirm the fundamentals of some of his stories'.[62]

Such a position was not without the fear of both criticism and ridicule, and in favouring Hary as a poet over Barbour, philogist and editor of the *Oxford English Dictionary* W. A. Craigie was aware that he did so in the face of 'the fierce blasts of the historian, and as if afraid of being caught resetting such dubious goods'.[63] With similar concerns expected for his *History of Wallace*, Alexander Brunton was compelled to dedicate the third part of his study to refuting many of the 'critical remarks of the English History'.[64] Similarly, the Rector of Aberdeen Grammar School James Moir was aware that his analytical edition of *Wallace* for the Scottish Text Society would 'offend all those who blindly believe that the Minstrel's story is veritable history', yet still he wished 'to clear his memory from the attacks made on him by some of our historians and literary critics'.[65] And yet both authors, and James Paterson from earlier in the nineteenth century, described Hary as the biographer of Wallace.[66]

*　*　*

The failure of modern historians to overwhelm Hary's narrative with empirical detail or to dismiss Gilbertfield's vernacular version of the epic poem or to insist on the patriot's superhuman powers being made mortal, ensured that the literary framing of episodes from the patriot's life not only persisted widely, but impacted outside the specific genre of the national tale. Alongside Gilberfield's text the tale appeared with many embellishments among the immensely abundant balladists and in the recovery of seemingly lost songs, a move which gathered momentum throughout the second half of the eighteenth century. This appetite for collecting pre-modern verse then grew with Hogg's two volumes *The Jacobite Relics of Scotland* (Edinburgh 1819–21), Motherwell's *Minstrelsy: Ancient and Modern* (Glasgow, 1827) and Child's *English and Scottish Ballads* (Boston, 1859).

The earliest-preserved ballads that mention Wallace are of doubtful antiquity and refer to the murder of Marion in Lanark.[67] The first is 98 lines in length, and, in the extract here, emphasises the patriot's brutal strength:

> He slew the captain where he stood,
> The rest they did quack an' roar;
> He slew the rest around the room,
> And ask'd if there were any more.[68]

The ballad entitled 'Sir William Wallace' is over 100 lines long, and Child's version came from 'an old gentlewoman in Aberdeenshire'. The first quarter of the poem shows the romantic Wallace unafraid of capture, taunting the English soldiers:

> Wo'd ye hear of William Wallace,
> An' sek him as he goes,
> Into the lan' of Lanark,
> Aman his mortal faes?
>
> There was fyften English sogers
> Unto his ladie cam,
> Said 'Gie us William Wallace,
> That we may have him slain.

'Wou'd ye gie William Wallace,
That we may have him slain,
And ye's be wedded to a lord,
The best in Christendeem.'

'This verra nicht at seven,
Brave Wallace will come in,
And he'll come to my chamber door,
Without or dread or din.'

The fyften English sogers
Around the house did wait,
And four brave Southron foragers
Stood hie upon the gait

On Wallace's arrival she repents: 'And for the ill I've dane to you, Let me burn upon a hill.' Wallace disguised himself in women's clothing, but 'yon lusty dame' was uncovered. The verse continues:

Then all the Southerns follow'd him,
And sure they were by four:
But he drew his trusty brand,
And slew them pair by pair.[69]

As regards the published poetry, one of the earliest references to Wallace comes in 'Symmie and his Bruther': 'Thair is no story that I of heir/Of Johnne nor Robene Hude/Nor zit of Wallace wicht but weir/That me thinks half so gude . . .'[70] The verse links Wallace to the outlaw tradition, as well as the ballad-creation of Robin Hood.[71] In one undated eighteenth-century account, probably from the 1740s, the Duke of Perth was reminded of the freedoms Wallace secured:

Design'd from Mankinds loyal nameless Crowd
To raise the Humble, and to check the Proud,
To stop the baseful Growth of lawless Power
And render injur'd Innocence secure.[72]

In 'An honorable achievement of Sir William Wallace', published in Edinburgh around 1745, stress is placed on Wallace's superhuman powers and on his Scottish lineage at a time of Jacobite political and military manoeuvrings towards the British throne:

Then Five he sticked where they stood,
And Five he trampled in the Gutter,
And Five he chas'd to yon green Wood,
He hang'd them all out o'er a Grain
And 'gainst the Morn at Twelve o' clock
He din'd with his kind *Scottish* men.[73]

Dated to the mid-eighteenth century, yet not collated until decades later, this verse is less concerned with biographical certainties in order to project the leadership powers of the patriot. These verses valorise cunning over tenacious and cruel opponents, and always Wallace's ability to overcome superior numbers is stressed. Undoubtedly, it would only be betrayal, not physical or military defeat, that could bring about his end. And once that end has come, the verse tends then to dramatise the emotions of his execution: 'He got a priest the book before him hauld/While they to him had done all that they would do.'[74] That edition of Hary from the 1790s includes William Birrell's engraving of the execution scene. Others use well-known identifiers to hang their verse on, the sword symbolising Wallace's political struggle, his martyrdom and his spiritual struggle:

Thou Sword of true valour! Tho' dim by thy hue,
And all faded thy flashes of light
Yet still my mem'ry thy sight shall renew
The remembrance of WALLACE that night! [75]

The final verse of the *Shade of Wallace* (1807) made a plea for Wallace's continued life in heaven. Despite the blood that so obviously was shed by his sword of valour, the higher virtues of his actions, domestically and for the nation, sets Wallace aside from the judgement given to others:

When I throw off this mortal coil,
Fly from a world of wrongs and toil
Where me themselves in cares embroil
Grant me this solace
Once more, on heaven's exalted soil,
To see great Wallace.[76]

Despite such compassion in his death, baseness was as much an excuse for poetry as spiritual advance. Holford's *Metrical Romance*

(1809) was described by Walter Scott as not one to please the Scots simply because Wallace was a character not suited to poetry, although still Scott suggested it would be better appreciated in England.[77] This was poetry reminiscent of Hary's gruff style:

> A king in chains – a trampled land;
> Our chiefs, a pale, desponding band;
> A people, wrong'd, despoil'd bereft
> Nor courage, zeal, nor honour left!
> Stewart I scorn to boast – ''Twas I'
> I rallied around her banner'd tree

Yet there were examples of anti-Englishness being maintained, most notably Burns' *Parcel of Rogues*, which he never owned up to in his lifetime, and, much less well renowned, *The Tragedy of the Valiant Knight Sir William Wallace*, from 1815:

> *Parcel of Rogues*
> Oh would, or I had seen the day
> That Treason thus could sell us,
> My auld grey head had lien in clay
> Wi' Bruce and loyal Wallace!
> But pith and power, till my last hour
> I'll mak this declaration;
> We're bought and sold for English gold –
> Such a parcel of rogues in a nation!

> *The Tragedy of the Valiant Knight Sir William Wallace*
> Behold! Who tramples on the Lion bold?
> A patriot greater than the heroes of old:
> Treach'ry alone o'er him gave England pow'r
> In death doth Edward's spite show to this hour.[78]

But most of the nineteenth-century verse looked to avoid crude anti-Englishness and remain supportive of the crown and the Union. When *Wallace and Bruce, a poem* (1825?) was published in the years immediately after George IV made the first visit to Scotland by a Hanoverian monarch, George was depicted as one of the strangers who had now come north to pay homage to 'Scotia's Patriot Knight':

> While amply broad the firm foundation lies,
> And rare devices ev'ry side emblaze

For shall the top ascend the yielding skies,
The statue, stern, sublime in air to raise,
And strangers oft will come, in future days,
Here to contemplate Scotia's Patriot Knight,
Whose glorious aim (that yet commands our praise)
Was always to secure his country's right,
By wisdom in debate, by valour in the fight.[79]

Throughout this period, and into the twentieth century, a contemporary political reading of the Wallacian nation tale was rarely consumed by late medieval machinations. In J. Morrison Davidson's collection of patriotic Scots' biographies, published on the eve of World War I, Wallace embodied the national *Geist*:

Of 'Wallace' to be found, like a wild flower,
All over his dear country; left the deeds
Of Wallace, like a family of ghosts
To people the steep rocks and river banks
Her natural sanctuaries, with a local soul
Of independence and stern liberty.[80]

The inclusion of verse in the national tale is important for the ease with which it could develop the narrative through listening and recitation, and without the empirical angst that beset the historical as well as the literary prose. Indeed, patriotic verse took the Wallace narrative into the wider politics of the nation, confirming the story's centrality to the national psyche. It is clear that, when the tale was evoked on national occasions, the story – the collective national memory – was of significance to nationalism. Two examples illustrate this transition well. In the first, dating from the push for franchise reform in 1832, a political squib framed against William Dundas is presented to the tune of 'Scots Wha Hae':[81]

Tories, – Friends of Bill D—s,
Sycophants of every class,
Rats, we're sore beset, alas!
Whisk your tails round me.–

Now's the day, an' now's the hour,
See her frown Britannia's lour,
See approach Truth's awful power,
Honour and Honesty.

In the second, relating to another important date in Scotland's constitutional history – the failure of the referendum in 1979 to secure devolution – a similar use is made of song and tune. From the fall-out of that event, splits appeared within the Scottish National Party:

> Wha will find the Labour knave,
> Infiltratin' oor conclave?
> 'For God's sake, man. Come on! Behave!
> 'A socialist? No' me!
> Tell the workers no' tae mourn;
> Freedom's cause is no forlorn!
> Maybe no' the morn's morn,
> But in Eternitie![82]

Juxtaposing Burns, Wallace and contemporary politics through cultural transition, satire is deployed to assist the non-literate and the non-political mesh with the politically engaged opinion makers, just as the chapbooks offered cheap publications for the growing consumer public, often in patriotic tones, mixing emotive colloquialisms alongside more authoritative polysyllabic words.[83] Brought into the tenets of the narrative through these means, nationalism's 'people' inculcated the national tale in ways that were less anti-English and less oppositional than the tone of Hary.

In the nineteenth century, the prose and verse that depicted Wallace's superhuman strength and charismatic leadership did so in term of Scotland's contribution to Britain's imperial might. The episodic retelling of his tale through six straightforward stories of 'Wallace's masks' – his physical size, the murder of Heselrig at Lanark, the battles of Stirling Bridge and Falkirk, and his betrayal and execution – opened Wallace's biography up to ideological capture. This transition from national tale to nationalism happened within a different political and constitutional context from the pre-modern past, and took place against the backdrop of a new dominant text. William Hamilton of Gilbertfield's shortened prose had been largely superseded, with the tone of the national tale and the social memory of Wallace it instilled in the nation, led by the voice of Jane Porter. *The Scottish Chiefs* took the tale forward in the age of nationalism, and did so with a contemporary rather than a historical conviction.

NOTES

1. *From Max Weber: Essays in Sociology*, trans. and ed. H. H. Gerth and C. Wright Mills (London: Routledge, 1948), p. 245.
2. *Lives of Scottish Poets*, ed. Robertson, p. 55.
3. R. J. Goldstein, *The Matter of Scotland: Historical Narrative in Medieval Scotland* (Lincoln, NE and London: University of Nebraska Press, 1993), pp. 220.
4. S. J. Brown, '"Echoes of Midlothian": Scottish liberalism and the South African War, 1899–1902', *Scottish Historical Review*, Vol. LXXI, 1, 2: Nos 191/2 (1992), p. 158.
5. *In Memory of Sir William Wallace: Address by Lord Rosebery* (Stirling: Eneas Mackay, 1897), repr. in *Wallace, Burns, Stevenson: Appreciations by Lord Rosebery* (Stirling: Eneas Mackay, 1905).
6. This is the key passage from Fordun, see: Cowan, 'The Wallace Factor in Scottish History', p. 7; Rosebery, *Appreciations by Lord Rosebery*, pp. 12–16.
7. P. Hume Brown, *History of Scotland to the Present Time* (Cambridge: Cambridge University Press, 1911), Vol. I, pp. 117–22, 123–37.
8. I. Pears 'The Gentleman and the Hero: Wellington and Napoleon in the Nineteenth Century, in R. Porter, *Myths of the English* (Cambridge: Polity, 1993), pp. 216–22.
9. K. McKay, *Mel Gibson* (London: Sidgwick & Jackson, 1988), p. 11; Morton, 'Review: Sir William Wallace and other tall stories (unlikely mostly)', pp. 103–15. Doubts on the great size of Wallace are raised in C. Knightley, *Folk Heroes of Britain* (London: Thames & Hudson, 1982), p. 158.
10. Book 9, lines 1,918–34, *Wallace; or the life and acts of Sir William Wallace, of Ellerslie. By Henry the Minstrel. Published from a manuscript dated M.CCCLXXXVIII*, ed. J. Jamieson (new edn, Glasgow, 1820, 1869).
11. *The Tragedy of the Valiant Knight Sir William Wallace to which is prefixed a brief Historical Account of the Knight, and his Exploits for the Delivery of Scotland, and added a more particular Account of the way which he was betrayed into the hands of the English* (Glasgow: Hutchison & Co., 1815?), p. 9.
12. A. Keith, *Several Incidents in the Life of Sir William Wallace, with an account of Lanark, the theatre of his exploits, and a description of the romantic scenery in the neighbourhood* (Lanark, 1844), pp. 3–6, 9–10.
13. J. S. Watson, *Sir William Wallace, the Scottish Hero: A narrative of his Life and Actions, chiefly as recorded in the Metrical History of Henry the Minstrel on the authority of John Blair, Wallace's*

Chaplain, and Thomas Gray, Priest of Liberton (London: Saunders, Otley & Co., 1861), pp. 2–3.

14. A. F. Murison, *Sir William Wallace* (Edinburgh: Oliphant, Anderson & Ferrier, 1898), p. 152

15. Ibid., pp. 152–3.

16. *Scotland Yet! An Address Delivered by the Rev. James Barr, B.D., at the Wallace Monument, at Elderslie, on 27th August, 1921; and now re-printed from the 'Forward' of 3rd September, 1921* (Glasgow: Scottish Home Rule Association, 1921), p. 3.

17. *Wallace Commemoration Day, Saturday 26th August 1933. Held at Wallace Monument, Elderslie, Official Souvenir Programme.*

18. *700th Anniversary Guide to Events: Easter to Autumn, 1997.*

19. S. Schama, *History of Britain*, BBC Television, 18 October 2000.

20. J. Fergusson, *William Wallace: Guardian of Scotland* (London: Alexander MacLehose & Co., 1938), p. 20.

21. Watson, 'Sir William Wallace', p. 29.

22. *Wallace, the Hero of Scotland; or Battle of Dumbarton, A historical Romance in which the love of liberty and Conjugal Affections are exemplified in the characters of Sir William Wallace and Lady Wallace, with the unparalleled Bravery of the former against a band of Ruffians in the rescue of the Earl of Mar, and his revenge on the governor of Lanark for the Murder of Lady Wallace* (London: Thomas Redruffe, 1825?), pp. 5–6.

23. L. G. M. G., *Authentic Life of Sir William Wallace; with chapter on Traditional Wallace. Compiled from the best authorities* (Dundee: George Montgomery, 1877), p. 20.

24. *History of Sir William Wallace: The renowned Scottish Champion* (Glasgow, Printed for the Booksellers, c.1840), p. 4.

25. G. Alexander, *Sir William Wallace: the Hero of Scotland. A historical Romance* (London, 1903), p. 13.

26. *Wallace, the Hero of Scotland, a drama, in three Acts: Adapted to Hodgeson's Theatrical Characters and Scenes in the Same* (London: Hodgeson & Co., 1822), pp. 8–10.

27. P. Donaldson, *The Life of Sir William Wallace, the Governor General of Scotland and Hero of the Scottish Chiefs. Containing his parentage, adventures, heroic achievements, imprisonment and death; drawn from authentic materials of Scottish History* (Hartford: Silus Andrus, 1825), p. 128.

28. D. Macrae, *The Story of William Wallace, Scotland's National Hero* (Scottish Patriotic Association, 1905), p 9.

29. *Wallace's Women*, a play in two acts by Margaret McSeveney and Elizabeth Roberts, 31 Oct.–2 Nov. 1997, Smith Art Gallery and Museum, Stirling.

30. Donaldson, *The Life of Sir William Wallace*, p. 84.
31. P. R. Sawers, *Footsteps of Sir William Wallace. Battle of Stirling: Or, Wallace on the Forth* (Glasgow: Thomas Murray & Son, 1856).
32. A. Brunton, *A New Work in Answer to the Pamphlet, 'Wallace on the Forth', proving the stratagem at Stirling Bridge and that the Bridge was at Kildean, etc. Also the history of the famous battle of Stirling Bridge, to which is added two letters written by Sir William Wallace himself, and Wallace's charter to Scrymgeour of Dundee* (Dunfermline: W. Clark, 1841, Stirling, R.S. Shearer, 1861), pp. 3, 4; G. F. T. Jones, 'Arms and the man: how the Scots who bled with Wallace fought in Braveheart and in history', *Journal of the Sydney Society for Scottish History*, 5 (1997). RCAMHS, 'Stirling Bridge', NS79SE 1 7972 9461 and for the later bridges, NS79SE 2 and NS79SE 185; R. Page, 'The ancient bridge at Stirling: investigations, 1988–2000, *Scottish Archaeological Journal*, 23 (2001), pp. 141–65.
33. Brunton, *A New Work in Answer*, p. 16.
34. Fergusson, *William Wallace*, p. 54.
35. R. Page, 'The archeology of Stirling Bridge', *One Day Wallace Conference*, 17 May 1997, Smith Art Gallery and Museum, Stirling.
36. Schama, *History of Britain*; E. Ewan, 'Braveheart', *The America Historical Review*, 100, 4 (October 1995), 1, pp. 219–21.
37. J. C., *Life of Sir William Wallace*, 3rd edn (London: Griffen & Co., 1849), p. 105.
38. *William Wallace: National Hero of Scotland, Special Commemorative Publication to Mark the 650th Anniversary of his Martyrdom* (Glasgow: Scots Secretariat, 1955), p. 11.
39. Macrae, *Story of William Wallace*, p. 15.
40. Anon, *The Life of Sir William Wallace, the Scots Patriot* (Edinburgh: Oliver & Boyd, 1810), pp. 3–4.
41 Ibid., pp. 24, 93.
42. J. C., *Life of Sir William Wallace*, p. 122.
43. *William Wallace, Special Commemorative Publication to Mark the 650th Anniversary of his Martyrdom*, p. 13.
44. Ibid., p. 15.
45 J. Sibbald, *Chronicle of Scottish Poetry from the thirteenth century to the Union of the Crowns, to which is added a glossary*, 4 Vols (London: Longman & Rees, 1802), Vol. 1, pp. 82ff.
46. *The Metrical History of Sir William Wallace, Knight of Ellerslie by Henry, commonly called Blind Harry: carefully transcribed from the MS. copy of that work in the Advocates Library under the eye of the Earl of Buchan. And now printed for the first time, according to the ancient and true orthology. With Notes and Dissertations*. 3 Vols (Perth: Morison, 1790), Vol. III.

47. Ibid., pp. 370–2.
48. Fergusson, *William Wallace*, pp. 217–18.
49. McDiarmid, *Hary's Wallace*, Vol. I, p. xciv.
50. *Wallace, or, the Vale of Ellerslie with Other Poems* (Glasgow: Chapman & Lang, 1802), pp. 9–10.
51. J. Paterson, *Wallace and His Times* (Edinburgh: William Paterson, 1858), p. xx.
52. My thanks to Linas Eriksonas for this point and for hinting at his own fascinating researches into heroic Wallace.
53. The quotations refer to the 1890s, M. Ash, 'William Wallace and Robert the Bruce', in R. Samuel and P. Thompson (eds), *The Myths We Live By* (London: Routledge, 1990), p. 92.
54. P. Traquair, *Freedom's Sword* (London: HarperCollins, 1998), p. 124.
55. Fergusson, *William Wallace*, p. ix.
56. Murison, *Sir William Wallace*, p. 56.
57. W. A. Craigie, 'Barbour and Harry as Literature', *The Scottish Review*, Vol. XXII (1893), p. 176.
58. Craik, *A Compendious History*, p. 389.
59. Henderson, *Scottish Vernacular Literature*, p. 74.
60. *Documents Illustrative of Sir William Wallace, his life and times*, Maitland Club 54, ed. J. Stevenson (Edinburgh, 1841), p. xi.
61. *Calendar of Documents Relating to Scotland*, ed. J. Bain (Edinburgh, 1887), ii, p. xxix, xliv.
62. Brown's critique; Hill Burton, *History of Scotland*, Vol. II, p. 183.
63. Craigie, 'Barbour and Harry as Literature', pp. 201, 174; Indeed, Walker argues that in his defence of Hary, Craigie was too quick to denigrate Barbour. I. C. Walker, 'Barbour, Blind Harry, and Sir William Craigie', *Studies in Scottish Literature*, 1, 3 (1963–4), pp. 202–6.
64. A. Brunton, *A New Edition of the Life and Heroic Actions of Sir William Wallace, Knight of Elderslie: in three parts* (Glasgow, 1881), part III.
65. Moir, *Sir William Wallace*, preface, p. 11.
66. Paterson, *Wallace, the Hero of Scotland*, pp. xii–xiii.
67. F. C. Child's, *English and Scottish Ballads* (Boston: Little, Brown, 1859), Vol. VI, pp. 231–2.
68. Ibid., 'Gude Wallace', lines 51–74, pp. 234–5.
69. Ibid., 'Sir William Wallace', lines 1–20, 39–40, 65–8, pp. 237–42.
70. *Early Popular Poetry in Scotland and the Northern Border*, ed. D. Laing in 1822/6, rearranged and revised with additions and glossary by W. Carrew-Hazlitt, 2 Vols (London: Reeves & Turner, 1895), Vol. II, p. 6.

71. Holt, *Robin Hood*; Keen, *The Outlaws of Medieval Legend*; Seal, *The Outlaw Legend*
72. *To His Grace, James, Duke of Perth, &c. Lieutenant General of His Majesty's army, under the command of His Royal Highness Charles, Prince of Wales, &c.* (n.p., c.1745?.) [NLS: Mf.SP.159(14)].
73. *Four new songs, and a prophecy: I. A song for joy of or ancient race of Stewarts. II. The battle of Preston, that was fought by his Royal Highness Prince Charles, the 21st of September 1745. III. On an honorable achievement of Sir William Wallace, near Falkirk. IV. A song, call'd, The rebellious crew. V. A prophecy by Mr. Beakenhead*, Song III (Edinburgh?, 1750?) [NLS: Ry.1.2.85(21); F. C. Child, *English and Scottish Ballads* (Boston, 1859), vi, 232.
74. From Harry's *The Wallace*, Book VI, line 1400. *The Metrical History of Sir William Wallace, Knight of Ellerslie, by Henry, commonly called Blind Harry*, frontispiece to volume III.
75. 'The Sword of Wallace' found within *Wallace, or, the Vale of Ellerslie* (1802).
76. *The Shade of Wallace: A poem* (Glasgow: D. Mackenzie, 1807), p. 11.
77. M. Holford, *Wallace; or, the Fight of Falkirk; a Metrical Romance* (London, 1809), Canto 1, CH XXXII, 24–5; Letter of Sir Walter Scott to J. Baillie, 20 February1810, *The Letters of Sir Walter Scott*, ed. H. J. C. Grierson (London: Constable, 1932–7), Vol. II, p. 302.
78. *The Tragedy of the Valiant Knight Sir William Wallace to which is prefixed a brief Historical Account of the Knight, and his Exploits for the Delivery of Scotland, and added a more particular Account of the way which he was betrayed into the hands of the English* (Glasgow: Hutchison & Co., 1815?), p. 2.
79. *Wallace and Bruce, a poem* (n.p., 1825?), p. 96.
80. J. M. Davidson, *Leaves from the Book of Scots, The Story of William Wallace, Robert the Bruce, Fletcher of Saltoun and Other Patriots*, first Published by the Civic Press, Glasgow, 1914 (Penicuik: Scots Secretariat, 1971), p. 9.
81. 'Political Squibs, Edinburgh 1820–21', Edinburgh Public Library, YJN1213.820, A106X.
82. C. Baur, 'Lament to the Seventy-niners after R. Burns', cited in Mitchell, *Strategies for Self-government*, p. 228.
83. E. J. Cowan, 'William Wallace: "The Choice of the Estates"', in E. J. Cowan (ed.), *The Wallace Book* (Edinburgh: John Donald, 2007), p. 14.

Chapter 6

The Scottish Chiefs

The contribution to the national tale of Jane Porter (bap. 1776–1850), acknowledged as a minor novelist who produced a contemporary stir with three of her works before slipping steadily into the literary margins and the marginalia of history, has remained opaque.[1] Her failure to conform to the tenets of the historical novel and to the political opposing of nations characteristic of the literary national tale has, as Chapter 2 maintained, misplaced her centrality to contemporary nationalism.

The Scottish Chiefs was one of the most widely read novels of the Romantic period, and the novel's widespread cultural impact throughout the diaspora is the subject of the chapter that follows.[2] Published in the five-volume format popular in that day, *The Scottish Chiefs* built on the reputation of Porter's first novel, *Thaddeus of Warsaw* (1803), and found itself a ready market.[3] Longmans printed 2,000 copies in 1810, 1,500 the next year, and 750 in each of 1816, 1819 and 1825.[4] These impressions were below the peak sales for Scott, which touched 12,000 in the 1820s, but on a par with the 1,500 to 2,000 generally retained for established authors, and well above the norm of 500–750 copies for most first impressions.[5] *The Scottish Chiefs'* impact overseas was immediate. There were editions in Philadelphia and New York in 1810, and between 1811 and 1822 further impressions were published in Baltimore, New York, Hartford (Connecticut) and Brattleborough (Vermont). As the Napoleonic Wars reached a conclusion, a French edition, *Les Chefs Écossais: roman historique*, was published in 1814 – its ban by Napoleon I serving to confirm a reading of Porter's work as British patriotism. Once peace was established, though, a dramatised version of the tale was performed on stage in Paris in 1819 as part of a fad for Scottish theatre, and in 1824 a dramatic treatment of the work was performed in Scotland.[6]

Porter's success even spawned the spurious novel *Bannockburn*, printed in London by J. Warren in 1821 and promoted as a 'sequel' in the Philadelphia edition of that year.[7] Not from the pen of Jane Porter, it came from an opportunist cashing in on her popularity. Success also led to *The Scottish Chiefs* being carried by *Mackay's Edinburgh Circulating Library*, along with at least fourteen other circulating libraries across the British Isles, and at least five subscription libraries in Scotland and England between the years 1814 and 1838.[8] Both Porter's first novel, *Thaddeus of Warsaw*, and *The Scottish Chiefs* were presented as 'Companions to the Waverley Novels' for subscribers to the Standard Novels in 1831, published by Henry Colburn and Richard Bentley, and sold by Bell & Bradfute in Edinburgh.[9] Thereafter, at least ten further impressions of the 1831 standard edition were produced in the period up to 1900, including an imprint published in Dublin, with Irish and Russian translations made, and publishers offering variations of title or subtitle. *The Scottish Chiefs* was serialised in the *London Journal* in 1854; the first part was given away free, and then sold every Saturday for one penny.[10] Destined for the lower-middle-class market, a new single-volume edition was advertised in 1859 by a group of publishers in Edinburgh, Glasgow, Aberdeen, London and Manchester for sale at two shillings.[11]

The Scottish Chiefs went through around seventy-five editions and reprintings in the nineteenth century, and *Thaddeus of Warsaw* achieved around eighty-four editions and reprintings,[12] yet it was the publishing houses, not the author, who profited.[13] As a follow-up, Porter published the moderately well-received *The Pastor's Fireside* in 1817, for which she received 200 guineas. Its success, and the lustre from her earlier two novels, was sufficient for Longmans to offer her £100 in 1823 as an advance on her next romance, making the amount up to 600 guineas upon publication. The publisher noted: '. . . should the work meet with the anticipated success you will probably hear still further from us.'[14] This advance was much less than Scott was earning and less than half of what Maria Edgeworth was being offered, but it was at the higher end of the norm for most novelists and well above the meagre £10 to £20 with which the Minerva Press was rewarding its writers.[15] In 1824, Longmans considered the copyright of *The Scottish Chiefs*, along with Porter's other writings, as being of 'much value', and it was therefore not disposed to 'deligate [*sic*] the right of printing an edition to anyone, yet [we are] prepared to allow an edition of 1000 to 2000 copies to be printed'.[16] Her editor, Owen Rees, warned Jane, when she was looking to earn income from publishers elsewhere, that '[w]e purchased of you the intire of your interest in the copyright of your novels'.[17] In part because Porter's *Duke Christian of Luneburg* (1824) was no success, Rees continued to dash the hopes of the increasingly impoverished Miss Porter. She received nothing from the many reprints of the first two romances; Rees pointed out that when sales had warranted it the publisher had sometimes paid out more, but '[t]he demand for the last we are sorry to say does not admit of this'.[18] Longmans eventually sold the whole of Jane Porter's works and those of her younger sister Anna Maria, and copyright, to Colburn & Bentley in 1831, prompting their novels to be marketed at less than the regular price.[19]

* * *

Presented as an episodic narrative freed from the incremental chronology of history, developed from a literary and conjectural marshalling of the evidence, with the ascription of superhuman powers, Wallace's biography came to dominate the national tale. Hary's *Wallace* took the tale beyond the chroniclers and William Hamilton of Gilbertfield modernised its consumption through the narrative form, contracting the account and deploying the Scots vernacular. Anglicisation and further shortening followed to add readership to stories that had once been recounted orally, a process furthered by the romanticisation of the biography within contemporary international relations by *The Scottish Chiefs*. The impact of Porter can be measured though sales of her book and her cultural impact in Scotland and overseas – with the novel the leading point of access to the Wallace story for generations of English readers.[20] The focus of this chapter is on examining how this authoritative voice became a declaration of authenticity, further securing Porter's hold over the national tale. By deploying the concept of social memory, I aim to demonstrate how the presentation of Porter's biography mirrored that of Hary and *Wallace* for its use of episodic juxtapositions sustained by false claims to historical veracity.

Within disciplines other than history, the concept of social memory has been used to study the communal response to death and trauma, moral knowledge and practice, as well as the historical basis of economic and political strategies.[21] Social memories have greatest impact when personalities and lives, physical artefacts and structures adhere to hagiographic or critical narratives to communicate understanding and knowledge. The British monarchy's claim upon the historical past to manufacture social memories has not been lost on commentators, who have demonstrated through a range of national narratives how symbolic authority is rooted in wider culture from which 'the nation' comes to represent *our* social life.[22] Within the dynamic interplay of history, culture and cognition that connects monuments and other markers of the national past is the pull of individual memory. The mix of individual cognition with history and culture legitimates social memories against the authenticity of written records. By allowing the researcher to include the atypical and transcendent memories of the individual in the analysis, social memories work differently from static collective memories which offer dominant understandings and are isolated from personal agency.[23] In Charles Withers' study of the nineteenth-century Highland clearances, for example, it is demonstrated through Donald MacLeod's publication of his own lived experience of these events in Sutherland, and the letters he received from others who concurred with his *Gloomy Memories*, that a social memory was formed.[24] This mix of living memory with the weight of second-hand memories comprised fluid evidence that converged as 'fact' for MacLeod and, once established, this 'fact' was used to compromise historical knowledge gained from written sources.[25] As with the case of Donald MacLeod, Jane Porter's contemporaries knew her as a carrier of 'fact' through her narrative of William Wallace, along with a presentation of her public self marked by opportune ties to historical authenticity, literary leadership and British military success. When a particular story, trope, or symbolic representation gains authority over another at a particular time, to the extent that it appears to transcend the told narrative 'out of its history', the concept of social memory directs attention to the processes behind individual cognitive memories, and the resources employed to transfer those memories more widely in society.[26] The authority of *Wallace* came from its being labelled contemporary with its hero executed in 1305, and later generations assigned Hary individual consciousness from the poem's origins in oral traditions and its substance based on a 'Latin Buk' maintained by Wallace's chaplain, John Blair. Manufactured as these memories and claims were, they professed their derivation from contemporary experience and as such claimed legitimacy.

In order to further situate *The Scottish Chiefs* within the national tale, attention is directed towards a set of stories formed in Porter's own cognition. These living memories were forged in her childhood experiences of a new life in Scotland; her claim to have pioneered the historical novel; her personal, familial, and fictional projections of her public self; and how contemporaries returned to her, and made known to society, their reception of her personality, her deportment, and her fiction. It was in combination that a leading social memory of the nation's tale was formed out of living memory that could not have transcended time and place.

One can postulate that creativity might come from being born on the border between two nations (England and Scotland), or growing up in 'debatable lands'. Such has been an inspiration ascribed to both Scott and Porter. Jane Porter was born in Durham of mixed Irish and English parentage (another border). Upon the death of her father William Porter (1735–79), Jane's mother, also Jane Porter, née Blenkinsop (1745–1831), her sister Anna Maria (1778–1832), and her brothers John (1772–1810), William (1774–1850) and Robert (1777–1842), went north in 'wretched poverty', primarily in search of better and cheaper schooling, which they found at George Fulton's Edinburgh school.[27] However much Mrs Jane Porter valued this instruction, it was Scotland's fights for monarchical and political independence that filled the future storyteller's head. The 1831 standard edition of *The Scottish Chiefs* provided its author with the opportunity to reassess her famous work and to explain the memories that inspired its composition and the structure she employed, and, ultimately, to stake her claim as the creator of the historical novel. Reliving how the story of Wallace formed in her mind, she recalled, 'there is a spirit of wholesome knowledge in the country, pervading all ranks, which passes from one to the other like the atmosphere they breathe'. 'Nowadays', she disclosed:

> To wander in these memories has, however, a pleasure of its own, many pleasant places presenting themselves to stop at, and thence to review with a sweet sadness, through the long vale of past days, some distant, lovely scene, under the soul-hallowed twilight of time. Such scenes are peopled with beloved forms, living there before our heart's eye; but, in reality, long removed from us into an eternal paradise.[28]

She tells us that her sister's nurse, Bell Johnstone, sang of Wallace, and that her humble neighbour, Luckie Forbes, told the children stories of the Scottish heroes.[29] As Jane remembered, she had heard of Wallace from six years of age:

> not from gentlemen and ladies, readers of history; but from the maids in the nursery, and the serving man in the kitchen: the one had their songs of 'Wallace Wight!' to lull my baby sister to sleep; and the other his tales of Bannockburn and Cambuskenneth, to entertain my brother, – keeping his eager attention awake evening after evening, often till a late hour, and sending him to bed, still asking for more, to see the heroes in his dreams.[30]

Added to this jumble of historical episodes and tales of valour, around the closes of Edinburgh's High Street she heard of past times from Jacobite widows she met. She was fortunate, Jane claimed, that in Edinburgh there were still many of the 'celebrated persons who had distinguished themselves by a brave and devoted attachment to the cause of the unhappy race of royal Stuarts'. Flora Macdonald, the Drummonds, the Lockharts and others 'in their storied old age' came to visit 'the English widow and her bairns'.[31] In her recollections Porter recounts the visit of an old stranger to her house – someone who left a white rose symbolic of Bonnie Prince Charlie. This character, whom she wrongly supposed to be a man, was Jeannie Cameron, wearing the scarf that Charles Edward Stuart had folded round her neck one stormy night at sea.[32] And of greater repute still, the celebrated Flora Macdonald came to the Porter household to view Robert's drawings.[33]

Jane Porter's youthful experiences when living in Scotland between the ages of four and eighteen led her to layer the individual memories of others upon wider social memories. She claimed these mediaeval and Jacobite reminiscences as her own when, aged thirty-four and having lived in England for the past sixteen years, she put down her pen upon completion of *The Scottish Chiefs*. One commentator described the impact of Porter's childhood Jacobite stories as '[t]he flame that prepared her to be the future "epic historian" (for so some of our contemporaries have denominated her style of writing)'. They continued: 'in the year 1745 [*sic*], all the disasters of the narrator's were consummated at the fettle battle of Culloden'.[34] By coincidence, Jane Porter's mother was born in 1745, and it was through Mrs Porter's friendship with Walter

Scott's mother Anne (née Rutherford, 1739?–1819) that the young Walter became a frequent visitor to the Porter home.[35] It was a friendship Jane tried hard to cultivate right up to the end of Scott's life, writing to him with her concerns for his health, and bringing to mind her recently deceased mother's delight in conversing on his works, and remembering his days as a boy visitor to their home. In 1831, Jane Porter hoped to meet with Sir Walter on his way through London to Italy in search of health-restoring weather. While her concern was genuine, she still found time to enquire if he had received copies of *Sir Edward Seaward's Narrative*, so keen was she to have his approval of the text.[36] Later reflections by Douglas Percy Bliss, published in the *Scotsman* in 1936, claimed that the younger Scott 'took pleasure in visiting these infant prodigies and alarming them with tales of warlocks and witches',[37] but there were few signs of his affection.

Claiming memory as innate, part of one's very being, Jane Porter added gravitas and Highland lineage to open *The Scottish Chiefs* with an epigraph attributed to Ossian: 'There comes a voice that awakens my soul. It is the voice of years that are gone; they roll before me with their deeds.' With mention of Macpherson's fragmentary fabrications, she places the Scottish Homer alongside Wallace's domesticity and Charles Edward Stuart's failure, to further feminise an ahistorical pathway to Scotland's constitutional present. In *The Scottish Chiefs*, Porter had fashioned a successful means of communicating the social memory of a national tale that would resonate widely.

This all appears very calculating, yet when the contract was being drawn up for Longmans in 1808, there was no mention of Ossian or Wallace, and indeed no confidence that Porter had any definite plans for her follow-up to *Thaddeus of Warsaw*. It was to be a 'novel or romance', in four volumes, for the sum of £300.[38] In preparation Porter had conducted some research, but she was lingeringly vague about what this entailed. Like Blind Hary, who had claimed a 'Latin Buk' by Wallace's chaplain John Blair, in her retrospective introduction to the 1840 edition Porter professed to have consulted many authorities – 'our old British historians' – and that she herself had added nothing new 'excepting where time having made some erasure, a stroke was necessary to fill the space and unite the outline. Tradition has been a great assistance to me in this respect'.[39] It was the poet Thomas Campbell who is credited with providing Jane, who had left Edinburgh for London in 1794 and was residing in Thames Ditton in Surrey at time of writing, with many of these historical materials. But by 'wandering in these memories ... living there before our heart's eye' and basing her characterisations on 'tradition', she proposed the connection from her own living memory to the individual consciousness of Wallace, Blair and Hary.

* * *

As Jane Porter's reputation and output waned over her long life, she took every opportunity to promote her own role in opening the pages of the historical novel. Staging the social memory embodied by *The Scottish Chiefs* was based on a value-laden and intellectual bond between herself, her character of Wallace, and Sir Walter Scott. Porter shared Longmans as publisher with Scott and could do nothing but acknowledge the latter's fame and talent: in her letters to him she describes him as 'the mighty magician' who 'has made all Scotland a sort of sacred shrine'. 'I can earnest say', she wrote, 'that your portraits of these times have brought my sister and myself to live amongst them.'[40] She writes to request permission to invite her friends to see him.[41] Indeed, she jokes that '[a]t sight of this, perhaps you will think my little notes of introduction haunt you like a ghost!'.[42] When she was not making overtures on behalf of others to her famous friend, she clearly hoped to gain his approval for her novels. She wrote to Sir Walter Scott in 1828 asking him to give attention to 'a little work recently brought out by my sister and myself, a novel on existing manners – the third volume entirely mine: and because it is a kind of trespass on ground you have so completely made your own, it comes in the light of a tribute, ever humble the offering, to the rightful Lord of the soil!'.[43] In the same year she again wrote to Scott, saying that she had resisted reading his *Peveril of the Peak* (1823) and *Woodstock* (1826) before completing her own volume. Yet, when addressing her readers in 1831, she describes Sir Walter as 'he who did me the honour to adopt the style or class of novel of which *Thaddeus of Warsaw* was the first – a class which, uniting the personages and facts of real history or biography, with a combining and illustrative machinery of the imagination, formed a new species of writing in that day'.[44] She engineers her own *Waverley*-like mystery in *Sir Edward Seaward's Narrative*, the story of a shipwreck and simple utopian society, contracted to Longmans in 1831 for £300.[45] Jane Porter is credited as editor and claims in the preface to have received the manuscript from a representative of Sir Edward Seaward, and that the Admiralty had tried to locate the (nonexistent) 'Seaward Islands'. *The Spectator* described it as '[t]he most curious and instructive work that has appeared since the first dawn of discovery, and in the history of navigation'. The *New Monthly Magazines*, meanwhile, suggested there had never been '[a] more attractive personal narrative . . . issued from the press'.[46] Mrs Fletcher, formerly Miss Maria Jane Jewsbury, could not make up her mind 'whether the "Narrative" be truth touched by fancy, or fancy working on truth, [but] the result is equally captivating'; it prompted her to produce eighty-eight lines of verse as a tribute.[47] In response to the probing of *The London Quarterly Review* as to the authenticity of the piece, Porter replied that 'Sir Walter Scott had his great secret: I must be allowed to keep this little one'.[48] But the real secret was that her brother William, a former naval surgeon, was the author.[49] Presenting fiction as fact, and being mysterious and evasive about it, was indicative of her determination to latch on to the success of *Waverley*'s creator and the burgeoning demand for historical fiction.[50]

Porter's retrospective claims to have blazed the path for the historical novel were of sufficient currency to raise a scurrilous comment from *Fraser's Magazine* in 1835: 'She may parody Bishop Hall, and tell Sir Walter – I first adventured – follow me who list/And be the *second* Scottish novelist.'[51] And if one fake novel (*Bannockburn*) and one fabricated authorship (*Sir Edward Seaward's Narrative*) was not enough, there is a spurious letter which purportedly comes from Jane saying that she *and* her sister had just finished *The Scottish Chiefs* and would like Sir Walter to help with its climax to 'write the last sheets'.[52] Perhaps her contemporaries had noticed the tendency to hang, as best she could, on to the coat-tails of the northern wizard and use her association with him to seek authority for her writing. It is perhaps also telling that within the Porter family correspondence there is nothing extant from Scott.[53] And while Scott is recorded by James Hogg as suggesting he might have attempted his own 'life of Wallace' had it not been for the one written by Porter, it was not out of admiration:

I am grieved about this work of Miss Porter! I cannot describe to you how much I am disappointed, I wished to think so well of it; and I

do not think highly of it as a work of genius. But, Lord help her! her
Wallace is no more our Wallace that Lord Peter is, or King Henry's
messenger to Percy Hotspur. It is not safe meddling with the hero of a
country; and, of all others, I cannot bear to see the character of Wallace
frittered away to that of a fine gentleman.[54]

Others compared her Wallace unfavourably to what it was imagined Scott would do with such material. Thomas Carlyle, in a letter
to Robert Mitchell in October 1814, noted that he was reading
both Porter's *The Scottish Chiefs* and Scott's *Waverley,* and that
the latter was 'the best that has been published these thirty years'.[55]
Later, in 1821, when reflecting on the fate of Wallace in the hands
of the latest 'vulgar rhymer' (Joanna Baillie), Carlyle asks, 'Why
does not the author of *Waverley* bestir himself?'[56] Baillie's 'William
Wallace' gives credit to Porter for its inspiration, and while some
were prepared to accept the latter's role as John the Baptist in the
historical novel debate, criticism would accuse Jane of dragging
down Scotland's national hero.[57]

Nevertheless the link to Scott was vital for Jane Porter's reputation and authority as narrator of Scotland's national tale. In a
collection of eminent personages of the nineteenth century, the
accompanying memoir states that 'it is known that Sir Walter Scott
generously admitted to his late Majesty, one day in the library
at Carlton-palace, that this work [*The Scottish Chiefs*] was the
parent, in his mind, of the Waverley Novels'.[58] A year later, *Fraser's
Magazine* reiterated Scott's debt to Porter: 'It is to her fame that
she began the system of historical novel-writing, which attained
the climax of its renown in the hands of Sir Walter Scott; and no
light praise it is that she has thus pioneered the way for the greatest genius of our time.'[59] Significantly, both these summaries were
published after Porter's introduction to the 1831 standard edition
of *The Scottish Chiefs*, where she is at her most forthright in claiming Scott's embellishment of a genre she had begun. She herself did
most to set free the hare and watch the literary hounds take chase.
The conclusion of Mona Wilson, writing nearly a century later,
is that the story of Sir Walter telling George IV that *The Scottish
Chiefs* was the inspiration behind *Waverley* may be dismissed as
apocryphal. But there is some record of Scott and Hogg visiting
Jane in London in 1815, and Sir Walter would no doubt have
talked about the sensational reception of *Waverley*. Indeed, there is

evidence that he had discussed it with the Prince Regent at Carlton House at this time.[60] But as is so often the case with such matters, the actual detail is less relevant than the story, and it remained a mystery that reflected well on Jane Porter.

The *Monthly Mirror* asserted that 'it is not in Scotland alone that Miss Porter is greeted with the warmest applause, her work is generally read throughout the kingdom, and has fixed her as it were in an exalted hemisphere, where her *imitators*, as minor planets, shine with diminished brightness'.[61] James Paterson, Wallace historian and contemporary of Porter, concluded that since Hamilton of Gilbertfield's text had lost its place among the reading public, *The Scottish Chiefs* 'may be said to have assumed the position once occupied by the Minstrel'.[62] Others marvelled at the novel's 'electric effect', with rings and crosses carved from the surviving fragments of Wallace's Oak sent to its author along with other relics of even more dubious authenticity, giving credence to Penny Fielding's argument that antiquarianism and the written word were inextricably entwined in this period.[63]

Adding to this eminence was Jane Porter's success in advancing her social position through royal association. Robert Ker Porter's early art was in such vogue that Sir Sidney Smith had brought Prince William of Gloucester into the family's parlour to be introduced. Jane was reportedly tongue-tied and unable to make the kind of positive impression she might have hoped.[64] Yet her reputation endured, and *Duke Christian of Luneburg* was written at the behest of the future William IV in the hope of securing royal preferment to ease her financial worries.[65] The queen was then sent a 'fine copy' of *Sir Edward Seaward* upon its publication in 1831; one of a number of complimentary copies that had also been sent to Sir Walter Scott, the United Services Club and the Athenaeum Club.[66]

Certainly, Robert and his literary sisters had secured social prestige early in their careers. Lady Charlotte Bury, whose own writings and acquaintance with Scott gave her more than a passing interest in new Scottish literature, and who was appointed lady in waiting to the future Queen Caroline in 1810, recorded in her diary that 'Madame de C[–] praised Miss Porter's "Scottish Chiefs", and said, it quite *monté* her imagination about Scotch persons of Scotland'. Lady Charlotte continued her careful acclaim by noting that '[h]ad she known the high-minded authoress, she would have added an additional note of praise for the rare character of the writer'.[67] *The*

Monthly Mirror described her publication of *Thaddeus of Warsaw* as a 'new species of composition; an harmonious union between the heroic matter of ancient romance, and the domestic interest of a modern novel'.[68] Much contemporary observation coupled innate literary talent with the character and attractiveness of Jane Porter – a common experience for the literary ladies of the period.[69] This was comment that tended to be second-hand and retrospective. It even started before Jane was recognised for anything but being connected to a fashionable artist. Another who published with Longman & Rees, the poet Mary Robinson, wrote to Samuel Jackson Pratt on 31 August 1800, to note: 'I expect the Miss Porters, the beautiful sisters of the painter of the Seringapatam Picture with their mother.'[70] But few would depict Jane as attractive once seen. Her portrayal at the morning soirée of Mrs Leo Hunter, where celebrities gathered together ('without the slightest power of appreciating anything but the celebrity'), was not complimentary. Lady Morgan compared Jane Porter to 'a shabby canoness',[71] and also recorded her disgust that Jane had been mistaken for her: 'She is tall, lank and lean, and lackadaisical, dressed in the deepest black, with rather a battered black gauze hat, and an air of a regular Melpomene. I am the reverse of all this, *et sans vanité*, the best dressed woman wherever I go.'[72] Having written Irish romantic novels as Sydney Owenson before her marriage to the newly knighted physician Thomas Morgan in 1812, most notably *The Wild Irish Girl* (1806), Morgan was an author and wit who used her talent to overcome her small stature and slight facial deformity.[73] Yet her less than complimentary depiction of Porter was also echoed by Lord Abercorn. Having asked to meet them at the time of *Thaddeus of Warsaw*, and they being unable to afford the cost of travel, he sent them a cheque; they duly arrived. But on spying the sisters come through the hall he is recorded as taking the private staircase, crying to his wife, 'Witches my Lady! I must be off.'[74]

One persistent image of Jane Porter came after she had been made a Lady of the Chapter of St Joachim and had received the Gold Cross of the Order of Württemberg following the German publication of her first two novels.[75] With the option from the former of styling herself 'Lady Jane Porter', she instead chose the sombre costume of a 'Lady Canoness'.[76] The award inspired the sketch of Jane Porter found in the National Portrait Gallery's collection of eminent persons,[77] and she was known for wearing a black habit to literary gatherings.[78] Despite the positive comments on her Teutonic honour, the reflective on Jane Porter published in *Fraser's Magazine* in 1835 focused mostly on how well her looks had survived the ravages of time: 'Handsome the face is *still*. We hope that Miss Porter has sufficient philosophy to pardon us for that fatal adverb.'[79] A likely more favourable recognition received by the novelist came from the booksellers who had profited most from her popularity overseas. During his year as mayor of New York in 1844, the publisher James Harper organised a special presentation – 'A Votive Present to Miss Jane Porter'[80] – of a luxurious easy chair, richly carved and covered with crimson velvet.[81] Likely modelled on James Fraser's published sketch of 1834, the accompanying line drawing shows the author with head covered, nun-like and suitably *religieuse* to appeal to her German chivalric benefactors, taking coffee seated in a substantial high-backed chair.[82]

Jane Porter not only projected virtuousness through her sombre and at times shabby dress, and the patronage of those who remembered her heyday, but also through her personal and family life, including her love and admiration for those whom she no doubt realised were unattainable. The first edition of *Thaddeus of Warsaw* was dedicated to Admiral Sir Sidney Smith, victor at the Siege of Acre (1799) and a celebrated subject of her brother's portraiture. Failing to ensnare his affections she maintained a sycophantic correspondence until his death in 1840,[83] whereupon she proposed the construction of a monument in his honour, beginning the campaign with £10 in the name of 'Sir Robert Ker Porter, K.C.B.' and £1 in the name of 'William Wallace' – 'just to show that so minor a sum would be acceptable'.[84] In her diary she acknowledged that physical love was not for her, despite her claiming many letters and locks of hair gifted from various eligible men:

> Oh, not the Rose d'Amour for me!
> Too many thorns that rose surround:
> These thorns will pierce, these thorns will wound
> How sweet soe'er the flower may be![85]

Admiration had come from Willis, and there was a certain infatuation towards the young American author and critic that lasted until the day of her emotional entry recording his marriage to another.[86] Being the eldest daughter, Jane had taken to looking after her mother, who would be widowed fifty years – a choice that did little to reduce her distance from marriage. Contemporaries attributed this shaping of Jane's character to her filial self-sacrifice, although the indications are that it was a sacrifice that suited her: 'A mother's soft sorrows, to her led the way.'[87] Her mother's death in 1831 was followed the next year by Jane's concern over the increasingly recurrent illness of her 'dearest sister', whom she noted in her diary was at times too unwell to accompany her to church.[88] Illness and fatigue were constant themes in these entries, and on 21 June 1832 there was finality: 'My blessed sister was taken by her saviour this day around noon.'[89] Dead from typhus despite the efforts of William, with whom the sisters were then staying, Anna Maria was buried beside their mother at St Paul's churchyard in Bristol.[90] With her immediate household taken from her when aged fifty-six, Jane Porter was to remain unmarried, spending another eighteen years of long visits to friends and family to best stretch her meagre funds while struggling to maintain a home in London.[91]

Spinsterhood, and the commitment she had made to her mother, confirmed the presentation of piety with which Jane became known, and which in turn helped confirm the authenticity of her literary characterisations. This was what one publisher advertised as the 'sentiment of Jane Porter' – an idealised religiosity fixed in manners and mores, with her 'devoting her mornings to the prayer book, and her evenings to the *conversazione*'.[92] Reflecting her demeanour, commentators reminisced mawkishly about her characterisations of Wallace as 'a sort of sentimental dandy who, if we mistake not, faints upon occasion, is revived by lavender water, and throughout the book is tenderly in love'.[93] Such a memory, we recall, is evocative of her 'fine gentleman Wallace' that Scott (according to Hogg) railed so firmly against, yet could not suppress. In Hary's epic, Wallace was the seducer, but with Porter's pen he is 'unsexed by his patriotic crusade'.[94] And when contrasting the domestic bliss of Wallace at the start of her story, where he was to be found living quietly with his wife (defying historical knowledge that he was never married), it becomes a book about conjugal not national revenge.[95] In *The Scottish Chiefs* Wallace is a Christian gentleman idealised by and for his author's piety. Porter emasculated and depoliticised her hero, and by shifting focus from a diminished past to a diminished present she led the way for a wider narrative of Scotland and England entering union as equals, making monarchical or political reparation irrelevant.[96]

To her last, Jane Porter hung on to her role as the harbinger of the historical novel, writing to her friend Mr Litchfield just three months before her death:

> I own I feel myself a kind of sibyl in these things: it being fully fifty years since my 'Scottish Chiefs' and 'Thaddeus of Warsaw' came into the then untrodden field. And what a splendid race of the like chroniclers of generous deeds have followed, brightening the track as they have advanced! The author of 'Waverley' and all his soul-stirring 'Tales of my Landlord', &c. Then comes Mr James, with his historical romances on British and Foreign subjects, so admirably uniting the exquisite fiction with fact, that the whole seems equally verity.[97]

Like her sister, Jane died in the home of her brother William, succumbing to a second attack of apoplexy on 24 May 1850. She was identified in the death notices of the English regional press as 'The talented authoress of "Thaddeus of Warsaw", [and] "The Scottish Chiefs"', with '&c' accounting for her later works.[98] *The Pastor's Fireside* was added to the first two 'well known to our readers' by the *Aberdeen Journal*, which noted her passing under English domestic news.[99] In death her lineage was tied not to Scotland but to her birthplace of St Mary-le-Bow and her late parents' connection with Durham Cathedral.[100] She was suitably worthy to be listed alongside Patrick Fraser Tytler and Sir Marc Isambard Brunel among the 'Deaths of Public Men' [sic] in both *The Times* and Dublin's *The Freeman's Journal*, while *The Illustrated London News* carried her portrait.[101] To some she was simply the 'well known authoress'; to others she was appropriately and solely 'Miss Jane Porter'.[102] There was little to suggest she was ever a nationalist totem, excepting recognition that *The Scottish Chiefs* had been of great influence within society. The sentiments of the novel reflected many conventional mid-Victorian norms, and Scottish nationalism had not yet acquired associational expression at this time for Porter to be bracketed with Scottish–English conflict. *The Glasgow Herald and Mail* cited only the Wallace narrative from her opus, and stressed the 'cheerfulness and disposition for which she had been so much admired over her long life'.[103] The Edinburgh *Scotsman* did not mark her passing. Quoting personal comment published in the *Athenaeum*, it remembered Jane as amiable rather than brilliant: '. . . there was a touch of old world and sentimental eloquence in her manner.'[104] This is a fitting précis of how her life and her literary creation came to be embodied in a historical narrative that lasted well beyond her passing.

A moderate talent from an English–Irish family of some repute, with modest physical beauty hidden beneath a veil, and both a public and a private stress on piety and financial probity, Jane Porter was in many ways an unlikely carrier of Scotland's national tale. Yet from the first publication of *The Scottish Chiefs*, through its standard edition in 1831 to Virtue's fine reprint in 1840, a social memory formed that mirrored Hary's authenticity. The authenticity which failed so completely in her later works, but was widely sustained in her transmission of the Wallace tale into a pervasive social memory, had come from a series of connections, some remarkable, some less so: the childhood stories that came with the cross-border move from England to Scotland, the Jacobite romancing of the '45, and her mother's relationship with Scott's family. Together, they ensured an association with the greatest character of the day that she would cling to without abatement. Her favourite brother's diplomatic, military and artistic life, his royal connections, and his familiarity with both Sir John Moore and Sir Sidney Smith had led Jane to link Wallace's stand against the tyranny of Edward to the Siege of Acre and the Scottish line in the Peninsula Wars. In her pronouncements she claimed the historical novel for her own. Although never accepted without question, the claim was sufficiently credible to produce a decisive connection with Scott. This pairing, and the repackaging of her literary role, were of greater significance than their veracity. By these means of affirming authenticity, her literary and personal paradigm of the national tale prevailed as the social memory of the age.

NOTES

1. Her major works include the following unidentified contributions: A Society Gentleman [J. Porter], *The Quiz* (1797); Anon [J. Porter], *A Defence of the Profession of an Actor* (1800); I. Porter [J. Porter], *The Two Princes of Persia, Addressed to Youth* (1801). She claimed as her first romance *Thaddeus of Warsaw* (1803), and there then appeared *Aphorisms of Sir Philip Sidney, with Remarks* (1807); *The Scottish Chiefs* (1810); *The Pastor's Fire-Side* (1817); *Duke Christian of Luneburg: or Tradition from the Hartz* (1824); and,

with Anna Maria Porter, *The Field of Forty Footsteps* (1828). She is also credited along with William Ogilvy Porter with the editorship of *Sir Edward Seaward's Narrative of His Shipwreck and Consequent Discovery of Certain Islands in the Caribbean Sea* (1831). Full details in Robert Tate Irvine Jr, 'The Life of Jane Porter', unpublished MA thesis (University of Virginia, 1942), pp. 254–5.

2. Gary Kelly, 'Introduction', *The Scottish Chiefs* (London: Pickering & Chatto, 2002), p. vii.

3. Critically, her first historical romance is her best. It tells the story of the contemporary Polish freedom fighter Thaddeus Kościuszko (1746–1817), whom her brother Robert had met and whom she transformed into the fictional Thaddeus Sobieski – a fabricated descendant of John Sobieski of the Sobieski-Stuart line, whose travels to England were framed as a sympathetic tale of Polish refugees fleeing Napoleon's expansions into Europe. Polish émigrés lauded the tale's accuracy and Kościuszko let the author know of his praise for the German translation. See Dorothy McMillan, 'Porter, Jane (*bap*. 1776, *d*. 1850)', *Oxford Dictionary of National Biography*, Oxford University Press, 2004; online edn, May 2008, http://www.oxforddnb.com/view/article/22571 (accessed 17 July 2012). Correspondence relating to the reception of this work is to be found in Bristol, Bristol Record Office, Acc 5097, Ref 8032/88: Jane Porter to Eliza Vanderhorst, 1837; and Ref 8032/98: Jane Porter to T. C. Vanderhorst, 4 April 1845.

4. *Longman Impression Book* No. 4, fo. 31, fo. 107; *Longman Impression Book* No. 6, fo. 11; *Longman Impression Book* No. 7, fo. 39v; *Longman Impression Book* No. 8, fo. 69v, cited in 'Publishing Papers' for Jane Porter's *The Scottish Chiefs* (1810), *Database of British Fiction, 1800–1829* [DBF]: 1810A070.

5. Garside, 'English novel in the Romantic Era', pp. 38–9.

6. René-Charles Guilbert de Pixérécourt, *Les chefs écossais mélodrame héroïque en trois actes et en prose* (Paris, 1819). Pixérécourt's melodrama premiered at the Théâtre de la Porte-Saint-Martin, Paris, in Sept. 1819; and an engraved double portrait, 'Costume de Mme. Dorval, rôle de Lady Helène, et de Mme. St. Amand, rôle de Genevieve, dans les Chefs Écossais' was also produced at this time.

7. See the record for Anon's *Bannockburn* (1821), *DBF*: 1821A001. The 1822 edn published in Philadelphia is subtitled 'Being a sequel to the Scottish Chiefs by Miss Jane Porter'. A. D. Hook, 'Jane Porter, Sir Walter Scott, and the historical novel', *Clio* 2 (1976), p.184.

8. Given in 'Contemporary Libraries' for Jane Porter's *The Scottish*

Chiefs (1810), *DBF*: 1810A070; Garside, 'English novel in the Romantic Era', pp. 39, 44.

9. *Scotsman*, 8 June 1831, 7 September 1831. *Thaddeus of Warsaw*, *The Scottish Chiefs*, *The Pastor's Fireside*, and *Hungarian Brothers* by Anna Maria Porter, were the sisters' contribution to the forty-five 'Standard Novels and Romances' advertised by Richard Bentley, *Scotsman*, 13 May 1835.

10. This advert was placed under the heading 'Scottish Rights', in *Scotsman*, 6 May 1854; G. Morton, 'Scotland is Britain: the Union and Unionist-Nationalism, 1807–1907', *Journal of Irish and Scottish Studies* 1 (2008), pp. 127–41.

11. *Scotsman*, 4 January 1859.

12. Looser, *Women Writers and Old Age in Great Britain*, p. 166.

13. Her constant struggles with financial difficulty can be seen in her correspondence with Anna Maria. Durham, Durham University Library Archives and Special Collections [DULA], Porter Family Correspondence, MSS GB-0033-POR, A, 63–6.

14. Reading, Reading University Library [RUL], Longman Group Collection, MS 1393, Longman I, 101, No. 141: Owen Rees to Miss Porter, 26 May 1821; MS 1393, Longman I, 99, No. 229: Owen Rees to Miss Porter, 31 May 1816; MS 1393, Longman I, 101, No. 421A: draft letter 11 September 1823; Jane Porter, *Diary*, 1832; Jane Porter Papers, No. 715, Box 1: Longman & Co. to Miss Porter (at Mrs Gills, Carisbrook, Isle of Wight). Thanks are due Karen Racine for her insight into the Porter siblings.

15. Garside, 'English novel in the Romantic Era', p. 82.

16. RUL MS 1393, Longman I, 101, No. 459B: Longman & Co. to Mr Barclay, Liverpool, 12 August 1824.

17. RUL MS 1393, Longman I, 101, No. 480: Owen Rees to Miss Porter, 17 December 1824.

18. RUL MS 1393 Longman I, 101, No. 519B: Owen Rees to Miss Porter, 10 December 1824; Longman I, 10, No. 507B: Draft Letter to Miss Porter, 17 May 1825; Longman I, 101, No. 520C: O. Rees to Miss A. M. Porter, 24 December 1825.

19. RUL MS 1393 Longman I, 102, No. 166A: Longman, Rees & Co. to Mrs Opie, 7 April 1831; Longman I, 102, No. 195H: Letter from Mr Owen Rees, 29 April 1833.

20. C. Kidd, 'The English Cult of Wallace and the Blending of Nineteenth-Century Britain', in E. J. Cowan, *The Wallace Book* (Edinburgh: John Donald, 2007), p. 144.

21. M. Halbwachs, *On Collective Memory*, ed. and trans. L. A. Coser (Chicago: University of Chicago Press, 1992); M. G. Cattell and J. J. Climo, 'Meaning in Social Memory and History: Anthropological

Perspectives', in J. J. Climo and M. G. Cattell (eds), *Social Memory and History: Anthropological Perspectives* (Oxford: Rowman & Littlefield, 2002), pp. 3–5.

22. H. Bhabha's 'Narrating the Nation', in Homi Bhabha (ed.), *Nation and Narration* (London: Routledge, 1990); Linda Colley, 'The apotheosis of George III: loyalty, royalty and the British nation 1760–1820', *Past and Present*, 102 (1984), pp. 94–129; P. A. Scholes, *God Save the Queen! The history and romance of the world's first national anthem* (Oxford: Oxford University Press, 1954); J. S. Ellis, 'The prince and the dragon: Welsh national identity and the 1911 investiture of the Prince of Wales', *The Welsh History Review*, 18 (1996), pp. 272–94.

23. Blaikie, *Scots Imagination*, p. 11; D. S. A. Bell., 'Mythscapes, mythology and national identity', *British Journal of Sociology*, 54 (2003), pp. 65–6, 72.

24. C. W. J. Withers, 'Landscape, memory, history: gloomy memories and the 19th-century Scottish Highlands', *Scottish Geographical Magazine*, 121, 1 (2005), p. 35; D. Macleod, *Gloomy Memories in the Highlands of Scotland: Versus Mrs. Harriet Beecher Stowe's Sunny Memories* (Toronto, 1857).

25. Withers, 'Landscape, memory, history', p. 38.

26. C. Cairns Craig, *Out of History: Narrative Paradigms in Scottish and English Culture* (Edinburgh: Edinburgh University Press, 1996) is important for analysing how the historical novel, as represented by Scott, was based less on linear progress than on devices and tropes. These observations can also be applied to Porter.

27. George Fulton was also the author of a number of school books.

28. Jane Porter, 'Introduction', in her *The Scottish Chiefs* (London, 1831), p. i.

29. M. Wilson, *These Were Muses* (London: Sidgwick & Jackson, 1924), p. 119.

30. Porter, 'Introduction', in her *The Scottish Chiefs* (London, 1831), pp. iii–iv.

31. G. Harlowe, 'Miss Jane Porter', in W. Jerden (ed.), *National Portrait Gallery of Illustrious and Eminent Personages of the Nineteenth Century; with Memoirs*, 5 vols (London, 1834), v, n.p. (biographical entry paginated 1–8).

32. 'Yell a' ha'e heard tell o' Bonnie Jeanie Cameron,/How she fell sick, and she was like to dee/And a' that they could recommend her/Was ae blithe blink o' the Young Pretender./Rare, oh rare, Bonnie Jeanie Cameron!/Rare, oh rare, Jeanie Cameron!', in G. Eyre-Todd (ed.), *Ancient Scots Ballads, with their traditional airs to which they were wont to be sung* (Glasgow, n.d.), 7–12. Eyre-Todd came upon the

ballad, and its air, from William V. Jackson, 'in whose family it has been handed down by tradition from Jacobite times', and who told the story of an elderly Cameron dressed in men's clothing; a tale sufficiently well-known to be repeated in Robert Chambers, *Traditions of Edinburgh*, 2 vols (Edinburgh: Chambers, 1825), ii, pp. 190–1.

33. *Scotsman,* 29 July 1936.
34. Harlowe, 'Miss Jane Porter', p. 2.
35. Hook, 'Jane Porter, Sir Walter Scott, and the historical novel', 181.
36. Edinburgh, National Library of Scotland [NLS], MS 5317, fo. 185–6: Jane Porter to Walter Scott, 5 October 1831.
37. *Scotsman,* 29 July 1936.
38. DULA MSS GB-0033-POR, Vol. E, 45–6: Copies of contracts with Messrs Longman by Jane Porter and Anna Maria Porter.
39. This claim to authenticity was repeated as late as 1903 in a reprint forming part of the Collins' Imperial library series: Jane Porter, *The Scottish Chiefs* (London and Glasgow, 1903), pp. 1–2.
40. NLS MS 3906, fos 196–7: Jane Porter to Walter Scott, 8 Apr. 1828.
41. 'I cannot have the satisfaction of making the pilgrimage myself to Melrose, or rather to the mighty magician, which has made all Scotland a sort of sacred shrine. I send my friends, whose taste and hearts are ready to be my representative. Allow(?) me to present to you Captain Montgomery, a brave and accomplished man; and his fair daughter whose beautiful mind, was once cased in as lovely a form, until sickness and sorrow paled the rose and withered the lily. But to see Sir Walter Scott would be a rich satisfaction to them both! Captain Montgomery has seen much foreign service; and is now returning to the West Indies, by the way of Scotland, to his native country, Ireland. A brave man, suffering under service, is worthy indeed a candid grasp of the hand from the Chivalry poet of Dear Old Caledonia.' NLS MS 3896, fos 183–4: Jane Porter to Walter Scott, 31 May 1823.
42. NLS MS 3901, fos 118–19: Jane Porter to Walter Scott, 10 September 1825.
43. NLS MS 3906, fos 196–7: Jane Porter to Walter Scott, 8 April 1828.
44. Wilson, *These Were Muses*, 125; Hook, 'Jane Porter, Sir Walter Scott, and the historical novel', p. 183.
45. RUL MS 1393, Longman I, 102, No. 165D: Owen Rees to Jane Porter, 29 March 1831.
46. As advertised in *Scotsman*, 21 March 1832.
47. Mrs. Fletcher, 'Lines Written After Reading *Sir Edward Seaward's Narrative*', *Athenaeum* 1 December 1832.
48. Wilson, *These Were Muses*, pp. 135–6.
49. See Fiona Price, 'Jane Porter and the authorship of *Sir Edward*

Seaward's Narrative: previously unpublished correspondence', *Notes and Queries* (March 2002), pp. 55–7. The scam was, of course, not a new one, and her sister had toyed with anonymously publishing *The Hungarian Brothers* before quickly adding her name. Quayle, 'Porter, Anna Maria (1778–1832)'.

50. NLS MS 3906, fos 196–7: Jane Porter to Walter Scott, 8 April 1828.
51. Maginn, 'Miss Jane Porter', p. 404.
52. NLS MS 23118, fos 22–3: Jane Porter [spurious?] to Walter Scott, 12 December 1820.
53. DULA MSS GB-0033-POR, vols A–F.
54. James Hogg, *Domestic Manners of Sir Walter Scott* (Stirling, 1909), p. 112.
55. Quoted in Hook, 'Jane Porter, Sir Walter Scott, and the historical novel', pp. 184–5.
56. Thomas Carlyle, 'Miss Baillie's Metrical Legends', *New Edinburgh Review* I (1821), pp. 402–3, quoted in Price, 'Resisting "The Spirit of Innovation"', p. 638.
57. Harlowe, 'Miss Jane Porter', p. 5.
58. Ibid.
59. Anon, 'Miss Jane Porter', *Museum of Foreign Literature and Science* XXVII (1835), p. 113.
60. Hook, 'Jane Porter, Sir Walter Scott, and the historical novel', 181. Details of Sir Walter's dinner with the future King are found in John G. Lockhart, *The Life of Sir Walter Scott* (London, 1906), pp. 269–73.
61. Anon, 'Memoirs of Miss Porter (with a Portrait)', *The Monthly Mirror* (December 1810), pp. 404.
62. James Paterson, *Wallace and His Times* (Edinburgh, 1858), p. xx.
63. Harlowe, 'Miss Jane Porter', p. 5. Wallace's Oak was located at Torwood Forest and reportedly cut down in 1790, with only its roots remaining at this time for souvenirs such as, in addition to Porter's gift, a musical box presented to George IV; J. D. Carrick, *Life of Sir William Wallace of Elderslie* (London, 1840), p. 96; Penny Fielding, *Scotland and the Fictions of Geography. North Britain, 1760–1830* (Cambridge, 2008), p. 102.
64. White, 'Selections from a diary of Miss Jane Porter', pp. 226–7.
65. Hook, 'Jane Porter, Sir Walter Scott, and the historical novel', p. 181; Looser, *Women Writers and Old Age in Great Britain*, p. 29.
66. DULA: Porter Correspondence B [1831]: 'A note on the binding of presentation copies of Sir Edward Seaward's narrative'.
67. Lady Charlotte Bury, *The Diary of a Lady-in-Waiting*, ed. A. F. Stuart, 2 vols (London, 1908), i, 295, cited in 'Anecdotal Records' for Jane Porter's *The Scottish Chiefs* (1810), *DBF*: 18100A070.

G. C. Boase, 'Bury, Lady Charlotte Susan Maria (1775–1861)', rev. Pam Perkins, *Oxford Dictionary of National Biography*, Oxford University Press, 2004, http://www.oxforddnb.com/view/article/4147 (accessed 17 July 2012).

68. Anon, 'Memoirs of Miss Porter (with a Portrait)', p. 403.

69. Anon [William Maginn], 'Gallery of Literary Characters. No. 59: Miss Jane Porter', *Fraser's Magazine* 11 (1835), p. 404.

70. Mary Robinson to S. J. Pratt, 31 August 1800, cited in Kenneth Neill Cameron (ed.), *Shelley and His Circle 1773–1822* (Cambridge, 1961), pp. 231–5. The picture refers to the panoramic 'The Storming of Seringapatam' by Robert Porter.

71. 'Personal reflections of Lady Morgan', *New York Times*, 26 July 1874.

72. Wilson, *These Were Muses*, p. 128.

73. Dennis R. Dean, 'Morgan , Sydney, Lady Morgan (*bap.* 1783, *d.* 1859)', *Oxford Dictionary of National Biography*, Oxford University Press, 2004; online edn, January 2008, http://www.oxforddnb.com/view/article/19234 (accessed 17 July 2012); Ina Ferris, *The Romantic National Tale and the Question of Ireland* (Cambridge: Cambridge University Press, 2002).

74. Wilson, *These Were Muses*, pp. 127–8.

75. S. C. Hall, 'Memories of Jane Porter', *Harper's Magazine*, 1 (1850), p. 435; I. M. White, 'A diary of Jane Porter', *Scottish Review*, 29 (1897), p. 329. Until legislation in 1823 regulated the recognition of foreign knighthoods, Jane and Robert were entitled to call themselves 'Lady' and 'Sir'. Admiral Lord Horatio Nelson was wearing the breast cross of a Knight Grand Commander of The Order of Saint Joachim when he fell mortally wounded at the Battle of Trafalgar in 1805.

76. *The Herald – Communications of the Order of St Joachim*, Summer 2006, p. 8.

77. Harlowe, 'Miss Jane Porter', p. 5.

78. Thomas Sadler (ed.), *Diary, Reminiscences, and Correspondence of Henry Crabb Robinson*, 3 vols (London, 1872 edn) i, p. 202.

79. Original emphasis. Maginn, 'Miss Jane Porter', p. 404.

80. DULA MSS GB-0033-POR, Vol. B, 295–6; *The Gentleman's Magazine* XXIII January–June (1845), p.173.

81. *The Times*, 16 January 1845. The signatories, in addition to Harper, were: W. H. Appleton, Charles S. Francis & Co., Harper & Brothers, Daniel Appleton, S. B. Collins, and N. Authours.

82. Maginn, 'Miss Jane Porter', p. 404.

83. Devoney Looser, 'The Great Man and Women's Historical Fiction: Jane Porter and Sir Sidney Smith', *Women's Writing*,

19 (2012), pp. 293–314; Roger Morriss, 'Smith, Sir (William) Sidney (1764–1840)', *Oxford Dictionary of National Biography*, Oxford University Press, 2004; online edn, May 2009, http://www.oxforddnb.com/view/article/25940 (accessed 17 July 2012). Various likeness of Smith then followed in the style of Sir Robert Ker Porter, one notable example being produced by the engraver Anthony Cardon in 1804, London, National Portrait Gallery: D6794.

84. UVL, Papers of Jane Porter, Acc. No 1625-A, Box No. Wf1588-a: Letter from Jane Porter to Henry Robinson, 29 November 1840.
85. White, 'Diary of Jane Porter', pp. 325, 326, 333.
86. White, 'Diary of Jane Porter', pp. 331, 333.
87. Harlowe, 'Miss Jane Porter', p. 1.
88. RUL Jane Porter, *Diary*, 26 February 1832.
89. RUL Jane Porter, *Diary*, 16 March 1832, 21 June 1832.
90. Quayle, 'Porter, Anna Maria (1778–1832)'.
91. Irvine, 'Life of Jane Porter', pp. 207–8.
92. The publisher was Derby & Jackson for their mid-century edition of *The Scottish Chiefs* (New York, 1856); Anon, 'Miss Jane Porter', *Museum of Foreign Literature and Science* XXVII (1835), p. 113.
93. Ibid.
94. Dennis, *Nationalism and Desire*, p. 20.
95. Hence in *Wallace, the Hero of Scotland* (1822), for example, the eponymous protagonist believes himself a warrior sent by Marion and inspired by conjugal affection within a narrative structure indebted entirely to Porter.
96. Dennis, *Nationalism and Desire*, p. 44.
97. Anon, 'Miss Jane Porter', *The Gentleman's Magazine* XXIV, July–December 1850, pp. 220–1.
98. *The Hull Packet and East Riding Times*, 31 May 1850.
99. *The Aberdeen Journal*, 5 June 1850.
100. *Newcastle Courant*, 7 June 1850.
101. *The Freeman's Journal*, 28 May 1850; *The Illustrated London News*, 8 June 1850.
102. These sobriquets were used by the English provincial papers, including *The Bristol Mercury and Western Counties Advertiser*, 25 May 1850, *The Manchester Examiner and Times*, 14 August 1850, and *The Leeds Mercury*, 1 June 1850, which also adds *Thaddeus of Warsaw* and *The Scottish Chiefs* to help identify the deceased.
103. *The Glasgow Herald and Mail*, 31 May 1850.
104. Anon, 'Miss Jane Porter', *Gentleman's Magazine* XXIV, July–December 1850, p. 222.

Chapter 7

A Distant Tale

In 1900, under the title 'Some Famous Old Maids', the *Western Mail* recorded that 'Jane Porter lived and died an old maid. The children of her busy brain were "Thaddeus of Warsaw" and the "Scottish Chiefs", which have moved the hearts of millions to excitement and tears.'[1] Following the National Portrait Gallery's acquisition of the portraits of Jane and Anna Maria Porter in 1898, the *New York Times* recorded that Jane wrote *The Scottish Chiefs* while her younger sister 'made books, but she is forgotten'.[2] It was a significant turn-around. Anna Maria was first to find fame with *Artless Tales* in 1793 and it was she whose talents were recognised as the greater; her literary output the more prodigious.[3] The sisters flirted with the fashionable parlours of their day, but neither seemed entirely comfortable with the attention that brought. It was suggested the somewhat plain Misses Porter were unpopular among their contemporaries, with Miss Mitford and Lady Morgan saying '*nasty* things about them. And yet, *The Scottish Chiefs* and *Thaddeus* are still read'.[4]

That discussion of their writings and character continued for such a length of time after death – Anna Maria in 1832, Jane in 1850 – gives some clue to the Porters' cultural relevance. In scholarly analysis, the sisters secure a place in the literary canon at the development of the historical novel, yet it is in her transformation of the national tale that Jane's influence was greatest.[5] *The Scottish Chiefs* gained authenticity as a national narrative because it fitted the contemporary social memory of the nation. This connection was formed in Porter's lived memory, the memories she reproduced from others, and in how she projected her own life to her readership: together it sustained a reading of Scotland's past that vindicated the contemporary political nation. In 1831, *The Manchester*

Times reproduced an extract from Porter's introduction to provide its readers with sketches of Scottish character.[6] It told mainly of Porter's interest in Wallace, but singled out her portrayal of Scotland as 'the land of enthusiasm for all gallant and disinterested emotions'. The newspaper worried that support for the underdog was not always conducive to national progression, but could readily connect *The Scottish Chiefs* to Scotland's political fate. Affirming her personal opposition to the darker side of nationalism, Porter fused an ensemble of heroes to précis Scotland's place within Britain: Thaddeus Kościuszko, Sir Philip Sidney, Sir John Moore, Sir Sidney Smith, and Sir William Wallace. Explaining why nations must commemorate their champions, she counsels:

> For let us remember that when a nation ceases to recollect the great and the good amongst their own forefathers, they soon cease to be a people of much account at home; and in proportion to that internal decline, they sink in the estimation of the nations abroad.[7]

Can it be said that Porter's historical romance achieved this very sentiment for the Scottish nation in the estimation of people abroad? For sure, no one was able to rival *The Scottish Chiefs* for telling the Wallace story in this period; Scott never produced a play or narrative dedicated to the story, and the many chapbooks, poems, and plays printed in the nineteenth century failed to match the numerous editions, and sales, that Porter achieved. The authority garnered for this version of the nation was a debate internal to Scotland's place within Union, but one where Porter's influence came by means of her personal authenticity.[8] Despite her novel lacking a historical understanding rooted in Enlightenment modes of progress, through the coupling of the national tale with the contemporary nation Porter's sway was enhanced, a position promoted further by her success distant from Scotland. To explore why Porter's Scottish nation should gain such credence internationally, two themes are examined. The first charts the cultural penetration of her most popular novel to delineate the worldwide appeal of its sentiment; the second gives focus to her poverty and piety, and to the connections – and poverty – of her siblings. The Porter family, as with her own social memory, played an important role in Jane's presentation of self, and from that the wider acceptance of her characterisation of Wallace as a pious self-made man of honour.

* * *

Having already followed her sister into print with some trivial contributions, Jane Porter began her career in earnest with the romantic novel *Thaddeus of Warsaw* (1803). Based on the life of Polish military hero Thaddeus Kościuszko (1746–1817), fictionalised with Scottish royal lineage as Thaddeus Sobieski, it would remain her most critically acclaimed work. Polish émigrés lauded its accuracy; she was sent a lock of Kościuszko's hair and a gold ring with a miniature of the General. Kościuszko read the German translation and let Jane know his praise for it.[9] Academically, *Thaddeus* is the root to Porter's claim – such as it is – to the historical novel before the Waverley series began in 1814: Polish and French editions were produced in 1803 and 1809 respectively, and it would go through ten editions over the next seven years.[10] Following her compendium *Aphorisms of Sir Philip Sidney, with Remarks* (1807), Porter's next full-length novel, *The Scottish Chiefs*, was contracted with Longman in 1808 and published two years later.[11] The new novel kept up her fascination with the Stuart line through its characterisation of King Robert I, but its focus fell on the medieval patriot and Guardian of Scotland, William Wallace. Written in the style of the historical romance, it eschewed blood lust to contrast the domestic bliss of its protagonists with the union of England and Scotland, making the story one of feminine intrigue and revenge.[12] With a print run of 3,500 copies over the next eighteen months Longman kept it in circulation with further modest impressions, insisting that the book, as with all her works, was a prized part of their catalogue.[13] But it was valuable to others, too, and her publisher was powerless to prevent sales being lost to Irish and American printing houses. This, the consequence of weak copyright laws, gained Porter renown but not royalties from the abundant editions that then ensued. Some concerns were raised over the popularity of the poorer productions, where price was fixed to nothing but the thickness of the spine, but better-quality editions later appeared from various London publishers.[14] Fredrick Warne published *The Scottish Chiefs* in 1886 and the newly established J. M. Dent & Co. chose a revised edition for the Christmas market of 1900, with illustrations by T. H. Robinson, priced at five shillings.[15] The book's marketing would even stretch to a colourfully illustrated version published by Hodder & Stoughton in 1921, with images by the American illustrator N. C. Wyeth brightening the story to meet the expectations of a twentieth-century audience.[16] In each instance, and repeated elsewhere, as the centenary of *The Scottish Chiefs* was passed, Jane Porter was being read, being discussed, and continued to delineate the cultural roots of Scotland's political nation.

The American publications, and those of Ward Lock of London and the Strathmore Press in Scotland, found their way to New Zealand and Australia.[17] There were French translations published in 1814 and 1820.[18] The book was a staple of circulating libraries in Scotland and England, as well as overseas.[19] Mr R. Campbell of Bligh Street in Sydney used the classified advertisements of *The Sydney Gazette and New South Wales Advertiser* in January 1814 to declare that he was missing the first volume of *The Scottish Chiefs*, and 'whomever may have [it] was requested to send it immediately' to him.[20] Aitken's Circulating Library in New Zealand advertised the work of Jane Porter to its South Island readership throughout October and until Christmas 1854.[21] Indeed, a performance of the play in the Scottish settlement of Otago in 1863 was denounced as overly sensational when 'a gory head, intended to be a striking resemblance of the actor, was raised by the executioner' upon the fall of the axe. The audience were not calmed until the actor appeared from behind the curtain with the promise that the offensive incident would not be present in future performances.[22]

Along with the many reprints, a number of citations can be found that reflect the infiltration of Porter's work into popular culture. In a review of the America historical novelist James Fenimore Cooper's *The Water-Witch* (1830), the prevailing influence of the Scottish story is noted:

> It would probably be found on inquiry, that there are few romances of which a larger numbers of copies have been, and continue to be sold, than *The Scottish Chiefs*; which, after the strange enthusiasm which attended its first appearance had subsided, was not estimated very highly by those who wish to see the faithful representation of character and manners together with a tolerable adherence to correct taste.[23]

Porter elicited comparisons that mixed praise with disappointment. In 1831, *The North American Review* would welcome a second reading of Scott, but not of Porter, although still it acknowledged

The Scottish Chiefs' success.[24] In *The Liberal*, published the same year, *The Scottish Chiefs* is described as a work 'no woman should be without', pointing plainly to the gender of its core readership.[25] Even at the century's end, Porter was important enough to be one of only seven women included in Edmund Gosse's review of English literature for a New Zealand audience.[26] More particularly, *The Scottish Chiefs* was part of the reading matter compiled by child prodigy Sallie Marvine Demaree of Kentucky,[27] and cited when a half-century of women's writings was reviewed in 1907 – although the American readership was warned that Porter's five-volume output was rather more fearsome than welcoming.[28]

Research on the impact of women's writing identifies a number of influences lasting long after Porter's death that would fan out into popular culture. Thackeray makes J. J. Ridley, the romance-addicted schoolboy in *The Newcomes*, a devotee of Porter.[29] Among the various aliases of Helen Jewett, a New York prostitute whose murder in 1836 made headline news, was 'Helen Mar', the heroine of *The Scottish Chiefs*.[30] Both examples are evidence that Porter's appeal stemmed from the simplicity of her emotional message, and the ease with which it could resonate. According to *The North American Review* in 1844, a young lady would read *The Scottish Chiefs* with great delight because its sentiments were refined, the incidents pleasing and the whole work '*so* interesting!'.[31] And somewhat bizarrely, *The Scottish Chiefs* was credited with prompting the oldest convert to Catholicism in Providence, Rhode Island, in 1879. The convert's inspiration came directly from Porter's description of Helen Marr praying for the safety of Bruce.[32]

The international interest in *The Scottish Chiefs* did not end with its author's death, itself an occasion recorded widely. She was one of the literary stars to drop from the hemisphere, according to Auckland's *Daily Southern Cross*.[33] It was as the authoress of *The Scottish Chiefs* that the *New Zealander* recorded her loss.[34] The *Scientific American*, noting that the English papers of the Atlantic states had announced her death, claimed Jane Porter was familiar to all as the author of *The Scottish Chiefs* among other novels and romances, while internationally she and her family were described as names England has good cause to hold in grateful remembrance.[35] If for many editors the death of Maria Edgeworth in May 1849 overshadowed that of Jane one year on (almost to the day), the latter was still presented to the American reading public as one of the most distinguished novelists England had produced, principally for introducing historical fiction to the literary world.[36]

Whatever the level of admiration, gossip or recall, Jane's life and irregular forays into essays and romances were generally known points of British social memory. When the corporation and people of Belfast prepared the local arrangements for the Queen's Diamond Jubilee in 1897, the death of Jane Porter was highlighted in extracts from the annals of Victoria's reign.[37] Porter could be and was remembered as being English, Scottish, British, and, given the interest in her books by the Dublin printing presses, and given her father's parentage, Irish. She was also an Anglo-Scot – an incomer writing Scotland's national history, but having returned south before penning *The Scottish Chiefs*.[38] Furthermore, she was a product of the provinces in England: who could best declare Jane Porter their local daughter was a matter of debate. In death she was claimed by Durham, the town in which she was born and where her mother was the daughter of a chorister at Durham Cathedral.[39] Yet Jane and family were local worthies in the *Newcastle Courant*'s guide to the North Country (12 September 1879), reproduced again the next year.[40] And while a report in the *Bristol Mercury* in 1880 rather reluctantly acceded to this, still the town claimed the authoress as one of their own through her place of residence, and that of her brother William Ogilvie Porter, as well as being the place where she died.[41] Jane Porter was included within the town's exhibition of modern women's work, adding to her association with the area and the recall of its residents.[42]

* * *

With an overtly sentimental account of human relations in the face of national adversity that was more popular with the reading public than the reviews by literary critics might suggest, *The Scottish Chiefs* enjoyed success beyond its geographic and temporal boundaries. Benefiting from the acclaim heaped upon Sir Walter Scott, Jane Porter was one of only a few contemporaries working within this genre. For critics, her work was too emotional, its merit dull, her style merely competent, yet still she was a literary star universally praised at her death. Along with demand for the historical romance, the appeal of Jane Porter came from knowledge of the life she led as a self-sacrificing spinster whose personal

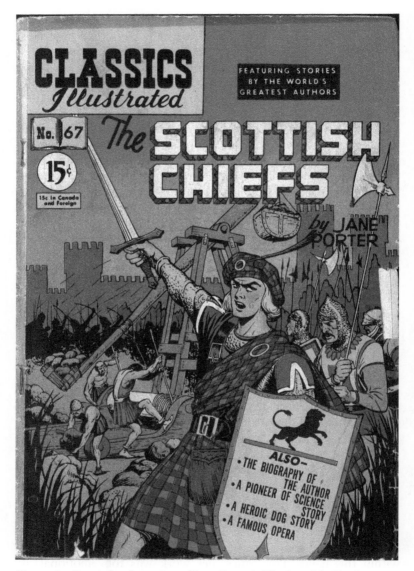

Figure 1 *Comic book version of Jane Porter's* The Scottish Chiefs
*(1950). © Dundee Art Galleries and Museums, Albert Square, Dundee
DD1 1DA. Licensor www.scran.ac.uk*

experiences contrasted with the characters of her imagination, yet author and creations alike maintained a central morality in their conduct. Not only was Jane's life (and death) recorded, but so also were those of her siblings, whose own talents, travails and international lives shaped the interplay of novelist and novel in the popular imagination.

Among these, it was the reputation of her brother Robert which was to the fore. As the literary sisters' careers began to take off, it was their youngest brother whose life course was first to stretch into Europe and beyond. Robert Ker Porter found fame first under the tutelage of Benjamin West as an artist of grand epics, notably his 'Storming of Seringapatam' of 1800, when he was aged only 23. Completed over a six-week period, it is 120 feet long and 21 feet in height, covering 2,550 square feet of canvas. So well-received was the epic that his 'Siege of Acre' (1801) and 'Agincourt' (1805) were soon brought to life.[43] Robert's renown opened up for him the opportunity to travel – he was appointed historical painter to the Russian Emperor Alexander I and invited to paint Admiralty Hall in St Petersburg. In Russia he met and married a Russian Princess, Mary van Schertbatoff, was knighted by Gustavus IV of Sweden in 1806, and became a knight of St Joachim of Württemberg in 1807; upon restabilising his home in England he was knighted by the Prince Regent in 1817.[44] His *Travelling Sketches in Russia and Sweden* (1808) did not signify great penmanship, the *Quarterly Review* concluding '[it] may lie without offence on a table'.[45] But it was Robert's travel with Glasgow-born Sir John Moore into battle at Corunna (1809) during the Peninsula Wars which fed Jane's passion for British patriotism. She would later associate the Scots who died there with those who died in the battles of Stirling Bridge (1297) and Falkirk (1298), connecting the tyranny of Napoleon I to Edward I and contrasting each as threats to a British future secured under the House of Hanover.[46]

For his diplomatic role as British consul to Venezuela (1825–41), notably for his support of the non-Catholic overseas community, in 1832 Robert was appointed Knight Commander of the Royal Hanoverian Guelphic Order by George IV.[47] When stationed in Caracas, Robert would write regularly to Jane with information on the social and economic development of South America. Jane was also included among her brother's own correspondents, including Colonel Belford Hinton Wilson, who wrote to her off Cape

Horn with information on the wildlife and territorial claims of the Falkland Islands.[48] Robert was the one sibling with a degree of financial stability. For 1830, Jane lodged £921 7s 6d on Robert's behalf with the bankers Wright & Co. of London, with steady and substantial deposits thereafter.

Robert and Jane Porter: Income and Expenditure Record, 1830–9

For the Year Ending	Income
1831	£1,300 5s
1832	£1,221 17s 6d
1833	£1,228 8s 5d
1834	£1,030
1835	£1,373 16s
1836	£1,585 3s 6d

For the Year Ending	Expenditure
1830	£183
1831	£931 19s 25d
1832	£167
1833	£104
1834	£200*
1835 (until September)	£165
1836	£201 18s

* This was recorded as '£200 and odd', indicating further small sums not accounted for in these accounts.

The expenditure refers to what Jane herself withdrew from these monies, and what she knew of Robert's spending,[49] all, it must be said, being very modest. The expenditure in 1831 is made distinct primarily for the £400 invested in 'Powles' (the British firm Powles, Lord, Weymar & Co., which was still active in Venezuela in 1842 but had failed by 1849).[50] Jane wrote in her account book for 1836 'Thank God for His Bounty!', and in that for 1838 that the sums 'show God's infinite goodness'. She was dependent on it, for there appears little income of her own in these records. When, in December 1839, she could finally add £100 of her own money to the total, her Royal Bounty, she gratefully wrote, 'Thank God!!!'[51]

The persistent need for funds, the push for a pension, and the adoption of the Lady Canoness as her public image ensured knowledge of Jane Porter's pecuniary straits never strayed far from her presentation of self. Jane appreciated the dangers of poverty and wrote often of its effects on her life. Despite the financial help he provided for his sister, and despite what these summary accounts recorded by Jane might indicate, Robert's expenses were great and complex, a fact that came to light after his death when Jane took on the onerous task of executing his tangled estate.[52] There can be little doubt that the Porters were aware that regardless of their various successes around the Empire, financial fragility was a companion for them all. It was the early death of the father, William Porter, in 1779 which caused the family to relocate to Edinburgh in search of greater economy to stretch an army widow's pension, a move that set in train so much of what followed in the lives of the children, and a story Jane often recounted to her readership of *The Scottish Chiefs*. A review of Robert Porter's life provided by *The Scotsman* highlighted the blight of poverty that the family had faced.[53] With a bankrupt business partner in 1817, William Ogilvie Porter took a number of years to overcome the loss of £3,000: '. . . my all – my profession and half pay excepted.'[54] By 1820, he was paying off his debt yearly from his income as a physician,[55] which amounted to around £1,000 in that year, but only £700 and £800 in the next two years.[56] This debt was a struggle to manage along with the purchase of a Commission for his son Charles.[57] Jane recommended Edinburgh for her nephew's education the next year, and while his father agreed, he retained a preference for Haddington. Either way, he calculated he could afford to subsidise Charles to the sum of £60 per year, yet was canny enough to insist on paying the sum in quarters.[58] For whatever reasons this educational jaunt was not to last, and Charles prepared to set sail for America in the spring of 1830 as another male member of the Porter family sought to revive his fortunes overseas.[59] Jane's least successful brother was her eldest, John, although he still rose to the rank of Colonel and was a merchant in the West Indies. John was not favoured among his siblings, dying relatively young in 1810, aged 38, while incarcerated in Castle Rushen Jail on the Isle of Man.[60] In 1806, he had written to his sister to say that a writ of execution had been taken out against him unless the sum owing be paid in full.[61] He was imprisoned as a debtor and left a wife and infant child in such poverty that her bed was sold to fund the purchase of a coffin. John seemed not to have been much loved outside the family either. When the minister issued a letter asking for charity, all declined. When, twenty years

later, Jane prepared her mother's tombstone, she would not include
John's name among the list of her mother's children,[62] although his
name is later inscribed alongside Jane, William and Anna Maria
in Bristol Cathedral in 1851.[63] Care with expenses and attention
to any path that might earn a little extra income was a habitual
struggle for the Porters.[64] Part of the rationale for William's silent
role in the creation of *Sir Edward Seaward's Narrative* was to
channel funds to Jane.[65] It is perhaps well that when Jane was asked
to reflect on 'Independence', her perspicacity was not a reflection
on the politics of the nation, but the independence that came from
financial and personal probity: 'To be truly and really independent,
is to support ourselves by our exertions', she wrote.[66] It would not
be implausible to suggest that this statement was a conscious reflection of the trope of 'Self Help' which so shaped the Victorian cult
of Wallace the self-made man.[67]

The entrepreneurial publisher George Virtue temporarily revived
Jane Porter's finances in 1840 after reclaiming copyright to her
romances.[68] He had approached her through Willis to produce
new, de luxe editions, filling Jane with great hope:

> ... last October, entered into an agreement with Mr Virtue (Please
> Heaven and as far as my recovered copyright allows) to furnish him
> a new Preface and additional notes to *The Scottish Chiefs* – at the end
> of 3 months or within 6 months – when he will give me Bill for £200,
> payable at 3 months; God in his gracious mercy grant I may be able to
> do it within the 6 – that will be the middle of April.[69]

Similar editions of *Thaddeus of Warsaw* and *The Pastor's Fire-Side*
were produced, giving Porter a modest sum for her old age while
the standard editions for which she was not recompensed continued
to flow forth.[70] But for all that genteel poverty came to characterise
her public persona and a steady decline in creative imagination less-
ened her output, Jane remained a personage of international repute.
The colourful talent and career of her brother Robert brought her to
royal notice, and her admiration for and friendships with Sir Sidney
Smith and the American writer and critic Nathan P. Willis were
known beyond literary circles.[71] Her movements were recorded,
whether overseas in St Petersburg accompanying Robert on his
final visit,[72] or touring the cathedral towns of England with some
antiquarian friends before spending the winter in Chester.[73]

It is ironic that the many editions produced royalty-free by publishing houses, in America especially, maintained Jane Porter's popularity and intellectual value. It is ironic also that the wider appeal of the author lay in her Christian forbearance and graceful frugality rather than her literary talent and the pecuniary success that might have come from it: 'A cheerful temper spreads like the dawn, and all vapours disperse before it', she is quoted as saying.[74] In the year her mother died, Jane returned to *Aphorisms of Sir Philip Sidney*, offering two translated letters showing the virtues of the sixteenth-century courtier and author travelling through Continental Europe, published within a collection of religious lives.[75] The public inevitably envisaged her, pictured with religious headdress or politely sipping tea seated in a gifted high-backed chair, as 'Miss Jane Porter', connecting her sentimental treatment of Wallace with the sentiment of her biography and that of her family. It was this association which helped to ensure that Jane Porter's reflection of post-Union Scotland in the mirror of its medieval hero was so eagerly consumed, to an extent beyond its literary or historical merit. Porter's gender and her genre were also part of this appeal. Her life of royal connections and the internationalism of her brother Robert kept Jane's name known in various parts of the world.

For Scots more than many other nationals, identity is forged in the cradle of emigration. Along with Ireland and Norway, Scotland may be said to have led the European exodus of people to North America, the Antipodes and many other parts of the modern world, if exodus is measured per head of the population.[76] Yet the meaning of diaspora is not forged in the numbers who left, but in the orientation of those migrants back to their homeland.[77] The international publishing history of *The Scottish Chiefs* enabled an account of Scotland's national patriot to be known in nations abroad, as it was at home. By taking the Scottish nation into the imagination of the wider world, Porter's historical romance authenticated its place within the minds of the domestic reading public of the day. After all, Scotland's national tale is a diasporic tale, because that is Scotland's history.[78]

NOTES

1. *Supplement to the Western Mail*, 10 February 1900. The list also included Queen Elizabeth, Maria Edgeworth, Joanna Baillie and Florence Nightingale.

2. *New York Times*, 5 February 1898.
3. Anna Maria Porter published *Artless Tales* when aged only thirteen and, among shorter works, went on to pen *Walsh Colville* (1797) and *Octavia* (1798), achieving around fifty publications in total.
4. *New York Times*, 5 February 1898.
5. Price, 'Resisting "the spirit of innovation"', pp. 638–51; McLean, 'Nobody's argument: Jane Porter and the historical novel', pp. 88–103; Hook, 'Jane Porter, Sir Walter Scott, and the historical novel', p. 184.
6. *The Manchester Times*, 24 September 1831, p. 722.
7. Ibid.
8. Ferris, *Literary Authority*, pp. 10, 105–22, 195–222.
9. Letter from Jane Porter to Eliza Vanderhorst [1837], thanking her for 'the images of Kościuszko and his kind friend', Bristol Record Office [BRO], Acc 5097, Ref 8032/88; Jane writes for the date of Kościuszko's visit in Bristol, Letter from Jane Porter to T. C. Vanderhorst, 4 April 1845, BRO, Acc 5097, Ref 8032/98; R. T. Irvine, JR, 'The Life of Jane Porter' (MA thesis, University of Virginia, 1942), p. 88.
10. McLean, 'Nobody's argument', pp. 94–7.
11. Copies of contracts with Messrs Longman by Jane Porter and Anna Maria Porter, one dated 1 June 1808 on verso of a prospectus printed by J. Catnach of Alnwick and dated 1805, Durham University Library [DULA], Porter Family Correspondence, GB-0033-POR, MS. E, 45–6.
12. Dennis, *Nationalism and* Desire, p. 15; P. Beasley, 'Georgiana Molloy, Jane Porter and the significance of exploration narratives for new beginnings in a strange land', *Victorian Network*, 1, 1 (2009): 60; Hook, 'Jane Porter', p. 189.
13. Longman Impression Book No. 4, fo. 31, fo. 107, and No. 6, fo. 11, Database of British Fiction, 1800–1829, DBF: 1810A070; Owen Rees to Miss Porter, 17 December 1824, URLA, MS 1393, Longman I, 101, No. 480.
14. *The Atlantic Monthly*, 40, 241 (November 1877), pp. 619–20.
15. *Pall Mall Gazette*, 1 December 1900, p. 5.
16. In the twenty-first century, Wyeth's images have been presented, with musical accompaniment from *Braveheart* (1995), on the video-sharing site YouTube.
17. *The Scottish chiefs by Jane Porter*; adapted by John H. O'Rourke; illustrated by Alex A. Blum (Sydney, NSW, 19—).
18. *Les chefs écossais mélodrame héroïque en trois actes et en prose* by R.-C. Guilbert de Pixerecourt; Alexandre Piccinni; Théâtre de la Porte-Saint-Martin (Paris, 1819).

19. 'Contemporary Libraries' for Jane Porter's *The Scottish Chiefs* (1810), *DBF: 1810A070*; *New York Times*, 2 August 1902.

20. *The Sydney Gazette and New South Wales Advertiser*, 29 January 1814, 2.

21. *Nelson Examiner and New Zealand Chronicle*, XIII, Issue 674, 11 October 1854, 2; *Nelson Examiner and New Zealand Chronicle*, XIII, 14 October 1854, 1; *Nelson Examiner and New Zealand Chronicle*, XIII, 18 October 1854, 1; *Nelson Examiner and New Zealand Chronicle*, XIII, 21 October 1854, 1; *Nelson Examiner and New Zealand Chronicle*, XIII, 25 October 1854, 1; *Nelson Examiner and New Zealand Chronicle*, XIII, 28 October 1854, 1; *Nelson Examiner and New Zealand Chronicle*, XIII, 1 November 1854, 4; *Nelson Examiner and New Zealand Chronicle*, XIII, Issue 688, 29 November 1854, 1; *Nelson Examiner and New Zealand Chronicle*, XIII, Issue 695, 23 December 1854, 1.

22. *Otago Witness*, Issue 627, 5 December 1863, 2.

23. *The North American Review*, Vol. 32, Issue 71 (April 1831), pp. 508–9.

24. Ibid., p. 386.

25. *The Liberal*, 12 September 1833.

26. *Bruce Herald*, 13 July 1900, p. 7.

27. *Star*, 2 June 1900, p. 3.

28. *Star*, 10 May 1907, p. 3.

29. R. D. McMaster, *Thackeray's Cultural Frame of Reference* (Kingston: McGill-Queen's University Press, 1991), p. 59.

30. K. Peiss, 'Crime without punishment', *London Review of Books* (November 1998), p. 9.

31. *The North American Review*, 58, 123 (April 1844), p. 270.

32. *New Zealand Tablet*, 25 July 1879, p. 11.

33. *Daily Southern Cross*, 24 January 1851, p. 4.

34. *New Zealander*, 12 February 1851, p. 2.

35. *Scientific American*, 22 June 1850, 314; *The International Magazine of Literature, Art, and Science*, 1 , 1 (1 July 1850), p. 11.

36. Ibid., 10; Maria Edgeworth died 22 May 1849, Jane Porter died 24 May 1850.

37. *Belfast News-Letter*, 24 May 1897.

38. Despite only living in Scotland between the ages of 4 and 18, and not publishing until returning south in 1794, Porter lauded Scotland as the place that first formed her intellectual life; see J. Porter, 'Recollective Preface' (1840), *The Scottish Chiefs*.

39. *Newcastle Courant*, 7 July 1850, p. 4.

40. *Newcastle Courant*, 30 September 1880, p. 6.

41. *The Bristol Mercury, and West Counties Advertiser*, 8 June 1850, p. 8.

42. *The Leeds Mercury and Weekly Supplement*, 7 March 1885, p. 6.
43. H. de Almeida and G. H. Gilpin, *Indian Renaissance: British Romantic Art and the Prospect of India* (Aldershot: Ashgate, 2005), 160; 'Mr. Robert Ker Porter', in *Public Characters* (Dublin: J. Moore, 1801), pp. 140–1.
44. Eric Quayle, 'Porter, Anna Maria (1778–1832)', *Oxford Dictionary of National Biography*, Oxford University Press, 2004, http://www.oxforddnb.com/view/article/22559 (accessed 17 July 2012).
45. Anon [Reginald Heber], 'Art. V. *Travelling Sketches in Russia and Sweden, during the Years 1805, 1806, 1807, 1808*. By Robert Ker Porter, 2 vols 4to. pp. 600. London. Phillips. 1809', *Quarterly Review* II, 4 (1809), pp. 288–91, reproduced in *Romantic Circles*, 19 Feb. 2007, '*Quarterly Review*', ed. Gavin Budge.
46. *The Era*, 29 May 1842, 3; Hook, 'Jane Porter, Sir Walter Scott, and the historical novel', 187; Irvine, 'Life of Jane Porter', p. 113.
47. 'Death of Sir Robert Ker Porter, K.C.II', *Scotsman*, 1 June 1842; R. K. Porter, *Letters from Portugal and Spain written during march of British Troops* (London, 1809); *Caledonian Mercury*, 29 October 1836; *Notes and Queries*, 4 Ser., Vol. 3 (London, January–June 1869), p. 293.
48. Dated 19 January 1833, *The Porter mss., 1799–1850*, Lilly Library Manuscript Collection, Indiana University.
49. Porter (Jane), 'Expenditure Record and Note Book for the years 1830–1839', University of California [UC], Collection No. 715, Box 1, Folder 3.
50. S. Berglund, 'Mercantile credit and financing in Venezuela, 1830–1870', *Journal of Latin American Studies*, 17, 2, November 1985, pp. 377–9; M. Deas, 'Powles, John Diston (1787/8–1867)', in *Oxford Dictionary of National Biography*, ed. L. Goldman (Oxford: Oxford University Press, 2004).
51. Porter, 'Expenditure Record'.
52. DULA, MSS GB-0033-POR, A, 63–6. Jane Porter's close attention to her finances, reliance on Robert's government salary, and relief at securing funds from the Royal Bounty in 1839 are seen in her account book; California, University of California Archives, Collection No. 715, Box 1, Folder 3, 1–50: J. Porter, *Expenditure Account Book and Digest* (1830–9). The estate was eventually wound up in 1844 following the auction of his remaining art and possessions: T. Seccombe, 'Porter, Sir Robert Ker (1777–1842)', rev. R. Lister, *Oxford Dictionary of National Biography*, ed. H. C. G. Matthew and B. Harrison (Oxford: Oxford University Press, 2004).
53. *The Scotsman*, 29 July 1936.

54. W. O. Porter to Miss [Jane] Porter at Ditton, Kingston, Surrey, from Bristol, 7 March 1817, DULA, MSS GB-0033-POR, MS A.

55. W. O. Porter to Miss [Jane] Porter at Ditton, Kingston, Surrey, from Bristol, 31 May 1820, DULA, MSS GB-0033-POR, MS A.

56. W. O. Porter to Miss Porter at Ditton, Kingston, Surrey, from Bristol, 12 July 1822, DULA, MSS GB-0033-POR, MS A.

57. Ibid.; W. O. Porter to Miss Porter at Ditton, Kingston, Surrey, from Bristol, 30 August 1822, DULA, MSS GB-0033-POR, MS A.

58. W. O. Porter to Miss Jane Porter at Esher, Surrey, 12 April 1829, DULA, MSS GB-0033-POR, MS A.

59. W. O. Porter to Miss Porter from Bristol, 5 April 1830, DULA, MSS GB-0033-POR, MS A.

60. D. McMillan, 'Porter, Jane (*bap.* 1776, *d.* 1850)', *Oxford Dictionary of National Biography*. That this may be a case of mistaken identity, with John B. Porter named as dying in the jail, not Colonel John Porter, is raised by George Bryce in *Notes and Queries*, 3rd Series, 30 April 1864, p. 367. It is countered with the suggestion that the 'B.' stood for his mother's maiden name Blenkinsop, and that a letter from Jane Porter indicates the death was in 1811, *N & Q*, 3rd Ser. 30 April 1864, p. 529; later reproduced in *Gloucestershire notes and queries*, ed. Rev. B. H. Blacker (London: Wm Ken & Co., 1887), 3, p. 33.

61. John Porter to Miss Jane Porter, 14 May 1806, DULA, MSS GB-0033-POR, MS A.

62. Irvine, 'The Life of Jane Porter', p. 131.

63. McMillan, 'Porter, Jane'; *Gloucestershire notes and queries*, p. 31.

64. W. O. Porter to Mrs. Jane [Blenkinsop] Porter at Ditton, Kingston, Surrey, from Bristol, 20 May 1824, DULA, MSS GB-0033-POR, MS A.

65. Authorship of the book was left a mystery, with contemporary hints that Jane was behind it. W. Ogilvie Porter to Miss A. M. Porter [on paper with watermark date of 1830, with notes on payments relating to Miss Jane Porter dated 7 July 1826 on two small scraps of paper attached], MSS GB-0033-POR, MS B. Inserted note: 28 January 1846, 'There was a balance in my favour, in my banker's hand Mr Drummond of £76. Have since 7th January donated two cheques amounting together 16s 5d, leaving £59 15s.'

66. *Supplement to the Hampshire Telegraph and Sussex Chronicle*, 3 June 1893, p. 12.

67. G. Morton, 'The most efficacious patriot: the heritage of William Wallace in nineteenth-century Scotland', *The Scottish Historical Review*, 76, 2, No. 204 (October, 1998), pp. 224–5.

68. White, 'Diary of Jane Porter', p. 334.

69. Ibid., 334. Virginia, University of Virginia Library [UVL], Papers of Jane Porter, Acc. No 1625-A, Box No. Wf1588-a: Letter from Jane Porter to Henry Robinson, 29 November 1840.
70. Irvine, 'Life of Jane Porter', pp. 215–16.
71. White, 'Diary of Jane Porter', p. 334.
72. *Caledonian Mercury*, 6 September 1841, p. 1; *The Examiner*, 6 September 1841, 571; *The Bristol Mercury*, 11 September 1841, p. 2.
73. *The Preston Chronicle*, 24 December 1836.
74. Jane Porter quoted on 'cheerfulness' in *Supplement to the Hampshire Telegraph and Sussex Chronicle*, 9 June 1894, p. 11.
75. J. Porter, 'The Youth of Sir Philip Sidney', in *The Iris: A religious and literary offering*, ed. Rev. T. Dale (London and Philadelphia: Sampson Low, Hurst, Chance & Co., Thomas Wardle, 1831), pp. 303–12; H. R. Woudhuysen, 'Sidney, Sir Philip (1554–1586)', in *Oxford Dictionary of National Biography*.
76. D. Baines, *Migration in a Mature Economy: Emigration and Internal Migration in England and Wales, 1861–1900* (Cambridge: Cambridge University Press, 1985), pp. 59–61; T.M. Devine, *To the Ends of the Earth: Scotland Global Diaspora, 1750–2010* (London: Allen Lane, 2011), p. 87.
77. T. Bueltmann, A. Hinson and G. Morton, *The Scottish Diaspora* (Edinburgh: Edinburgh University Press, 2013), pp. 18–21.
78. G. Morton and T. Griffiths, 'Closing the door on modern Scotland's gilded cage', *The Scottish Historical Review*, 92, Supplement, No. 234, April 2013, pp. 49–69.

Chapter 8

The Feminised Nation

Darkness envelops the place of gender within nationalism; there are few instances to be found where their aspirations converge. Most commonly, the blindness comes from the nationalist side as the rights of women are made marginal to the agenda of the nation's needs (see pp. 10–11). So hidden have the claims of gender been that the leading nationalist theorists have only fitfully explored the interaction, and only recently have others taken up the challenge to reimagine what nationalism and national identity might have meant, and may mean, through the power relations that gender analysis unearths.[1]

It is by way of literary scholarship that the most extensive engagement with 'gendering the nation' is to be found.[2] Scrutinising the Scottish nation in communion with the core nation of England, and with the state nation of Britain, reveals results that are suggestive of both feminine and masculine outcomes.[3] Too easily, though, commentators are sucked into a shorthand characterisation of the Scottish nation that is male-dominated, chiefly in analysis of its popular culture.[4] Assuredly, whether a literary or historical approach is used, the popular nationalist canon is stubbornly male: Saint Andrew, William Wallace, Robert Bruce, Charles Edward Stuart, Robert Burns and Hugh MacDiarmid continue to dominate.[5] Indeed, these men are paraded within the national narrative for their excessive masculinity. The one place where the feminine has claimed a major symbolic presence is at the constitutional level, where the nations of Britain have been represented by the images of Britannia, Scotia and Hibernia. Yet there is irony here, for notwithstanding their gender, these are masculine symbols of authority. Representing 'women-as-nation', they are most often masculinised in times of opposition or international dispute.[6] If nothing else, this makes us aware that when national identity is privileged it is based on recurrent gender inequalities.[7] Governments have not been immune from legislating on women and men in ways that might seem to reflect constitutional rather than personal nationalism. Sex, itself, has been politicised. State (and church and institutional) control over sexual behaviour is the norm, with control over age of marriage, marriage to relatives, sodomy, bestiality, homosexuality, and masturbation.[8] It is unclear how much Victoria was aware of her Prime Minister's attendance at the culmination of her confinement to ensure the royal line was protected, although insistence that she be a virgin upon marriage would have been something she was, however subtly, reminded of.[9] Interest in the royal progeny was more than constitutional. With the birth of Princess Victoria in 1840, nine months after marriage, and then the future Edward VII in 1841, Victoria was both mother of the nation and symbol of bourgeois domesticity. She and Albert were depicted as Mr and Mrs Middle Class, and during the period when her infants were breast-fed this maternal activity became popularised as the domestic ideal of the nation.[10]

*   *   *

Broadly speaking, women's interaction with the state and the embodiment of women by the state is no different in Scotland from in the other nations of Britain. In this respect, the attempt to understand the inequalities of gendered nations is only taken so far by social theory, and that is why Romance, as a feminised literature (and specifically *The Scottish Chiefs*), can provide clues to the Scottish example. Yet we must take care that the symbols carried by Kailyard and Romantic fiction are not assigned a false place within Scotland's nationalism. This pathway comes not from any simplistic notion of femininity or domesticity, but because Romance is no literature of politics or state.[11] Even in core nations it is thus. Within its boundaries, Romance incorporates rural and parochial literature; a tradition can be traced in continuities over time, providing the patriotism of a national tale sustained in poetry and the historical novel.[12] In the second half of the nineteenth century the parochial element is transmitted through the literature of the Kailyard and the place that sentimentalised literature gained within the diaspora, sustaining a weakened narrative of nationhood at home.[13] As Christopher Whyte has noted in the case of Neil Gunn, the Kailyard literature further emasculates the nation in that it is a trope where women are 'ready to serve their husbands and sons', to be silently on hand, to be strong and resourceful but not to demand anything for themselves.[14] Such was the nationalist reaction to this literary style that it was consciously dismantled and masculinised in the writings of Lewis Grassic Gibbon and Hugh MacDiarmid at the start of the twentieth century.[15]

Yet we must take care that the Kailyard, the romance, and the symbols they carry are not wrongly assigned their place within Scotland's nationalism. It would be naive to straightforwardly bracket the literature of Kailyard as symbiotically reflected in the 'emasculated' settlements of 1603 and 1707. Scholars have argued that a feminised literature immersed in the restoration of the Scottish monarchy and pre-Union nation would lead not to modern Scotland but to an unreconstituted Scotland.[16] Alternatively, it is argued that the romanticisation of the Scottish Highlands in art – most dramatically represented by Sir Edwin Henry Landseer's *The Monarch of the Glen* (1851), and the cult of deerstalking – represents the constitutional incorporation of Scotland into England, forming a staple masculine element of an English and British identity.[17] There is some rhetorical power to both these reactions, yet they bookend a nationalism that is not to be found. Restoration of the Stuarts or an unreformed parliament were not on the agenda, other than for a very few. The symbols might be masculine, but again this is not the nationalism they reflected. It was Britain not England that contemporaries envisioned when blending the Scottish nation with English constitutionalism, a meld where the Union was inviolate.[18] Indeed, the construction of the Highlands or the kilted soldier was a contribution to the peripherality of the nation, forging a nationalism that was decidedly feminine despite its masculine motifs. In the antinomies of the Celt and the Anglo-Saxon, feminine and masculine are part constructs in the moral, personal, immediate and social opposites of *Gemeinschaft* and *Gesellschaft*.[19] To the anatomist Robert Knox, writing in 1859, the 'Caledonian Celt of Scotland' and the Lowland Saxon were as distinct 'as any two races can possibly be'. So too, from these observations, can it be explained that the nation is returned to its racial types, taking it further from hybridity or commonality, and thus accentuating difference.[20] This was a case of opposites attracting. The Scottish symbols were not appropriated by

England because they were masculine, but because they had been feminised. According to Ernest Renan in 1860, the Scotland of his day had become melancholy. Now, 'diminutive feminised pygmies' inhabited Scotland, once a land of masculine heroes.[21] In Matthew Arnold's analysis of social progress, a distinct Celtic identity was an essential component of, as well as counterpoint to, the British Empire.[22] And this thesis can be taken one stage further, to argue that consciously or not the Scots were complicit in this feminisation. Edward Said's influential theory of Orientalism teaches us that the culture of the periphery is consumed through the imperatives of the core, and that such culture is then assimilated within the periphery as if it were its own.[23] The darkness faced by studies of gender and nationalism comes from the struggle to make sense of privileging social constructions of sex, but no progress can be made until the nation's nationalism is imputed correctly. Scotland's was a feminine identity because it was the product of a peripheral nation in partnership with a core nation, a union envisioned, if not in actuality, as one of equality.

*   *   *

Out of 250 works of fiction thought worthy by the American Library Association in 1895, *The Scottish Chiefs* and *Thaddeus of Warsaw* were recommended to girls, women and their reading clubs.[24] Porter, certainly, created a feminine romance out of the most masculine of characters. The text, again without doubt, is melodramatic:

> At this sight, Helen, with a cry that was reechoed by the compassionate spectators, rushed to his bosom. Wallace, with a mighty strength, burst the bands asunder which confined his arms, and clasping her to him with a force that seemed to make her touch his very heart, his breast heaved as if his soul were breaking from its outraged tenement, and, while his head sunk on her neck, he exclaimed in a low and interrupted voice, 'My prayer is heard! Helen, life's cord is cut by God's own hand! May he preserve my country, and, oh, trust from my youth!' He stopped – he fell and with the shock the hastily erected scaffold shook to its foundation. The pause was dreadful.[25]

Here, the grisliness of medieval execution – the disembowelling while alive, the drawing and the quartering – is sanitised for sentimental effect, and the nation's destiny immediately transferred to

Bruce's chiefdom.[26] This, and the many comparable examples that can be identified, is how Porter's romantic literature fed historical events into the national tale. Yet the linguistic tone of *The Scottish Chiefs* is also shaped by Porter's juxtaposition of key names and terms, a process akin to that whereby historical events and epochs are foregrounded within nationalism.

Constructing a straightforward word concordance and text proximity test gives insight into the coherence and episodic structure of the language used.[27] The twenty most frequent words penned by Porter confirm the focus given to its hero, the list headed by the name 'Wallace', used on 2,209 occasions. This was over five times the frequency of 'Bruce' (479), a divergence that increased with the addition of their forenames. There are only eighteen occasions when Wallace and Bruce are mentioned in sentence proximity – confirming Wallace as the more heroic of the two 'Chiefs'. Ensuring, further, that the personal tie overshadowed the political bond, and that Wallace is the tale's domestic hero, is the fact that 'Helen' (647) is cited more often than 'Bruce' (479).

The deployment of the redemptive power of domestic love – inspired by a violation of that love – is similarly indicated by Helen's pre-eminence over the slain Marion (105), but this should not detract from the author's stress on patriotic bravery, with the characters being 'brave' on 265 occasions. 'Heart' was highlighted 476 times, and 'love' (189) won over 'honour' (172), but 'Wallace' and 'love' were only found in sentence proximity nine times.[28] Titles of honour and status were used frequently, whereas Wallace was only given the historically confirmed administrative title 'Guardian' on sixteen occasions. Curiously, despite the historical claims made by the author in successive introductions that she made use of 'the old standard historians', their names do not make it into the text, nor does Hary (or Harry or Harrie), other than in the preface to the first edition. Indeed, the blood spilling of Hary's *Wallace* is not there to flow in Porter's narrative: 'blood' was mentioned 194 times and was linked to ties of genealogy, but there were few other blood-related instances.[29] Instead, and presaging the people's claim to *The Scottish Chiefs*, the communitarian values of 'friend' (338), 'friends' (146) and 'friendship' (56) were to the fore.

The most sustained nationalist reading of the text comes from Ian Dennis, who comments on the contrast Porter draws between then and now, good and bad, the classic dualities of 'them and us' which maintain perceptions of the historical 'other'. Imagining the domestic bliss of Wallace at the start of the story, Porter depicts the hero living quietly with his 'wife', then contrasts this privatised domesticity with the public evil of Heselrig. Porter objects to the death of Marion at the hands of the English, and to allowing women in men's clothes to participate in warfare and national politics.[30] In this construction Porter makes the book a story about revenge for the ravished Helen and the murdered Marion on behalf of all 'outraged and violated womanhood'.[31] With such features to the fore, this is not a historical novel; this was no early Walter Scott, but it was a major contribution to the national tale. Wallace, like Thaddeus Sobieski, who appeared in Porter's first full-length novel, is portrayed as an ideal Christian gentleman.[32] And recent research has shown that Porter's female characters throughout her oeuvre have been drawn as strong and resourceful women, with Marion Wallace and Helen Marr in the forefront, maintaining domestic order in times of revolution and strain.[33]

While Porter maintains that '[t]he melancholy circumstances which first excited him [Wallace] to draw his sword for Scotland, though it may be thought too much like the creation of modern romance, is recorded as fact in the old poem of Blind Harrie', [34] still the power of her novel comes through personal romance, not historical fidelity. In *The Scottish Chiefs* Wallace is nobler because of his superhuman moral and religious purity, but less noble because he is only moved to action by the death of his wife, and because he is made the victim of a sentimental, feminine intrigue.[35] Yet this makes Porter no less a contributor to reading the nation than the historical fiction of Scott, and the life he led at the epicentre of the nation's introspection. Rather, she may be regarded as providing a nationalist reflection of the nation for the very reason that her most influential writing was so undoubtedly ahistorical. That, after all, is how the nation is popularly conceived: narrated in acceptable and legitimate pasts.[36]

*   *   *

The argument has been made that Porter gained authority for her tale by association with Walter Scott, the promotion of her connections with the heroes of the Peninsular Wars, and a presentation of self that foregrounded her own piety and patriotism. Her international reputation and that of her brother Robert then helped maintain this authority in the decades after *The Scottish Chiefs* was first published. Added to this is the appeal of the Romance in an age of increasing readership for novels, but so too the personal authority Porter claimed from association with the most powerful woman on earth, the woman who came to embody Scotland in Britain.[37] This bond was initiated when the Porter sisters were living in the village of Esher between 1822 and 1844, one mile distant from Claremont House where Prince Leopold, king of Belgium, uncle to both Albert and Victoria, was then residing.[38] The royal party often attended the parish church near the small cottage where the female Porters lived, their respective pews facing one another. The novelist spoke in 'rapturous tones of the beauty of Princess Victoria at this time' (in 1824, when Victoria was aged five).[39] The Porter sister and their mother had moved to Surrey from London once Robert had left for overseas. As an artist of grand military epics, Robert's work garnered the level of attention that reflected well on the family. It ensured the continuation of recently acquired royal patronage for the novelist, with Dr Clarke reporting her Majesty's pleasure with Miss Porter's 'historical fidelity' in the heroes she portrayed.[40] George also conveyed to Jane that *The Scottish Chiefs* had won her favour with the late William IV (r.1820–30), their onetime close neighbour in Thames Ditton.[41]

Of all, it was Victoria with whom Jane Porter looked to connect. Apparently writing from her own bed, possibly where she was confined after having waited in the rain for six hours at Pall Mall for the royal procession to pass, she sent six lines of verse to the royal couple on their wedding day in 1840. The lines 'were graciously acknowledged', although not published until Victoria's Golden Jubilee celebrations in 1887:

> Wake Albert, wake! from dreams of hope arise!
> And clasp with blissful arms the hovering prize;
> A lily from the highest Eden bends
> To seek thy bosom, and in light descends,
> Not cold, but chaste, and spotless as its hue,
> It breathes of Paradise, and breaths for you![42]

Jane had earlier, in 1831, sent Victoria a 'fine copy' of *Sir Edward Seaward's Narrative*, and in belated return the then monarch arranged for Prime Minister Lord Melbourne to forward Jane £100 from the Royal Bounty in 1839 (after much public entreating by the novelist).[43] The funds were sorely needed and likely delivered as great a fillip to Jane as did the monarch's kind regards for her improving health the next year[44] – a blessing described by Porter as 'proofs of the value her gracious sovereign set upon such talents so applied'.[45] Perhaps it is right to accept that as late as 1898, under the title of Ladies' Gossip, the *Otago Witness* notes that '[o]ne of the most favourite books of the Queen when she was a girl was Miss Jane Porter's "Scottish Chiefs" and Sir William Wallace, among these, her Majesty's pet hero'.[46] The latter claim, one might suspect, is unlikely, with the queen found to express publicly her lineage to Bruce, but the appeal of the romantic novelist is more believable.[47] This suggests some measure of royal connectedness not solely the creation of the authoress herself. Porter was acknowledged for her loyalty to and friendship with the hero from the Siege of Acre, Sir Sidney Smith. When it was learned that the sister of the great naval man was in London and found to be in destitute circumstances, it was to Miss Porter that Prime Minister Sir Robert Peel entrusted £150 from the Royal Bounty to pass on to Mrs Dwyer.[48] Government and monarch alike knew Porter, for all her marginality in the highest literary circles, and it helped spread the sentiment of her feminine nationalism.

* * *

Porter's erroneous claims to the origins of the historical novel have been shown, in default, to strengthen the authenticity of her voice, a narrative that gained authority from her interrelatedness with contemporary society.[49] And while she was no contributor to the nation's need for births to enhance its manpower against its enemies, her barren spinsterhood came to define her religiosity and the morality of her readership throughout the diaspora.[50] Thus, within the literary genre that is feminine, her contribution to framing the contemporary Scottish view of their nation was an influential one, reflecting the complexity of contemporaries' nationalism. Her ahistorical connections sidestepped the teleology of Union to produce an ascendant national tale. Neither political nor marital connections were necessary conditions for the Scotland she envisioned in her novel, and thus she went beyond the minimum structure of a Romance to make wider historiographical and episodic constructions. Her Wallace followed a higher morality of action forged in the events of the thirteenth and fourteenth centuries, yet one framed in the military heroism that so engaged Porter's passions in the nineteenth century.[51] Porter was writing Scottish history to reflect the Britain of her time. Born in England of Irish parentage, raised in Scotland, living and writing in England, known to Victoria and connected to the world through the travels of two brothers, so enmeshed in following the successes of Sir Sidney Smith and the military, she located Scotland in some of its deepest British moorings.

Throughout all this, Porter's centrality to Scottish national identity is strengthened because she used romance masquerading as the historical novel to produce a dominant national tale. If it is accepted that Scotland's contribution to British identity is that of a peripheral and feminine identity in commune with England's core and masculine identity, notwithstanding internal infractions to these broad characterisations, then Porter's appeal becomes evident. Feminising the most masculine of Scottish heroes ensured the greatest impact, dominating the literary output in this strongest phase of the Wallace cult. This caught the popular construction of Scottish nationalism like no other in the decades before political nationalism of the twentieth century. The life of Miss Porter and the literary style she adopted made it so. The lack of participation which elsewhere masks women from the state stands aside from a Scottish nationalism itself masked from the state. This nationalism, it would appear, was a gendered concept

NOTES

1. J. Heuer, 'Gender and Nationalism', in *Nations and Nationalism: A Global Historical Overview*, Vol. 1, ed. G. H. Herb and D. H. Kaplan (Santa Barbara: ABC-Clio, 2008), p. 43; D. McCrone, *The Sociology of Nationalism: Tomorrow's Ancestors* (London: Routledge, 1998), pp. 120–4; M. Guibernau, *Nationalisms: The Nation-State and Nationalism in the Twentieth Century* (Cambridge: Polity, 1996), pp. 54–5. An examination of gendered Scottish/British identification as revealed through survey data is found in D. McCrone, *Understanding Scotland – The Sociology of a Nation*, 2nd edn (London: Routledge, 2001), pp. 168–9.

2. C. Whyte (ed.), *Gendering the Nation: Studies in Modern Scottish Literature* (Edinburgh: Edinburgh University Press, 1995).

3. The less common masculine argument is proposed in M. M. Martin, *The Mighty Scot: Nation, Gender, and the Nineteenth-Century*

Mystique of Scottish Masculinity (Albany, NY: State University of New York Press, 2009).

4. E. Breitenbach and L. Abrams, 'Gender and Scottish Identity', in L. Abrams, E. Gordon, D. Simonton and E. J. Yeo (eds), *Gender in Scottish History since 1700* (Edinburgh: Edinburgh University Press, 2006), pp. 17, 19.

5. That Burns, Bruce and Wallace head surveys of the 'most important Scots' is shown and examined in M. Penman, 'Robert Bruce's bones: reputations, politics and identities in nineteenth-century Scotland', *International Review of Scottish Studies*, 34 (2009), p. 7ff.

6. J. Edmunds, 'Generations, Women and National Consciousness', in J. Edmunds and B. S. Turner (eds), *Generational Consciousness, Narrative and Politics* (Boston: Rowman & Littlefield, 2002), p. 46; A. Rauser 'Death or liberty: British political prints and the struggle for symbols in the American Revolution', *Oxford Art Journal*, 21, 2 (1998), pp. 151–2, charts the American challenge to Britannia's claim on liberty.

7. M. Molloy, 'Imagining (the) difference: gender, ethnicity and metaphors of nation', *Feminist Review*, 51, Autumn 1995, p. 105; J. Giles and T. Middleton (eds), *Writing Englishness, 1900–1950* (London: Routledge, 1995), pp. 111, 114–18; McClintock, 'Family Feuds', p. 61.

8. R. Davidson, '"The sexual state": sexuality and Scottish governance, 1950–1980', *Journal of the History of Sexuality*, 13, 4 (October 2004), p. 501; R. Davidson, *Dangerous Liaisons: A Social History of Venereal Disease in Twentieth-Century Scotland* (Amsterdam: Rodopi, 2000). The rise of first-cousin marriages in nineteenth-century England, including Charles Darwin's marriage to Emma Wedgwood and Victoria's marriage to Albert, is explored in Adam Kuper, *Incest and Influence: The Private Life of Bourgeois England* (Cambridge, MA: Harvard University Press, 2009). The Matrimonial Causes Act of 1857 allowed limited divorce in England, where the parties are domiciled in England; in Scotland divorce had been possible since 1560 and in 1830 the Court of Session oversaw divorce and issues of bastardy; the divorce procedure was updated in the Conjugal Rights (Scotland) Act of 1861. The debate in 1820 on the legality of marriage to the widow of a deceased brother under Scots law, when the marriage took place in North America, is examined in L. Leneman, *Alienated Affections: The Scottish Experience of Divorce and Separation*, 1684–1830 (Edinburgh: Edinburgh University Press, 1998), pp. 261–2.

9. J. Plunkett, *Queen Victoria: First Media Monarch* (Oxford: Oxford University Press, 2003), p. 29.

10. P. Schlicke (ed.), *The Oxford Companion to Charles Dickens: Anniversary Edition* (Oxford: Oxford University Press, 2011), p. 190. Plunkett, *Queen Victoria*, pp. 56, 138.

11. The theoretical debate behind this concept is laid out in 'Feminist Approaches to Romantic Literature', in C. J. Murray (ed.), *Encyclopaedia of the Romantic Era, 1760–1850, Vol. 1 A–K* (New York: Taylor & Francis, 2004), pp. 343–5; and the construction of the feminine sublime by Edinburgh-born Susan Ferrier (1782–1854) is analysed in A. K. Mellor, *Romanticism and Gender* (London: Routledge, 1993), pp. 103–5.

12. S. C. Behrendt, *British Women Poets and the Romantic Writing Community* (Baltimore: Johns Hopkins University Press, 2009), pp. 210, 213.

13. The conceptual value of the Kailyard in face of its wide cultural connotations is explored in A. Nash, 'The Kailyard: Problem of Illusion?', in I. Brown, T. O. Clancy, S. Manning and M. Pittock (eds), *The Edinburgh History of Scottish Literature. Volume Two: Enlightenment, Britain and Empire* (1707–1918) (Edinburgh: Edinburgh University Press, 2007), pp. 317–23.

14. C. Whyte, 'Introduction', in *Gendering the Nation: Studies in Modern Scottish Literature*, ed. C. Whyte (Edinburgh: Edinburgh University Press, 1995), p. xi.

15. R. Zumkhawala-Cook, *Scotland As We Know It: Representations of National Identity in Literature, Film and Popular Culture* (Jefferson, NC and London: McFarland & Co., 2008), pp. 91–3. In the language of Tom Nairn, the Kailyard represents a cultural neurosis, T. Nairn, *The Break-up of Britain* (London: Verso, 1977), p. 156.

16. Whyte, 'Introduction', p. xii.

17. Martin, *The Mighty Scot*, pp. 42, 79.

18. G. Morton, 'Scotland is Britain: the Union and Unionist-Nationalism, 1807–1907', *Journal of Irish and Scottish Studies*, 1, 1 (2008), pp. 127–41.

19. McCrone, *Sociology of Nationalism*, p. 58.

20. Quoted in C. Craig, *Intending Scotland: Explorations in Scottish Culture since the Enlightenment* (Edinburgh: Edinburgh University Press, 2009), p. 230. Knox believed that the races were inherently antagonistic, Clare L. Taylor, 'Knox, Robert (1791–1862)', *Oxford Dictionary of National Biography* (Oxford, 2004), http://www.oxforddnb.com/view/article/15787 (accessed 25 February 2010).

21. M. G. H. Pittock, *Celtic Identity and the British Image* (Manchester: Manchester University Press 1999), p. 69.

22. M. Arnold, *On the Study of Celtic Literature* (London, 1867), pp. xvii–xviii; Zumkhawala-Cook, *Scotland As We Know It*, p. 7.

23. Morton, *Ourselves and Others*, pp. 4–15; Craig, *Out of* History, p. 206.

24. *List of books for girls and women and their clubs: with descriptive and critical notes and a list of periodicals and hints for girls' and women's clubs*, ed. H. A. Leypoldt and G. Iles (Boston, 1895), p. 29.

25. J. Porter, *The Scottish Chiefs* [1841 edn], p. 312.

26. Ibid., pp. 370–2.

27. Where text proximity is indicated, this was limited to within three words of the search term.

28. Lord, 698; Lady, 508; Sir, 455; King, 406; Knight, 181; Chief, 173; Noble, 170; Chiefs, 102; Guardian, 16.

29. Bloody, 16; Blood-stained, 7; Blood-shed, 4; Blood-red, 3; Life-blood, 2.

30. S. Brown, P. Clements and I. Grundy (eds), 'Jane Porter' within *Orlando: Women's Writing in the British Isles from the Beginnings to the Present* (Cambridge, 2006), http://orlando.cambridge.org/ (accessed 16 August 2010).

31. Dennis, *Nationalism and* Desire, p. 15.

32. J. Porter, *Thaddeus of Warsaw* (London, 1803).

33. P. Beasley, 'Georgiana Molloy, Jane Porter and the significance of exploration narratives for new beginnings in a strange land', *Victorian Network*, 1, 1 (2009), p. 60.

34. J. Porter, *Preface* (1841) 'Preface to the First Edition' [1809], p. vi.

35. Hook, 'Jane Porter, Sir Walter Scott, and the Historical Novel', p. 189.

36. E. Renan, 'What Is a Nation?' [1882], in H. K. Bhabha (ed.), *Nation and Narration* (London: Routledge, 1990); McCrone, *Sociology of Nationalism*, pp. 52–63.

37. The most obvious reference point here is the purchase of Balmoral, and Victoria's wildly successful Highland Diaries, but there are many more points of connection that could be made here, Morton, *Ourselves and Others*, pp. 275–80.

38. J. L. Polasky, 'Leopold I (1790–1865)', *Oxford Dictionary of National Biography* (Oxford, 2004), http://www.oxforddnb.com. subzero.lib.uoguelph.ca/view/article/41227 (accessed 10 Feb 2010).

39. *The Childhood of Queen Victoria by Mrs Gerald Gurney (Dorothy Frances Blomfeld)* (London: Nisbet & Co., 1901), pp. 97–100.

40. Porter, *Preface* (1840), pp. xxxv–xxxvi; Hook, 'Jane Porter, Sir Walter Scott, and the historical novel', p. 181.

41. Porter, *Preface* (1840), p. xxxvi.

42. *The Graphic* 'Jubilee Number' 20 June 1887; Pope-Hennessy, *Agnes Strickland*, p. 8.

43. DULA MSS GB-0033-POR, Vol. B, 49–51 Vol. A, 63–6. Others to

get copies included Sir Walter Scott, who was third on the list after the United Services Club and the Athenaeum Club.

44. Irvine, 'Life of Jane Porter', p. 213; Hook, 'Jane Porter, Sir Walter Scott, and the historical novel', p. 181; Looser, *Women Writers and Old Age in Great Britain*, pp. 162–4.

45. Irvine J. R., 'The Life of Jane Porter', p. 213; Hook, 'Jane Porter, Sir Walter Scott, and the historical novel', p. 181; Porter, Preface (1840), p. xlv.

46. *Otago Witness*, Issue 2301, 7 April 1898, p. 43.

47. In Victoria's continuation of her highland journal she records seeing the National Wallace Monument in the distance, but no visit, and no other mention of the patriot, is recorded, *More Leaves from the Journal of a Life in the Highlands, From 1862–1882* (London: Smith Elder, 1884), ed. A. Helps, p. 121. The first journal notes that Wallace was incarcerated at Dumbarton Castle, but nothing else, *Victoria, Leaves from the Journal of Our Life in the Highlands from 1848 to 1861* (London: Smith Elder, 1868), ed. A. Helps, p. 78. Her lineage to Bruce was expounded in G. Russell French, *The Ancestry of Her Majesty Victoria, and of His Royal Highness Prince Albert* (London: William Pickering, 1841), Ch. 15.

48. 'English Extracts', *New Zealand Gazette and Wellington Spectator*, IV, Issue 262, 12 July 1843, p. 3.

49. Price, 'Resisting "The Spirit of Innovation"', pp. 638–51; McLean, 'Nobody's Argument', pp. 88–103; Hook, 'Jane Porter, Sir Walter Scott, and the historical novel', p. 184.

50. *Museum of Foreign Literature and Science*, XXVII (1835), p. 113 reproduced from *Fraser's Magazine* of the same year.

51. Although falling within the genre of the historical novel, Porter's ascriptions of 'feminine' motivations to Wallace – his love of his wife, of the ravaged Helen Marr, and of all womankind – undermines his morality, Dennis, *Nationalism and Desire*, p. 15.

Chapter 9

Tall Stories

With the absence of extant artefacts associated with the patriot, the Wallacian national tale has been mastered through the medium of text. The previous chapters charted the tale's evolution from limited contemporary citing through to the literary dominance by Hary and the many revisions to those texts in vernacular and Anglicised forms that reimagined the tale before Miss Jane Porter's *The Scottish Chiefs* fixed the patriot within a historical romance. What is more, this modern textual representation was formed alongside a contemporary passion for monument building. Contemporaries commemorated Wallace with more monuments in the nineteenth century than any other man or woman from the nation's past, and included among the patriot's honours was a national monument.

The monuments that have been built to commemorate Wallace were – and continue to be – points of heightened memory.[1] These sites are entrepôts from the present to what has gone before, and form part of a process whereby social memory is privileged and shared within the community. As static beacons for nationalism, monuments facilitate layers of experience to be added upon pre-existing narratives, creating ever-available claims to be recalled, consciously or not, whenever a national frame of reference is required.[2] Importantly, it is observed that the Scots were free from the kind of suppression that might have constrained monument building, whereas in other European countries, where different outcomes transpired, this was not the case.[3] That the British union-state eschewed such obvious restrictions contextualises the rhetoric of nationalism that surrounds monumental construction – one remembers, indeed, that there is a commemorative plaque to Wallace displayed in Westminster Hall itself, at the heart of the imperial state.

*   *   *

The commodification of the Wallace national tale in non-textual forms did, of course, involve statements of commemoration that were read, circulated and recited in order to solicit support. When the National Wallace Monument was opened in 1869 it was the culmination of fifteen years of campaigning led by Charles Rogers, co-secretary with Thomas L. Galbraith of the National Wallace Monument Committee.[4] The Duke of Montrose and the Earl of Elgin and Kindcardine were the joint presidents of the Acting Committee, and it was they who organised the pursuit of private subscriptions to fund the building and design work.[5] While providing a window on the past, the work of the committee was reflective of contemporary concerns, and the choice of design was not without disagreement. William Stirling feared 'It was most discreditable to the taste of Scotland, if, in the year 1859, Wallace and the Abbey Craig, were to be . . . pilloried in the fashion which, early in the century, befell Nelson and Calton Hill'.[6] In other words, he feared for a neoclassical design being chosen, for this would fail to capture Wallace's ordinariness. With similar resistance to a limited commemoration, the Glasgow lawyer William Burns was convinced of the propriety of the *people* of Glasgow taking part in the erection of a National Monument.[7] The organisers were keen that 'a special resolution for working men' be added to the programme when laying the foundation stone, a proposal supported by Rev. Alexander Low, Minister of Keig in Aberdeenshire, who stated 'the chief supporters of Wallace in his struggles for independence, being the Scottish peasantry, it is fully expected that this Class will cordially unite with their fellow countrymen in the present movement'.[8] Burns' and Low's instincts were proved right, and the lists of subscriptions from around the Glasgow area showed many small amounts. With a number of the lists also published as posters, it further spread the word that this was a monument reflective of the aspirations of the ordinary Scot.[9]

With the aim of cultivating literature, science and art, the Wallace Caledonian Institute held its first meeting on 24 June 1861 to coincide with the laying of the foundation stone to the monument.[10] And a series of episodes indicative of Scotland's wider history were brought together for the opening ceremony at the Abbey Craig. The event was scheduled for the anniversary of the battle of Bannockburn, not the battle of Stirling Bridge. There were five or six amateur bands playing the republican-inspired ode 'Scots Wha Hae' to an audience loyal to the Hanoverians, and many wore 'the garb of the auld Gaul' despite Wallace's lowland origins and personal geography.[11] Introducing the second resolution that day, Sheriff-Substitute Henry Glassford Bell declared that 'Scotland and England are now one. Any Scotchman who now entertained animosity towards England, or any Englishman who entertained animosity towards Scotland, would be set down as simply insane (hear, hear)'.[12] It was a sentiment Jane Porter would have endorsed, as would her Queen. Indeed, the drive to raise subscriptions for the monument would have stalled if the aims of those who campaigned for its completion had stood contrary to the national tale.

Links between the monuments to Wallace and textual representations of the tale were also seen in the contemporary chapbooks: Buchanan offered his best wishes for the Abbey Craig plan, while Hutchison celebrated the recent construction of the Barnweil monument in a play depicting the patriot's life.[13] The renowned European nationalists Giuseppe Mazzini (1805–72), Giuseppe Garibaldi (1807–82) and Louis Kossuth (1802–84) signed letters of support, planting the thirteenth-century patriot firmly within the modern nationalist crusade.[14] Garibaldi was the greatest icon, described as the 'Wallace of Italy' who inspired Scots to sign up for the British Legion mid-century.[15] *The Scotsman* reported Garibaldi's plan to visit Scotland, 'which had been intimated to a friend in the north of England', an indication of that patriot's appeal as the monument neared completion.[16]

With the architect J. T. Roachead's design chosen, upwards of 50,000 attended the laying of the foundation stone.[17] They were treated to much music and reminders of the peace Wallace and Bruce had now brought for Scotland.[18] The final verse of a poem by James MacFarlane – the winning entry to a competition to mark the day – stresses progress since the nation's early youth:

Though years like shadows fall
O'er the dial of stones of time,
Thy pulse o' freedom still shall beat
With the throb of manhood's prime,
Still shall they valour, love and truth
That shone on Scotland's early youth,

From Scotland ne'er disever
The Shamrock, the Rose, the thistle stern
Shall wave around the Wallace cairn
And bless the brave for ever.[19]

Subsequently, after many delays from rising costs, the monument was opened on 11 September 1869, but with little of the fanfare that accompanied its inauguration. The ceremony lasted only half an hour, and immediately the monument was put in the custody of the Town Council of Stirling.[20] On that Saturday morning a portrait was presented to Mrs Rogers, representing her husband who would not attend.[21] Rogers was accused of taking for his own expenses the subscription to the monument given by the Alloa and Tillicoultry Weavers, and he resigned his chaplaincy in 1863 and removed himself to London.[22] Within the monument's foundations a time capsule was buried that explained why the patriot was being commemorated at this point in Scotland's history, over five centuries after Wallace met his death. Yet even at this time of public memorialising, the dominance of the literary construction of the tale was confirmed with the decision to preserve beneath the ground two patriotic narratives of Wallace's life alongside the poetry of the nation's greatest writers, Burns and Scott.[23]

The monument has also been a successful visitor attraction. The *Stirling Observer* in 1887 expressed concerns over too many of the wrong sort of people being attracted to the Abbey Craig for the view, with a bottle of liquor in their hand.[24] Inside the monument there is the so-called Wallace sword, its authenticity the subject of much chapbook debate. Charles Rogers had affirmed that 'this great blade' was found on Wallace's pillow on the night of his capture in Robroystone in August 1305.[25] We know this to be no more than a story, but it has obvious symbolic importance. On the evening of Sunday 8 November 1936, four men used force to steal the sword, and despite a raft of expert opinion pointing out at the time of its theft that their bounty was fake, concluding that it was not made until the latter half of the sixteenth century,[26] there was much concern raised until its return (as there was in 1972 when it was again recovered after theft).[27] In the twentieth century, the National Wallace Monument acted as the key focus for much of Scotland's nationalist sentiment. Although an indication of revenue raised at the monument is available since its opening, it was not until the turn of the century that visitor figures were collated. In the period 1900–5, fluctuating numbers of between 22,111 and 25,113 visitors were recorded.[28] Middleton, the leasee in 1906, wrote to the railway companies to ask them to reduce fairs on excursions heading for Stirling in an attempt to attract more people to enjoy the facilities he established on the Abbey Craig.[29] If only he had had access to the 'Braveheart effect' he would have had no need to pressure anyone or any group. The number of visitors to the Wallace Monument rose from 50,173 in September 1994 to 128,638 in August 1996. Part of the growth can be attributed to the earlier refurbishment of the monument, at a cost of nearly £1 million, before it was reopened in May 1993, but the influence of the 1995 movie release is clear.[30] In neither period do these figures include those who climbed the Abbey Craig for free.[31] Keen to take advantage of this emerging market opportunity which the Hollywood film inspired, Stirling temporarily dispensed with the bureaucratic appellation of 'Central Region' and plumped for the rather more romantic 'Braveheart County' instead.[32] This has not always been successful in the past, as McCrone, Morris and Kiely show when the Conservatives gained control of Stirling District Council in 1992, and reassessed the value of the council's branding: 'A knight on horseback does not give the impression of an open accessible council that cares about its customers.'[33] But with a bandwagon to jump upon, others left such reticence behind. Sensing a marketing opportunity following the video release of *Braveheart*, the BBC Scotland Symphony Orchestra chose 1996 to release a recording of three romantic symphonic poems written between 1892 and 1909 by the patriot's namesake under the collective title of *William Wallace*.[34]

*   *   *

The monument at Abbey Craig cannot be seen in isolation, however, with the patriot commemorated by additional monuments that further projected Wallace as Scotland's national tale. Furth of Scotland, monuments to the patriot were established in Ballarat near Melbourne in 1889 and Baltimore in Connecticut in 1893 – each the result of a bequest by a wealthy Scottish migrant.[35] The first monument in Scotland to depict Wallace was commissioned by David Steuart Erskine, 11th Earl of Buchan, and built on his land at Dryburgh in 1814.[36]

Designed in red sandstone by John Smith, standing twenty-one-and-a-half feet high, the likeness was taken from a watercolour in Buchan's possession.[37] The monument was restored in 1991 in the face of high drama caused by high winds on the exposed site.[38] As the *Glasgow Herald* put it: 'His threatened downfall now is not in the hands of the English . . . [but he] is suffering from another relentless enemy – the elements.'[39] Similarly, the next in a line of monuments inspired by Buchan's creation has also required restorative attention. St Nicholas parish church in Lanark is the location for a statue of Wallace which was put in place in 1820.[40] Since 1985 the monument has been the focus for an annual Wallace Day Commemoration under the auspices of the SNP, although the event is intended to be a time of reflection 'for all local groups, regardless of political affiliation'.[41] Restoration of the Lanark sculpture by Ainsworth was carried out in 1993 at an estimated cost of £15,000: both monuments, it should be noted, were restored before the *Braveheart* mania began in earnest.[42] The places most associated with Wallace's life are where further statues are to be found. There were two built in Ayr town centre, the first a statue placed in a niche in Newmarket Street in 1819, the second attached to the Wallace Tower (1831, rebuilt 1833), which could be named after the patriot, or, in reality, his namesake who owned the structure previous known as the 'auld tour'.[43] The sculpture of Wallace was made by James Thom and is placed high up on the 113-foot-tall building.[44] In the Ayrshire parish of Craigie, the Barnweil Monument was the outcome of an appeal started in 1837 and completed just over a decade later.[45] A plaque at the base of the monument details its association with the patriot, marking the point where Wallace and his associates set fire to a barn full of sleeping Englishmen, shouting 'the barns of Ayr burn well'.[46] Inspired by what he saw, the Scottish nationalist Lewis Spence ended his biography of Wallace with another extract from that inscription:

> Centuries have not diminished the lustre of his heroic achievements; and the memory of this most disinterested of patriots shall, through all ages, be honoured and revered by his countrymen . . . Ever honoured by the memory of the matchless Sir William Wallace . . . From Greece arose Leonidas, from America Washington, and from Scotland Wallace, names which shall remain through all time the watchwords and beacons of liberty.[47]

There is a stone pillar at Wallacetown above Falkirk,[48] interesting for marking a point of defeat, but less obvious as a heritage site. Nor is Bruce forgotten, his heart buried in Dunfermline and the well-loved statue to him standing at the entrance to Stirling Castle, looking over to Abbey Craig.[49] In Stirling itself, on the corner of Baker Street and Spittal Street, sculpted by the renowned Alexander Handyside Ritchie in the 1880s, is another Wallace statue. It was paid for by William Drummond and provides a more imposing commemoration than the statues of Wallace and Bruce on the municipal buildings in Stirling (from 1855).[50] A picture of the Aberdeen Wallace Statue (built in 1888), with a historical description, formed the 1951 Christmas card from the Lord and Lady Provost of Aberdeen.[51] Constructed with money donated in the will of John Steill, the statue became notable as the spot visited each year by the high-profile romantic nationalist Theodore Napier, pursuing his quest for a Jacobite-inspired home rule movement.[52] By contrast, the monument at Robroyston marking the spot where Wallace was betrayed by Menteith has been more widely politically mobilised. It was unveiled in 1900, David Macrae using the occasion to link the betrayal of Wallace to the betrayal of the aristocracy, an analysis that joined a gamut of contributions on the same topic submitted to the letters page of the *Glasgow Herald*.[53]

Edinburgh failed in 1859 to get its monument to either Wallace or Bruce and had to wait until the twentieth century for this to be rectified, despite Edinburgh Council advertising in 1882 that 'a public competition for a Wallace and Bruce memorial under the terms of a bequest left by Captain Hugh Reid' was to be held, with £2,000 available for the project.[54] In 1929, statues to the two heroes were unveiled on the Esplanade of Edinburgh Castle by the Duke of York, soon to be King George VI.[55] The date was chosen to mark the 600th anniversary of the oldest extant Royal charter granted to the city, and Edinburgh's worthies mixed civic pride with Scottish and British patriotism to commemorate the city's and the nation's foundations. The Lord Provost, Sir Alexander Stevenson, claimed that Bruce had completed what Wallace had begun. The Duke of York, who wore the uniform of the Cameron Highlanders, proclaimed that 'it is always a source of pride to us that we [himself and his wife] are both descended from Robert the Bruce'. He framed the patriots in the recent experience of war:

Six hundred years have passed away, and those two countries, who were then the bitterest of foes, have become sister nations, linked together by the closest bonds of blood and affection, bonds which have been cemented by the most enduring tie of all – comradeship in war. Animated by the same spirit and ideals which inspired those two heroes of old, Scotsmen and Englishmen fought side by side in the Great War for justice and liberty; and side by side they endured hardship and suffering until victory had been won.[56]

The unveiling ceremony came two days before the General Election, and so precluded a number of notables from attending. Ramsay Macdonald blamed either Bruce or Baldwin for the closeness of the dates denying his attendance. Lloyd George was similarly absent, but offered his congratulations to the Scottish Capital from 'one of another people within the family of British races'.[57]

The calibre of the guests, and the location of the statues sited outside the ceremonial home of the British army in Scotland, indicates that this was a national occasion for both Scotland and Britain. While not as numerous as in the Victorian age, the remaining Wallace monuments inaugurated in the twentieth century focused much more on separating Scotland from Britain. Marking the patriot's birthplace, the monument at Eldeslie has been the focus of the nationalist movement's commemorations since its completion in 1912, including the rights of women to the vote. The site was included as part of the 650th anniversary of Wallace's death in 1995, along with a Wallace Memorial Service at Paisley Abbey which was addressed by a range of prominent nationalist speakers.[58] Also at this time, acclaimed sculptor Sandy Stoddard's depiction of Blind Hary, which so impressed the visitors to the *Brave Art* exhibition at the Stirling Smith Art Gallery and Museum in 1997, brought new authority to the poet's place in history, whereas another sculpture, presented to the National Wallace Monument in 1998, its likeness the face of Mel Gibson, has endured a more contentious search for authoritativeness.[59]

* * *

These monuments and sculptures are specific focuses of commemoration, Wallace being fêted at their foundation, in the appeals and supporting documents used to mobilise subscriptions, and at annual occasions thereafter. Added to this geographical spread of built commemorations are a range of fixed geological and physical markers that have intruded into Scotland's modern nationalism. At the height of the mid-nineteenth-century cult of Wallace, a survey carried out by Patrick Yule claimed there were over fifty sites associated with the patriot in Scotland, ranging from caves and trees to wells, cairns, hills and waterfalls.[60] Adding to the list, Charles Rogers identified a chair and quaich at Bonnington in Lanark, and a spring well – Wallace's well – situated about a quarter of a mile to the north-east of Robroyston,[61] along with a cleft in a rock at Garleton, East Lothian, known as 'Wallace's Hole' or 'Cave', 'Wallace's Know' at Loudon Hill, and 'Wallace's Butts' in the Lamond Hills.[62] Indeed, numerous other caves, camps, chairs, seats and stones named after Wallace have been identified as such by nineteenth-century commentators.[63] Those listed by Donaldson and Morpeth include 'Wallace's Beef-Tower' at Bothwell castle; 'Wallace's Larder' at the dungeon in Craig's Castle, Ardrossan (where Wallace is said to have thrown the bodies of the defenders after he captured the castle), and 'Wallace's trench', sixty-three feet in circumference, near Blair Drummond.[64] Using modern maps, Elspeth King identified eighty-three places named after Wallace, rightly indicating that many more references could be found in maps from earlier years. All but eight of these sites are in the central belt or the Borders.

There is also a range of tangential links that have gained credibility from association with the national tale. Crosbie House in West Kilbride is associated with Sir Reginald Crawfurd, an uncle of Wallace, although little remains of the building. The ruins of Gascon Hall in Perthshire, where Hary claims Wallace encountered the ghost of Faudon, is, unfortunately, not of sufficient age to be of Wallace's time.[65] Lamington Tower, though, is where some furniture associated with Marion Braidfoot is located, and a knocking stane (used for pounding grains) associated with Wallace, found in Longforgan, is now housed in the McManus Galleries in Dundee.[66] And, reputed to be where one of his arms is buried, Cambuskenneth Abbey is linked to Wallace's uncle, and Paisley Abbey is where the patriot may have been educated. Paisley Abbey, moreover, contains the Wallace Memorial window (1873) to mark the association, with the superhuman Wallace depicted as Samson.[67]

The existence of this heritage trail makes the association of ordinary Scots with Wallace all the deeper. Monuments and statues are especially suitable for heightened moments of nationalist

Figure 2   *Local associations with the national patriot: Wallace's Well, Royston Mains, East Dunbartonshire. Photograph, c.1911. © Glasgow City Archives. Licensor www.scran.ac.uk*

Figure 3 *Knocking stone from Longforgan on which William Wallace is reputed to have rested. © South Lanarkshire Libraries. Licensor www.scran.ac.uk*

expression. Nevertheless, these geographical and physical sites across the country provide a tangible link to the local communities – a sense of personal attachment to the national story, and a sense of inspiration:

> I would relate
> How Wallace fought for Scotland, left the name
> Of 'Wallace' to be found like a flower
> All over his dear country; left the deeds
> Of Wallace, like a family of ghosts
> To people the steep rocks and river banks
> Her natural sanctuaries, with a local soul
> Of Independence and stern liberty[68]

Turning now to the production of material culture, we can observe that a range of souvenirs were manufactured to fix personal memories of the hero. This began when the Goldsmith Company of Edinburgh presented a snuff-box made out of wood from Wallace's oak to the Earl of Buchan, who, highlighting his republican sympathies, passed the gift to George Washington in 1790.[69] In political contrast, a musical box produced for George IV on his visit to Scotland in 1822 was declared a memento of 'the root of that oak which had preserved the houseless patriot when outlawed by the enemies of his country [which] has gone to the legitimate descent of that race of kings for whose right he so nobly contended'.[70] In a similar vein, Joseph Train presented the 'Wallace chair' to the Tory and arch-Unionist Walter Scott in 1820, the chair, constructed from wood taken from the barn where Wallace was captured, being seemingly refashioned in this way without fear of desecration.[71]

Alongside such high-profile examples, the knowledge of which continued to a national sense of remembrance, it is the banality of mementos that marks the dispersion of Wallace-themed material culture. The *Caledonian Challenge Shield* from 1863 – an incredibly impressive shooting trophy, standing at a superhuman height of nine feet six inches, and made of oak – displays carvings of Wallace and Bruce. The Wallace sword brooch, alongside Wallace pin cushions, table centres, cups, saucers and spoons, was offered for collection from the shop of the National Wallace Monument in the late nineteenth century.[72] And to further turn history towards heritage, the monument gained a specially erected Tea Pavilion in 1936, situated in adjoining Pine Woods, which offered tea, cakes and scones 'at town prices'.[73]

* * *

There have been concentrated efforts since the 1820s to commodify and monetise the Wallace tale, as these examples have shown.[74] The heritage industry is a debate about the kind of history deployed to define and present the nation. The analysis includes awareness that Scotland's culture is influenced by those of other nations and of Scots émigrés, yet it stands in distinction to the 'new British history' – history without borders – which Pocock ignited and developed through an Atlantic perspective as the history of 'Greater Britain'.[75] Scotland being a 'stateless nation', and being dominated politically throughout the age of nationalism, its history has been shaped from internal debate, but without insularity. The situation in Scotland, Ascherson explains, is more like that in France, where it is assumed, and indeed expected, that any account of French history will reflect the political leanings of the narrator. Thus a Republican version of French history will be inherently different from that of a Communist or a Catholic monarchist.[76] And just as nationalism feeds off episodic history, so the nation's built heritage appeals not to 'authentic' history but to an 'ideological' presentation of the past, where competing narratives of Wallace comprise the national tale.[77] Multiple interpretations of the past dominate to an extent that makes them seem real, where heritage 'makes an apparently immutable history present in the now of society', and we should expect that the episodic nature of the nationalist past is perpetuated in heritage sites as much as in the history book.[78] The historiography of Scotland's national tale is not just about reading texts; it is also a matter of passive consumption through the tourist's gaze.[79] This is a promoted history, one packaged by the national tale to market to ourselves and to others, to maintain jobs and local economies, and to keep an estimated 185,900 people (2011) employed, in total adding over £4.3 billion directly to the Scottish economy.[80]

NOTES

1. J. Coleman, 'Unionist-Nationalism in Stone? The National Wallace Monument and the Hazards of Commemoration in Victorian Scotland', in E. J. Cowan (ed.), *The Wallace Book* (Edinburgh: John Donald, 2007), pp. 151–2.
2. D. Lowenthal, *The Past is a Foreign Country* (Cambridge: Cambridge University Press, 1988); E. W. McFarland, 'Commemoration of the South African War in Scotland', *The Scottish Historical Review*, 89, 2, October 2010, pp. 195–6; A. Blaikie, *The Scots Imagination and Modern Memory* (Edinburgh: Edinburgh University Press, 2010), p. 13.
3. In this period, for example, the Austrian government actively obstructed the construction of a monument in Prague to the nation's fifteenth-century reformer Jan Hus, L. Paterson, *The Autonomy of Scotland* (Edinburgh: Edinburgh University Press, 1994), p. 85.
4. Coleman, 'Unionist-Nationalism in Stone?', pp. 153–68.
5. 'Subscription Schedule for the National Monument of Sir William Wallace on the Abbey Craig, Near Stirling' (n.p., n.d.).
6. W. Stirling of Keir, 'The Designs for the Wallace Monument: a letter

to the Lord-Advocate of Scotland, convenor of the committee of the Wallace Monument', *Stirling Journal* 28 January 1859 (printed at the Journal and Advertiser Office, Stirling, 1859), p. 8.

7. 'National Wallace Monument Stirling: Minute Book kept by William Burns'. Minutes of the meeting held at Glasgow 1 May 1856.

8. Ibid.; 'Scheme of the Acting Committee', National Monument to Sir William Wallace on the Abbey Craig near Stirling (n.p., 1856).

9. *Wallace Monument. Official Papers and Newspaper Extracts relating to the Wallace Monument Movement kept by Wm. Burns.*

10. *The Scotsman*, 27 June 1861.

11. *The Scotsman*, 25 June 1856.

12. Ibid.

13. R. Buchanan, *Wallace: A Tragedy in Five Acts* (Glasgow, Griffen & Co., 1856); Hutchison, *Life of Sir William Wallace; or Scotland Five Hundred Years Ago* (Glasgow: Thomas Murray & Son, 1858).

14. See postcard produced by the Stirling Smith Museum and Art Gallery showing these letters of support preserved and framed in fragments of Wallace's oak.

15. Fraser, *Scottish Popular Politics*, p. 80.

16. *The Scotsman*, 7 July 1869.

17. *The Builder*, 28 January 1860.

18. A fuller description is found in Morton, *Unionist-Nationalism*, pp. 177–81.

19. http://www.nationalwallacemonument.com/downloads/laying-found ation-stone.pdf (accessed 25 January 2014).

20. *The Scotsman*, 13 September 1869; *Some Records of the Origin and Progress of the National Wallace Monument Movement, initiated at Glasgow in March 1856* (printed for private circulation, 1880), pp. 25–6.

21. *The Scotsman*, 13 September 1869.

22. M. Forrest, 'The Wallace Monument and the Scottish National Identity', unpublished BA (Hons) dissertation, University of Stirling, 1993, pp. 32–4.

23. The texts buried in the time capsule were: James Paterson, *Wallace and His Times*; *The Life of Wallace* (Murray & Sons); *The Poetical Works of our Immortal and National Bard, Robert Burns* (Inglis & Son); Sir Walter Scott, *Lady of the Lake*; David Campbell (ed.), *British and Masonic Calendar* (1861); Dr Charles Rogers, *The National Wallace Monument – the site and design.* http://www. nationalwallacemonument.com/downloads/laying-foundation-stone. pdf (accessed 25 January 2014).

24. Alcohol was not sold at the monument, Forrest, 'The Wallace Monument', p. 37.

25. *The Stirling Antiquary*, Vol. 1 (n.d.), p. 52. Rogers' claims here, contextualised within a wider debate on the veracity of the sword, are explored in D. H. Caldwell, 'The Wallace Sword', in E. J. Cowan (ed.), *The Wallace Book* (Edinburgh: John Donald, 2007), pp. 169–75.

26. Meeting of the Custodian's Committee [National Wallace Monument], 14 December 1936; *Glasgow Evening News*, 9 November 1936; *Record and Mail*, 10 November 1936.

27. A useful discussion on the patriotic belief in the authenticity of the Wallace sword, and that it may indicate Wallace was a large man, is found in Magnusson, *Scotland: The Story of a Nation*, pp. 126–8.

28. Morton, 'The heritage of William Wallace', pp. 246–7. It can be compared with visiting figures to Walter Scott's home, Abbotsford, produced by Durie, for the period 1838–98, which rise from something over 1,000–2,000 in the 1830s and 1840s to over 5,000 in 1858 and never below 6,000 through the remainder of the nineteenth century; A. Durie, 'Tourism in Victorian Scotland: the case of Abbotsford', *Scottish Economic and Social History*, 12 (1992), p. 45.

29. *Meeting of the Custodians' Committee* [National Wallace Monument], Stirling, 12 February 1906, p. 131.

30. *The Scotsman* 22 May 1993. Stirling District Council co-ordinated the restoration with financial help from the Scottish Tourist Board, Forth Valley Enterprise and the European Community.

31. See for example A. Keith, *Several Incidents in the Life of Sir William Wallace, with an account of Lanark, the theatre of his exploits, and a description of the romantic scenery in the neighbourhood* (Lanark, 1844), pp. 3–6, 9–10.

32. See the advertising packaged with the *Braveheart* video cassette upon its first release.

33. *Stirling News*, 13 August 1992, quoted in D. McCrone, A. Morris and R. Kiely, *Scotland – the Brand: the Making of Scottish Heritage* (Edinburgh: Edinburgh University Press, 1995), p. 191.

34. Compact Disc CD A66848. My thanks to Trevor Griffiths for this observation.

35. *The Glasgow Herald*, 8 July 1889; *Sunday Herald*, 1 December 1893.

36. R. G. Cant, 'David Steuart Erskine, 11th Earl of Buchan: Founder of the Society of Antiquaries of Scotland', in A. S. Bell (ed.), *The Scottish Antiquarian Tradition: Essays to Mark the Bicentenary of the Society of Antiquaries of Scotland, 1780–1980* (Edinburgh: John Donald, 1981).

37. 'Colossal Statue of Sir William Wallace', *Gentleman's Magazine*, Vol. lxxxvii (1817), p. 621.

38. G. Ainsworth, 'Repairing Wallace Monuments', paper presented

at One Day Wallace Conference, Smith Art Gallery and Museum, Stirling, 17 May 1997.

39. *Glasgow Herald*, 14 September 1991.

40. 'Wallace Statue Appeal by the Saltire Society, Edinburgh', designed and published by Clydesdale District Council (c.1992).

41. http://www.clydesdalewallaceday.info/index.html (accessed 31 January 2014).

42. Ainsworth, 'Repairing Wallace Monuments'.

43. *Look at Ayr* (Doncaster: Bessacarr Prints, 1985), p. 5; RCAHMS: Archaeological Notes NS32SW 14 3385 2179. http://canmore.rcahms.gov.uk/en/site/41775/details/ayr+high+street+wallace+tower/ (accessed 14 January 2014).

44. RCAHMS: Archaeological Notes NS32SW 14 3385.

45. Hutchison, *Life of Sir William Wallace*, frontispiece.

46. D. Ross, *In Wallace's Footsteps: A Guide to Places Associated with the Life of William Wallace* (Glasgow: The Society of William Wallace, n.d.), p. 14. Although Barrow is not alone in disagreeing with this story, Barrow, *Robert Bruce*, p. 451.

47. L. Spence, *Story of William Wallace: Little Stories of Great Lives* (London: Humphrey Milford, 1919), p. 94.

48. Ross, *In Wallace's Footsteps*, p. 20.

49. The casket containing the heart was examined by Historic Scotland's experts in a two and a half hour operation. It was later returned to Dunfermline. *The Scotsman*, 30 August 1996.

50. Ibid., p. 23; Ross, *Trail of William Wallace*, p. 77.

51. *Description of Wallace State, Aberdeen; Lord Provost's Greeting* (December 1951) [NLS: Pt.sm.1.(7)].

52. G. Morton, 'Returning Nationalists, Returning Scotland: James Grant and Theodore Napier', in M. Varricchio (ed.), *Back to Caledonia: Scottish Homecomings from the Seventeenth Century to the Present* (Edinburgh: John Donald, 2012), p. 122.

53. *Glasgow Herald*, 22 August 1900.

54. *Conditions Relative to Proposed Public Competition for the Wallace and Bruce Memorial*, Captain Reid's Bequest, City of Edinburgh (1882).

55. 'Index to the Inventory of Monuments maintained by the District', *Edinburgh District Council, Department of Architecture*; M. T. R. B. Turnbull, *Monuments and Statues of Edinburgh* (Edinburgh: Chambers, 1989), pp. 77–8.

56. D. Robertson, M. Wood and F. C. Mearns, *Edinburgh 1329–1929* (Edinburgh: Oliver & Boyd, 1929), p. li.

57. Robertson, Wood and Mearns, *Edinburgh 1329–1929*, pp. l, liii.

58. *William Wallace, Special Commemorative Publication to Mark the*

650th Anniversary of his Martyrdom (Glasgow: Scots Secretariat, 1955), frontispiece.

59. 'William Wallet wanted to buy Braveheart Statue', http://www.thefreelibrary.com/william+wallet+wanted+to+buy+braveheart+statue.-a0110838928 (accessed 26 January 2014).

60. 'A former Subscriber for a Wallace Monument' [Patrick Yule], *Traditions, etc., Respecting Sir William Wallace; Collected chiefly from Publications of Recent Date* (Edinburgh, 1856), pp. 6–8.

61. C. Rogers, *The Book of Wallace in Two Volumes* (Edinburgh: Printed for the Grampian Club 1889), Vol. II, p. 229.

62. Ross, *In Wallace's Footsteps*, p. 13,

63. L. G. M. G., *Authentic Life*, pp. 261–3; Yule, *Traditions, etc.*, pp. 6–19; Rogers, *Book of Wallace*, Vol. I, pp. 304–5.

64. G. Donaldson and R. S. Morpeth, *A Dictionary of Scottish History* (Edinburgh: John Donald, 1977), p. 223.

65. RCAHMS, Archaeological Notes, NN91NE 14 9862 1743, http://canmore.rcahms.gov.uk/en/site/25960/details/gascon+hall/ (accessed 25 January 2014).

66. E. King, 'The Material Culture of William Wallace', in E. J. Cowan (ed.), *The Wallace Book* (Edinburgh: John Donald, 2007), pp. 124–5.

67. D. R. Ross, *On the Trail of William Wallace* (Edinburgh: Luath Press, 1999), p. 32.

68. 'In sight of Wallace's Tower', William Wordsworth, *The Complete Poetic Works by William Wordsworth* (London: Macmillan & Co., 1888).

69. Rogers, *Book of Wallace*, Vol. II, p. 94; *Copy of Earl of Buchan's Letter to General Washington, President of the United States of America, send enclosed in the box of Wallace's oak, June 28th, 1791; contained in The Earl of Buchan's Address to the Americas at Edinburgh on Washington's Birth-day, February 22nd* (1811).

70. Carrick, *Life of Sir William Wallace*, pp. 96–7.

71. *The Letters of Sir Walter Scott* (London, 1932–7), vii, p. 176. More recently, the former owner of Harrods, and keen pursuer of British citizenship, Mohamed Al-Fayed, can still be found sitting in his own Wallace Chair.

72. *Shearer's Illustrated Souvenir of the National Wallace Monument, Stirling* (Stirling, 1896); Rev. J. Bain and J. Paterson, *The Surroundings of the Wallace Monument as seen from the top* (5th edn, 19—), 20; *The Sir William Wallace Album. Wallace Monument Stirling, Bridge of Allan, Dunblane, Doune, Callander, The Trossachs, and Loch Katrine* (Stirling, 1904?); *Illustrated Souvenir of the National Wallace Monument, Stirling* (Stirling: R. S. Shearer & Son, 1896).

73. *Guide to the National Wallace Monument* (n.d.), SPL, Box 19,

LC/SAL, 6/64, 16; The custodians bought the Tea Pavilion from their tenant, R. W. Salmond, in 1937 for £60, *Correspondence of the Custodians of the National Wallace Monument, 1836–1938,* 29 January 1837, 2 April, 1937, Stirling Council Archive [SCA], SB10/1/1-SB10/4/1; *Guide to the National Wallace Monument. Situated on the Abbey Craig near Stirling containing the Great Sword of Sir William Wallace. The Finest View in Scotland* (Stirling?: R. W. Salmond, c.1964), p. 16.

74. And this list is not exhaustive, as the work of Elspeth King has shown, E. King, 'The Material Culture of William Wallace', in E. J. Cowan (ed.), *The Wallace Book* (Edinburgh: John Donald, 2007), pp. 131–2.

75. J. G. A Pocock, 'The limits and divisions of British history: in search of an unknown subject', *America Historical Review*, Vol. 87, No. 2 (1982), pp. 311–36; J. G. A. Pocock, 'Conclusion: Contingency, Identity, Sovereignty', in A. Grant and Stringer (eds), *Uniting the Kingdom? The Making of British History* (London: Routledge, 1995); J. G. A. Pocock, 'The new British history in Atlantic perspective: an Antipodean commentary', *America Historical Review*, 10, 2 (1999), pp. 490–500; N. C. Landsman, 'Nation, migration, and the province in the first British Empire: Scotland and the Americas, 1600–1800', *America historical Review*, 104, 2 (1999), pp. 463–75; D. Armitage, 'Greater Britain: a useful category of historical analysis?', *America Historical Review*, 104, 2 (1999), pp. 427–45.

76. Ascherson, *Games with Shadows*, p. 153.

77. M. Crang, 'On the heritage trail: maps of and journeys to olde Englande', *Environment and Planning D: Society and Space*, 13 (1994), p. 341.

78. Lowenthal, *The Past Is a Foreign Country*, p. 211; For an extended discussion of these themes, consult McCrone, Morris, Kiely, *Scotland – the Brand*, pp. 1–48. The familial relationship between history and heritage is found at p. 12. Samuel, *Theatres of Memory*, p. 15; N. C. Johnson, 'Framing the past: time, space and the politics of heritage tourism in Ireland', *Political Geography*, 18, 2 (1999), p. 190.

79. J. Urry, *The Tourist Gaze: Leisure and Travel in Contemporary Societies* (London: Sage, 1990).

80. http://www.scotland.gov.uk/Topics/Business-Industry/Tourism (accessed 14 January 2014).

Chapter 10

The People's Tale

The network of monuments, the production of chapbooks and the sales of Porter foreground the vernacular in the wider Wallace narrative, advancing the tale to diverse audiences without undermining its principal tenets. The sundry poems, ballads and epitaphs focused upon critical biographical elements to submerge the narrative deeper into Scotland's national consciousness. Adding to this interrelatedness, local topographic markers shaped these connections at the level of the everyday. But no matter how intricate it had become, the story remained open to ideological capture. Much of what has been presented so far from the historiographical literature supposed Wallace to be the 'people's champion', a man who realised national success in the face of resistance from society's 'natural rulers'. In the twentieth century, Wallace became 'a victim of the class conflict and the conspiracy theory of historiography'.[1] The socialist Home Ruler and later Secretary of State for Scotland, Tom Johnston, writing in 1920, made much of 'the serfs' who fought under Wallace and Bruce:

> These poor people had associated with men of the towns, discovered what freedom meant, and developed on the battlefield a consciousness that they were the equals, in the last resort, of the knight and men at arms they speared at . . . it was unthinkable that when Bannockburn was fought and won they would go back to the old settled slavery.[2]

Writing in the shadow of a second Imperial conflict with Germany, the historian Agnes Mure Mackenzie, quoting Fordun, also observes a sense of newly realised injustice, where the people who flocked to Wallace's side did not need to be press-ganged: instead they comprised 'all who were in bitterness of spirit and oppressed by the weight of intolerable sovereignty of the English dominion'.[3]

These impressions of a heroic proletarian leader of men stand in contrast to the views of the Whig historians of the nineteenth century who placed Wallace within the tenets of modernity and so condemned him never to be free from his inferiority.[4] In Whig analysis, Wallace made only limited progress before the legitimate rulers brought forth constitutional monarchy and democracy, realised most completely in Britain's twentieth-century imperial peak.[5] Each characterisation, however broadly drawn, confirmed Wallace as a man of the people.

The existential appeal of nationalism works strongest as a plea to the folk of the nation that is forged in older loyalties to the fatherland and the motherland. As an articulation of nationalism, the existential iteration of the ideology is oriented towards the rural world, both for authenticity and to gather up the language of inclusive sociability.[6] The statues, monuments and heritage markers dedicated to Wallace in the modern age evolved symbiotically with a folk identity, and his political legacy has been similarly framed in folkish terms. The task for this chapter is, by foregrounding the concept of national tale, to examine how this identity was incorporated into Scotland's national ethos. Wallace's relationship with the nobility has already been highlighted, and the people's hand of restraint on the aristocracy developed from a political ideology associated with those times, but prioritised most strongly in the twentieth century, the 'community of the realm'. This conception leads into analysis of the antonymous contrasts between Wallace and Bruce drawn by contemporaries, ideological divisions that reflected long-standing and ingrained stratums within the national tale.

The contention that Wallace become the people's chief is given prominence by a narrative that stresses the 'betrayal' of the nation by the Scottish nobility at the battle of Falkirk in 1298. Reflecting on the importance of Wallace to ordinary Scots, Lord Rosebery concluded, in a speech given in 1897, that '[t]he People turned to the new man with a new hope and a new expectation; and as he was deserted by the aristocracy and the priesthood, he became essentially the man of the people'.[7] With equal condemnation of those who did not act as they should for the nation, Mackenzie confirms that 'it is from Falkirk that Wallace's martyrdom begins'.[8]

By showing the persistence of the antonyms of rebel/king, anarchy/authority in the analysis of Wallace and Bruce over the twentieth century, Jonathan Hearn is able to contextualise an anthropological study of the devolution movement as it developed in the 1980s and 1990s. If Wallace as 'the rebel military leader from a knightly family' and Bruce as the 'defender king' are contrasted, the betrayal of Falkirk becomes an episode to underpin nationalist conceptions of democratic deficit and renewal.[9] Balancing 'the people' against the authority of the monarch and the nation's ruling elite, this folk appeal of Wallace against the 'perfidiousness' of Bruce has been captured in the political concept of 'community of the realm'. This is a contentious and sometimes overly optimist abstraction, but one that carries the name of the people into the philosophical realm of king-making.[10] Commentators have made much of the supposed symbiosis of people, government and crown, where the king pays fealty to the people. The Declaration of Arbroath, and the political manoeuvring about it, marked an important period in the interdependence of the community and Robert I. Geoffrey Barrow has fixed the community of the realm as central to thirteenth- and fourteenth-century political theory. At its most inclusive, the concept gave leadership to 'the totality of the King's free subjects', and it was Bruce's innovative evocation of this concept which helped secure him the crown over Comyn. Yet while Bruce is constrained by this conception of kingship, and submits willingly, Wallace is taken out of his life course to join the 'hundred men alive' who compelled their monarch to act in their interests. There are, of course, those who see the community of the realm as a concept that was, in theory and in practice, less than complete. Archibald Duncan is one historian who has argued that despite contemporary rhetoric, there are clear doubts as to how open this political principle was in reality. Edward Cowan, too, has warned against taking too all-encompassing a view.[11] And the Declaration has had a mixed commemoration, its 650th anniversary marked with a commemorative stamp, but not the public holiday to match the commemorations of the 800th anniversary of the Magna Carta in 2015.[12] Yet, in the episodic constructions of nationalism, the theme of Scotland's democratic heritage stems from the Wars of Independence and the pivotal coupling of Wallace and Bruce. Like the Wallace narrative itself, this coupling has been the subject of ideological capture, even from the very beginning. Young, for example, presents a powerful corrective of our understanding of the Comyn family, the rivals to Bruce. His work delineates the construction of the Bruce and Wallace myths in the chronicles of Fordun, Bower and Wyntoun – and by contrasting the linguistic construction of these narratives, shows how John Comyn was undermined and subsumed within overly patriotic chronicles that accuse him of siding with Edward I against Robert I.[13] Watson, furthermore, has shown the potential benefits to Bruce contained within such patriotic wells, allowing him to channel his power in a number of different ways. The other side of this, and of Bruce's manipulation of the contemporary record, is the attractiveness of Bruce to later generations of nationalists.[14] That Bruce harboured his own doubts about changing sides – confessing anxiety over joining in with Edward in 1302 (a point made in documentary researches by Stoners) – is not a narrative that sits comfortably against the folk hero Wallace.[15] When Tom Johnston coupled the two patriots together, he proclaimed their inspiration to ordinary Scots, but if the integrity of Wallace was to be overshadowed by Bruce then he offered a terse corrective: 'In truth, the "Good King Robert" of our school books played a most despicable, vacillating, and traitorous part in the by no means clearly-defined drama of the times.'[16] Johnston continued this tirade by listing the many occasions Bruce had changed sides, or offered loyalty to Edward, or undermined Wallace, stating 'it has even been suggested, witnessing his trial'.[17] The supposed meeting after the battle of Falkirk or in the chapel in Dunipace has been essential to setting the relationship between the two patriots. Craigie has described these encounters as 'perhaps the most dramatic scenes in the whole of old Scottish literature', despite there being no documentary evidence that they ever met.[18]

The projection of folk hero was one that better fitted Wallace as martyr and underdog than the mendacious and victorious Bruce. Alexander Brunton dipped into the world of Blind Hary to protect the integrity of Wallace's military skills: 'If Robert Bruce excelled him in military glory, I do not place him in competition, because the former flourished after William's time'. Yet he was still compelled to add his own editorial retort, that, in any case 'this is not true. Wallace far excelled Bruce in military glory.'[19] Others have joined the defence of the patriot. As a reaction to Maxwell's *Life of Bruce* (1897), produced as part of the *Heroes of the Nations* series, in which Wallace is chastised as 'an outlaw, a thief, a brigand', McKerlie claimed the patriot's heroism was all the greater because he faced such turbulent opposition.[20] The contrast between the two kept legitimate interest in a patriot for whom only a few years of activity are known or could even be classed as influential. This worked all the more successfully because the rivalry was channelled into two parallel life courses which coalesce in 1305, when, upon the execution of Wallace, Bruce is fated to complete the destiny of the other. 'The road to miracle' is how Mackenzie summed up the nine years from 1305 until the battle of 1314.[21] Bruce 'fulfilling Wallace's dearest wish' is how Murison sought Bruce to walk in the dead man's shoes.[22]

* * *

In much of the literature that has been examined hitherto, the battle of Bannockburn has been presented as forever the epitome of Scotland's renowned military ethos. In 1930, inspired by such traditions, the Earl of Elgin helped raise funds for the purchase of fifty-eight acres of land to turn the battlefield into a heritage site.[23] Today, Bannockburn is in the care of the National Trust for Scotland. This means the site of Scotland's most important battle is not, unlike the battlefields of France and the USA, in the care of the state but of a voluntary institution.[24] Moreover, it can be observed that the NTS, a body whose ruling council has always had a strong aristocratic and landed presence, is caring for a visitor attraction which is so strongly identified with the aristocratic Bruce, whereas the National Wallace Monument remains the responsibility of Stirling Town Council.

First opened in 1964 by Queen Elizabeth I & II – an occasion when she also unveiled the statue to Bruce at Stirling castle – the Bannockburn Heritage Centre was soon attracting around 60,000 people per year. Thirty years later, post *Braveheart*, this number was estimated to have increased to around 250,000. Fast-forward another two decades, and as a mark of how much the narrative of Bruce still appeals in the twenty-first century, even more were expected to visit the redeveloped centre opened in 2014, pulled in by the nation's historic vote on independence and diaspora-oriented Homecoming events. The new Centre includes a 3D visualisation of the medieval battle designed to appeal to the young, the result of a partnership between the National Trust for Scotland and Historic Scotland with funding from the Scottish Government and the Heritage Lottery Fund.[25]

Before the heritage centre was constructed, the battlefield site had been used for a number of commemorations in the modern period. An estimated 15,000 turned up in 1814 to celebrate the 500th anniversary of the battle,[26] and the Good Templars – estimated at 6,000 in strength – descended on Bannockburn in 1897 to draw inspiration from Bruce to warn Scots off the evils of drink.[27] More politically, from the 1950s, the Scottish National Party began holding annual rallies at the sites as they had at Wallace's birthplace in Elderslie.[28] Confirming their support for the patriot king, the year of the 700th anniversary of the battle was chosen as the most opportune date to stage a referendum on Scottish independence.

Bannockburn, indeed, is an example of a tourist attraction whose selling power is based on the myth of the heroic patriot king. Its Rotunda is now the focal point in a tourist trail of the sites associated with Bruce's guardianship and kingship, just as those of Wallace's exploits have been documented (pp. 144–51).[29] The supposed meeting of Bruce and Wallace after the battle of Falkirk in 1298, despite there being no evidence of it taking place, has been promoted as the link between the two heroes, the aristocratic Bruce and proletarian Wallace, giving much-needed historical continuity to the nationalist vision of the long fight for independence.[30] With fact-based myth more powerful than that which is invented, it sustains the 'living history' that Samuel tell us is so important to the nation's 'theatres of memory'.[31]

*   *   *

The motif of Wallace's betrayal has long been sustained in the national tale. The story starts in Fordun, before being carried by Hary's embellishments and then being repeated by Hamilton and the nineteenth-century chapbooks, ballads and verse. When subscriptions were sought to fund monuments to Wallace, the appeal was made to the people that this was a man of the people. The organising committee of the National Wallace Monument made much of the many small donations received from ordinary working people. Early in its progress, though, it was feared that to build a national monument would create an opportunity for the aristocracy to shape the memory of the patriot. The mid-nineteenth-century nationalist John Steill denounced the inclusion of the nobility in the planned tribute: 'The ancestors of these men were the bitterest foes Wallace had to contend against ... No, it is the peasantry, mechanics, and the middle classes of Scotland who ought to take this matter into their own hands. They alone fought under Wallace's banner. It is for them he laid down his life.'[32] Adopting an equally doubting tone, the Scottish Home Ruler Charles Waddie sent a letter to the *Ayrshire Post* in 1896 which castigated the aristocracy for how they had represented Scotland:

> Their patriotism is of the sickly sentimental kind, reaching no further than singing a Scotch song, playing at golf, and wearing the tartan; but they never lift their little finger to stop the plundering of Scotland or the ruin of our national monuments. It is not to these snobs but to the people – the common people of Scotland – we must look for redress. History in this will but repeat itself. The nobles of Scotland deserted their country over and over again; the common people supported Wallace to free his country from English tyranny and the same people maintained their religious independence in the Covenant.[33]

The proletarian allegory has served to support a particular Scottish ethos, one claimed to be rooted in collective spirit and a greater (than in England) sense of community. Robert Burns, of course, provided much inspiration to this philosophy, but, as Angus Calder has shown through a close reading of *The Dumfries Volunteers*, the vision of liberty Burns ascribed to had been compromised:

> To thee, I turn with swimming eyes –
> Where is that soul of Freedom fled?
> Immingled with the mighty Dead!
> Beneath that hallowed turf where Wallace lies!
>
> Is this the ancient Caledonian form.
> Firm as her rock, resistless as her storm?
> Shew me that eye which shot immortal hate,
> Blasting the Despot's proudest bearing:
> Shew me that arm which, nerved with drunken fate,
> Braved Usurpation's boldest daring!
> Dark-quenched as yonder sinking star
> No more that glance lightens afar;
> That palsied arm no more whirls on the waste of war.[34]

Yet, and importantly for deepening the Wallacian national tale in Scottish national consciousness, this communitarian ethos has been inputted from a number of different directions. The Scottish Chartists of the 1830s and 1840s placed their political concerns in a historical context which made reference to Wallace. Without the English tradition of the Norman Yoke, Wallace's resistance to Edward's injustices provided their inspiration. More widely within the workers' movement, heroes like William Tell and George Washington were placed alongside the Scottish patriot as signifiers of how future aims might be realised.[35] Formed in communitarian values, Wallace was a hero who could motivate Scots to think beyond their immediate lives. John Maclean, writing a century after the Chartists, was convinced of this, and evoked Wallace to encourage Scots to raise support for Ireland's claims to home rule:

> My plea is that Britain has no right to dominate Ireland with constabulary armed with bombs and with an army and navy considered foreign to the Irish. We Scots have been taught to revere the names of Sir William Wallace and Robert Bruce because these doughty men of old are recorded as championing the cause of freedom when Edward I and Edward II tried to absorb Scotland as part of English territory. All Scots must therefore appreciate the plight of Ireland, which for over seven centuries has chafed under the same English yoke, and now ought to stand by Ireland in her last great effort for freedom; the last because triumph is bound to be hers very soon . . .[36]

Even the great industrialist and philanthropist Andrew Carnegie could maintain a preference for Wallace over Bruce – 'the laird over the king' – as a choice of aspiration and self-help, convictions rooted in the radical politics and unorthodox religion of his youth, and the kind of protestations that motivated his emigration to America.[37] Overwhelmingly, Wallace's communication ethos was mobilised in this century to fight the cause of the oppressed and also to support an increasingly interventionist social gospel that was emanating from within the Presbyterian churches. The Scottish nationalist James Barr, in his *History of the Covenanters* (1947), linked a radical religious ethos to the democratic cause of post-war Scotland. Barr was backed by the *Scots Independent*, and these attempts to foster democratic egalitarianism began to gain traction in the second half of the century.[38] The Home Ruler Lewis Spence, founding member of the Scottish National Movement in 1926, quoted with approval Garibaldi's warm sentiments on the international reputation of the Scottish patriot as a hero to all, young and old:

> The name of William Wallace has not only a British but a European reputation. Said Mazzini, the Italian patriot: 'Wallace stands forth from

the dim twilight of the past, one of the high prophets of nationality to us all; honour him, worship his memory, teach his name and his deeds to your children'.[39]

Linking Celtic culture and Celtic communism, the Scots National League claimed that the folk of Scotland were more socialist in their beliefs because they were the people 'from which Wallace drew his inspirations'. It is for this reason, they argued, that 'we who share his convictions and speak his tongue, will use both to work out freedom for our beloved land'.[40] Yet the socialism–nationalism link remained a difficult one to sustain. At the 1932 Bannockburn Day meeting organised by the National Party of Scotland in the King's Park at Stirling, John MacCormick's telegram of allegiance to the King was met by the many attendant miners removing their badges and trampling them into the ground.[41] Others, indeed, were wary of nationalism undermining the cause of socialism, which had its own patriotic content:

> It [Scottish radicalism] is far more concerned with Bannockburn, Stirling Bridge, Bruce and Wallace, than it is with the dictatorship of the proletariat and Karl Marx . . . The Scots Labour man sees himself and his party as the living embodiments of the age-old tradition born of ancestral soil. He loves to think that men of his own kin fought in the past for ideals that are now, however changed in outward guise, fundamentally his own. To him the defenders of Scottish freedom on the battlefield, in the Council Chamber, at the state, in the whelming flood, on the misty hillsides, in desolate hollows of the waste, in Tory-dominated Courts, in the mean rows where miners dwell, all these, and more than these, are brothers. And, indeed, though it is probable that a good deal of the historical detail of this view of Scottish history is not very accurate, who can deny the substantial truth of the main inference drawn from it.[42]

Throughout, the internationalism of Wallace's proletarian motif remained rooted to local issues and local constructions of nationalism – adding depth to the Wallace national tale from a mix of internal and external affairs. In John Stevenson's *A True Narrative of the Radical Rising* (Glasgow 1835), what is described as the most important comment on the nationalist content of the insurrection of 1820 is produced:

> John Morrison, who had fought and beat the French often in the Peninsular wars, laughed heartily at the idea of the yeomanry attacking

us, he said he would wager his head against a rotten apple, that twenty-five brave fellows like us would rout a regiment of such vermin; he likewise said, that Wallace and Bruce had often fought and conquered in the glorious cause of liberty, and that he was proud to see free Scotsmen leave their homes to tread in the footsteps of such illustrious men, and if we are to perish, let us do it nobly, our names will be recorded among Scotland's patriotic sons.[43]

This was heady stuff, although there is little evidence of overt nationalism projected any more widely than this in 1820. Yet when radicalism was channelled through the slow process of Whiggish reform, the patriot's symbolic influence was foregrounded to light the path to democratic gains, even if it did not result in working-class enfranchisement. When Scots gathered to celebrate the parliamentary reform act of 1832, which brought the middle classes – the £10 property holders – into the electoral process, and which offered the first glimmer of hope for the industrial and industrious classes, the Grand Procession and National Jubilee held to mark the occasion presented a mix of Scottish and British imagery:

> The business of the day shall be commenced by vocalists singing the grand national anthem of 'Rule Britannia'; after which the address to the House of Commons and his Majesty's Ministers, on the triumphant success of the great cause of Reform, will be read and submitted to the meeting, the approval whereof will be accompanied by the Band with 'God Save the King' and the business of the meeting being concluded with 'Scots, wha hae wi Wallace bled' . . .[44]

The fifty-third group to process that day was the Wallace Youths' Society, carrying two yellow banners, one with the Scottish arms, the other with Wallace's arms and the motto 'God Save the Patriot'. The Society members then carried a blue flag depicting Wallace and Bruce supporting the Scottish shield with the Royal Arms of Scotland.[45] Chairing the event, Francis Jeffrey, Lord Advocate of Scotland, declared, 'We confidently anticipate that we shall be able to record that the first popular election in Edinburgh has not been attended with a single act of intrigue, or any accident of a painful nature.'[46] This was constrained radicalism, where respectable behaviour was demanded by all sides in order to persuade government of the rights of the common man. Similarly marked by nationalist symbolism, mixed with peaceful celebrations, the passage of the second Reform Act in 1868 was marked in Scotland with banners displaying variations of the Scottish lion rampant and the bird of freedom and mottoes declaring loyalty to Queen Victoria and the British constitution. This was a respectable gathering – with no alcohol – again with the hope of furthering the artisans' claims to the franchise.[47]

Male universal suffrage was gained in 1918, and further examples of Wallace's evocation by radicalism in the twentieth century were sporadic. Research into the Independent Labour Party of the 1920s finds nothing of significance to report on the ideological influence of Wallace,[48] nor among the Red Clydesiders,[49] nor in radical Paisley.[50] This was also the conclusion from a comprehensive survey of the history of the Communist Party in Scotland.[51] Yet some evidence can be found in other political corners, notably in the feminist movement. Historians have found 'Scots Wha Hae' used as a song of personal independence in the early years of the women's movement, as well as Wallace being depicted in Scottish suffragette propaganda.[52] In 1909, suffragettes in Edinburgh took part in a mass demonstration, with women pipers accompanying the marches and a historical procession picturing famous Scottish women.[53] The highest-profile coupling of Wallace with women's rights came in 1912. Ethel Moorhead, who had been arrested in London for damaging two windows in March that year, was undeterred, and six months later she smashed the glass at the National Wallace Monument.[54] Upon arrest, using the false name Edith Johnstone, she stated that her aim was 'to draw the attention of the people to the fact that their liberty was won by fighting'. Moorhead was held in Stirling prison overnight, then Perth prison for seven days, although her complaints about the conditions she endured created just as much of an outcry as the broken glass.[55] Recalling her own imprisonment, the suffrage campaigner Dorothy Pethnick, on finishing her account of the pain and the horror of forced feeding, recounted, 'I used to watch the sunset going down the side of the cell – a streak of light – and I always had a very strong feeling of people like Garibaldi, Mazzini and Joan of Arc with me.'[56] Not Moorhead's Wallace, but the early modern French folk heroine joined Europe's greatest contemporary nationalists to inspire national change: 'We must have a thousand women on this deputation. Garibaldi with his thousand set a nation free. Remember, if we have a thousand, it will be impossible for the Government to punish any.'[57]

* * *

Historical strength, common action, a communitarian ethos – these were the claims made as Wallace's biography formed a suitable national tale for the Scottish folk. Wallace was recalled as a point of opposition to the misrule of the aristocracy, a challenge transferred to absolutist monarchs and the anti-democratic state, revolutionary ideas that burst into action so dramatically in eighteenth-century America and France and throughout Europe in 1848. In the transition out of the nineteenth century, Wallace had become a symbol of the fight for democracy. From kingship in the medieval years to radicalism in the eighteenth century and unionist-nationalism in the Victorian age, Wallace was a figure of suffrage and social inclusion. The socialist James Maxton used the occasion of the commemoration of Wallace in 1923 to castigate English people for the arrogance of their domination of the Scots as they had dominated India and Ireland.[58] In his discussions with Hugh McDiarmid, Lewis Grassic Gibbon declared his support for Wallace over the aristocratic Bruce because he looked for a saviour of the poor:[59]

> Centuries ago, Wallace, the proto-martyr of Scottish nationalism, laid down his life for an ideal. Throughout his all too brief career he fought, struggled, and lived for Scotland. His ideal was the freedom of our native land.[60]

This 'freedom of our native land' has, of course, changed from empowered local councils to federal, local-national, devolved and independence parliaments; but it also included the suffrage rights of non-property-holding men and all women. Cross-national issues and British-wide disjunctures have continued to enter the Wallace narrative and broaden the reach of the national tale. The people of the twentieth century had a new consciousness of their rights – of class and democracy, social insurance and healthcare provision irrespective of ability to pay. Their narrative was dominated by the coming of social democratic values and freedoms not seen in previous centuries, and the national tale had to speak to these affairs. With the social ethos of Wallace being framed in these terms, focus turns to the nationalists and those who have delved deepest into that communitarian national tale in order to politicise national identity.

NOTES

1. Ash, 'William Wallace and Robert the Bruce', p. 84.
2. T. Johnston, *The History of the Working Classes in Scotland* (Glasgow: Forward Publishing, 1920, 1929), p. 16.
3. A. M. Mackenzie, *Robert Bruce: King of Scots* (London: Alexander MacLehose, 1936), p. 96. Although not a view shared by the chroniclers presented in Ch. 3.
4. M. Fry, 'The Whig interpretation of Scottish History', in I. Donnachie and C. Whatley (eds), *The Manufacture of Scottish History* (Edinburgh: Polygon, 1992).
5. C. Kidd, 'Sentiment, Race and Revival: Scottish Identities in the Aftermath of Enlightenment', in L. Brockliss and D. Eastwood (eds), *A Union of Multiple Identities. The British Isles, c.1750–c.1850* (Manchester: Manchester University Press, 1997).
6. B. King, *The New English Literatures: Cultural Nationalism in a Changing World* (London: Macmillan, 1980), p. 42.
7. Rosebery, *Wallace, Burns, Stevenson: Appreciations by Lord Rosebery*, pp. 17–18.
8. Mackenzie, *Robert Bruce*, p. 117.
9. Hearn, *Claiming Scotland*, p. 102.
10. A. Broadie, 'John Duns Scotus and the Idea of Independence', in E. J. Duncan (ed.), *The Wallace Book* (Edinburgh: John Donald, 2007), pp. 82–5.
11. Ibid., p. 58.
12. Ibid., p. 41.
13. Young, *Robert the Bruce's Rivals*, pp. 2–6.
14. Watson, 'The Enigmatic Lion', pp. 28–30.
15. E. L. G. Stones, 'The submission of Robert Bruce to Edward I, c.1301–2', *The Scottish Historical Review*, 34, 118, October 1955, pp. 125–6.
16. Johnston, *History of the Working Classes in Scotland*, pp. 23–4.
17. The suggestion that Bruce was there has been comprehensively dismissed in Mackenzie, *Robert Bruce*, pp. 146–50.
18. W. A. Craigie, 'Barbour and Harry as Literature', *The Scottish Review*, Vol. XXII (1893), p. 199.
19. A. Brunton, *A New Edition of the Life and Heroic Actions of Sir William Wallace, Knight of Elderslie: in three parts* (Glasgow, Stirling, Dunfermline, Newburgh, Edinburgh, Inverkeithing: Porteous Brothers, R. S. Shearer, W. Clark & Son; J. Wood, J. Stillie, W. Pringle, 1881), p. 96.
20. P. H. McKerlie, *Sir William Wallace: the Hero of Scotland. Contains Fresh Information about the Traitorous Opposition he had to*

encounter in his struggle for Scottish Independence (Glasgow: Morrison Brothers, 1900), p. 18.

21. Mackenzie, *Robert Bruce*, p. 157.
22. A. F. Murison, *Sir William Wallace* (Edinburgh: Oliphant, Anderson & Ferrier, 1898), p. 150.
23. T. Edensor, 'National Identity and the politics of memory: remembering Bruce and Wallace in symbolic space', *Environment and Planning D: Space and Society*, 15, 2 (1997), p. 178; McCrone, Morris and Kiely, *Scotland – the Brand*, p. 188.
24. McCrone, Morris and Kiely, *Scotland – the Brand*, p. 104.
25. Ibid., p. 188; Edensor, 'National Identity', p. 177. http://battleofbannockburn.com/the-project/about-the-centre/ (accessed 14 January 2014).
26. T. C. Smout, *A Century of the Scottish People: 1830–1950* (London: Collins, 1986), p. 237.
27. Ibid., p. 146; Fraser, *Scottish Popular Politics*, p. 146.
28. Although the Scottish Home Rule Association had been holding demonstrations there from at least the 1890s, W. Mitchell, *Bannockburn: A Short Sketch of Scottish History* (Edinburgh: Scottish Home Rule Association, c.1893), p. 3.
29. Ross, *In Wallace's Footsteps*; Ross, *Trail of Wallace*.
30. Grant confirms the modern conception of Wallace as the commoner to Bruce's nobility, where the nobility is perceived as an 'other', A. Grant, 'Bravehearts and Coronets: Images of William Wallace and the Scottish Nobility', in E. J. Cowan (ed.), *The Wallace Book* (Edinburgh: John Donald, 2007), p. 86.
31. Samuel, *Theatres of Memory*, p. 259.
32. J. Steill, *Scottish Independence: Letter on the Necessity of Dissolving the Union Between England and Scotland, and on Restoring Scotland to Her Ancient Supremacy as an Entire and Distinct Nation* (Edinburgh, 1844).
33. *Ayrshire Post*, 22 May 1896.
34. A. Calder, *Revolving Cultures: Notes from the Scottish Republic* (London: I. B. Tauris, 1994), p. 77.
35. W. F. Fraser, 'The Scottish Context of Chartism', in T. Brotherstone (ed.), *Covenant, Charter and Party: Traditions of Revolt and Protest in Modern Scottish History* (Aberdeen: Aberdeen University Press, 1989), p. 73.
36. *John Maclean. In the Rapids of Revolution. Essays, Articles and Letters 1902–23*, ed. with introduction by N. Milton (London: Allison & Busby, 1978).
37. G. Donaldson, *The Scots Overseas* (London: Robert Hale, 1966), p. 118.

38. R. J. Finlay, 'Controlling the past: Scottish historiography and Scottish identity in the 19th and 20th centuries', *Scottish Affairs*, 9, Autumn 1994, p. 138.

39. Spence, *Story of William Wallace*, p. 92.

40. Quoted in Finlay, *Independent and Free*, p. 37.

41. W. Wood, *Yours Sincerely for Scotland: The Autobiography of a Patriot* (London: Arthur Barker, 1970), pp. 72–5.

42. *The Scottish Socialists: A Gallery of Contemporary Portraits* (London: Faber & Faber, 1931), pp. 22–3. My thanks go Linas Eriksonas for this citation.

43. Quoted in J. D. Young, *The Very Bastards of Creation. Scottish-International Radicalism: A Biographical Study, 1707–1995* (Glasgow: Clydeside Press, c.1996), pp. 58–9; P. B. Ellis and S. MacA'Ghobhainn, *The Scottish Insurrection of 1820* (London: Gollancz, 1970) do most to argue the nationalist angle, but few sustain this view for long. The balanced discussion comes from T. Clark and T. Dickson, 'The Birth of Class?', in T. M. Devine and R. Mitchison (eds), *People and Society in Scotland, Vol. 1, 1760–1830* (Edinburgh: John Donald, 1988).

44. 'Order of the Procession' (Edinburgh: Grand Procession and National Jubilee, n.d., c.1832). [NLS: RB.1.54(5)].

45. *The Only True and Correct Copy. Order of the Procession* (August 1832). [NLS: RB.1.54(17)]; *The Scotsman*, 11 August 1832.

46. *Chairing of the Lord Advocate and the Honorable Mr. Abercrombie* (c.1832). [NLS: RB.1.54(8)].

47. Morton and Morris, 'Civil Society, Governance and Nation', pp. 389–94.

48. See A. McKinlay and R. J. Morris (eds), *The ILP on Clydeside 1893–1932: From Foundation to Disintegration* (Manchester: Manchester University Press, 1991).

49. W. Knox, 'The Red Clydesiders and the Scottish Political Tradition', in Brotherstone (ed.), *Covenant, Charter and party*.

50. C. M. M. Macdonald, *The Radical Thread: Political Change in Scotland. Paisley Politics, 1885–1924* (East Linton: Tuckwell Press, 2000).

51. W. Thompson, *The Good Old Cause: British Communism, 1920–1991* (London: Pluto Press, 1992).

52. L. Leneman, *A Guid Cause: The Women's Suffrage Movement in Scotland* (Edinburgh: Mercat Press, 1991, 1995), pp. 116–17.

53. A. Raeburn, *The Militant Suffragettes* (London: Michael Joseph, 1973), pp. 124–5.

54. Leneman, *A Guid Cause*, pp. 266–7.

55. L. Leneman, *Martyrs in Our Midst: Dundee, Perth and the Forcible*

Feeding of Suffragettes (Dundee: Abertay Historical Society, Publication No. 33, 1993), p. 15.

56. Raeburn, *Militant Suffragettes*, p. 124.
57. Ibid., p. 164.
58. Quoted in Mitchell, *Strategies for Self-Government*, p. 78.
59. Calder, *Revolving Cultures*, pp. 141–2.
60. *Wallace Commemoration Day, Saturday, 26th August, 1933, Held at Wallace Monument, Elderslie. Official Souvenir Programme.*

Chapter 11

A Nationalist Tale

The filming of the Oscar-winning *Braveheart* (1995) sparked widespread fascination with the biography of Wallace. The cinema run was long, the video-release much anticipated, and with its transfer to DVD, Blu-ray and HD streaming the movie is now marked by its own anniversaries. Inspired by this cinematic depiction of Wallace, websites were published that enabled the folk of the late twentieth century to contribute to and shape the narrative. Representative of these interventions include *MacBraveheart* and *William Wallace: The Truth*, the latter established to foster 'the spirit of *Braveheart* (the best motion picture ever) and the interest in Scottish history, culture and politics which *Braveheart* has helped awaken'.[1] The impetus the film gave to Scottish tourism, and in visitors to the National Wallace Monument in particular, has been noted (p. 144). With roots firmly planted in the episodic national tale, the film also impacted on Scotland's political rhetoric. In the wake of the movie's release, all sides of the political spectrum made claims to Wallace's memory. The Scottish National Party worked hardest to capture this fertile ground, and despite concerns voiced by the film's star and director Mel Gibson, and apparently without permission, the SNP used the film's imagery in its (very successful) recruitment drives to proclaim 'Winning with Wallace' to be a realistic aspiration.[2] Andrew Welsh MP tantalised those gathered for the Wallace Rally in August 1995 with the prospect that Mel Gibson might yet be sharing the platform.[3] Undoubtedly, in the post-*Braveheart* decade, the Gibson narrative of Wallace became the defining version of Scotland's national tale. This was confirmed when the SNP leader Alex Salmond chose a copy of its movie poster as his contribution to definitive representations of twentieth-century Scotland in the Museum of Scotland.

Yet the SNP is not alone in avowing Wallace's guardianship and fight against the English as being symbolic of Scotland's constitutional position in the late twentieth century. Politicians of contrasting stripes evoked the *Braveheart* national tale to display their commitment to Scotland.[4] The then Secretary of State for Scotland, Michael Forsyth, used the movie to proclaim 'Be a patriot, not a nationalist' to garner support for the Conservative administration.[5] Forsyth produced an extra £100,000 of public funding to help the Scottish Tourist Board market the film abroad after emerging from a special screening with Mel Gibson, with special focus given to the potential audience in France and Germany.[6] This was money well spent, with the Scottish economy estimated to have received over £11 million worth of free advertising from *Braveheart* and *Rob Roy* (1995), with 11 per cent of visitors to Scotland that year, rising to 26 per cent in 1996 claiming they had journeyed in response to viewing the heroics of Gibson/Wallace or Neeson/Roy.[7] This appeal continued into the 2009 Homecoming events, which attracted north-European affinity Scots alongside roots tourists from North America and the diaspora.[8] Throughout these events, and through *Braveheart*'s popular sway, Wallace remained a folk hero who faced down unbending rule. On the tenth anniversary of the film's release, Salmond addressed a gathering at St Bartholomew's Church in London's Smithfield, the spot where the patriot was executed. With inverted pride, the commemoration presented Wallace as the outlaw, a man revered by an outlaw nation:

> Seven hundred years on and William Wallace still has the establishment scared stiff. Note the absence of any official commemoration planned for today, the anniversary of the execution of Scotland's greatest national hero. And yet the event has been marked, not by official ceremony, but only by the activities of the many grassroots Wallace societies, which still flourish the length and breadth of Scotland.[9]

* * *

This interpretation of the national tale by nationalist groupings has had a longer heritage than the modern-day SNP. The first of such movements in the modern age, the National Association for the Vindication of Scottish Rights (1852–6), cherry-picked elements of the historical past to seek restoration of Scottish rights.[10] In today's language, this association would be called cross-party, such was the heterogeneous composition of its leadership. The brothers

James and John Grant used their literary skills to produce a myriad pamphlets, petitions and newspaper contributions to build the case that Scotland's rights as a nation, not a region of Britain, should be recognised in complete equality with England in matters of taxation, public expenditure and parliamentary time.[11] Their chairman was the Earl of Eglinton and Winton, and the Association gained representation from town provosts ranging from Ardrossan to Stirling and from subscribing representatives of numerous other town councils. The wider membership came from the professional classes, but this was never a mass movement despite the spread of affiliated branches.[12] With Eglinton – known for having hosted a medieval tournament on his lands in 1839 – at its head a chivalric interpretation of Wallace was not anathema to their aims.[13] Yet for all their romantic leanings, it was stated, at the first public meetings to launch their claims, that it was not domesticity that brought Wallace to his nation's hour, but heroics akin to more recent military endeavours: 'We glory in the triumph of a Marlborough, a Nelson and a Wellington, but might we not look with pride to the achievements of a Wallace and a Bruce?[14] This evocation was not to further sentimentality, but to make detailed judgements on past and future trends in Scotland's governance. Their nationalism, which was framed within explicit loyalty to the Union, focused on how Scottish rights had been established on a par with those of England in the Union of 1707. Now it was argued that those rights were lost because Westminster was too large and unwieldy, insensitive and unaccountable to local representatives and local needs: '. . . the crushing policy of centralisation . . . has placed Scotland in a position little better that Yorkshire or any other English country'.[15] In one contemporary analysis, the problem with the modern state came from a civil service recruited to serve political interests, not to achieve efficiency.[16] This was representative of a type of contemporary analysis that supported the nationalists' assertions that the political integrity of Britain had been compromised by undermining municipal government. In these debates, it was how Scotland achieved equality with England that carried the Wallace myth. Indeed, the link was explicitly made between Wallace (d. 1305), Bruce (d. 1329) and their 'results in' the union of Scotland and England in 1707. Four centuries of discord were wiped from the chronology as the medieval patriots were fêted for bringing the two nations together into peaceful eighteenth-century partnership. This juxtaposition of the past was explicit in an attempt to build a monument to Wallace and Bruce in Edinburgh in 1859, when 'It is the deliverance and its results, as distinguished from the Deliverers' that was looked to.[17] Linked to the tone and argument of the chapbook and subscription appeals outlined in the previous two chapters, the rhetoric of this period was far removed from the anti-English wrath that marked the early-modern *Wallace* and its vernacular reprints. In this construction of the national tale the great medieval patriots achieved Scotland's freedom, which four centuries later allowed the Union to be negotiated between independent nations. The outcome of that union – so the argument developed in the Victorian age – was that the nation's freedom would advance still further, if only political equality between Scotland and England were adhered to.

This mid-Victorian nationalism developed out of the Wallacian national tale that had been spread so vicariously through *The Scottish Chiefs* and other media. By 1850 Porter was dead, but her book continued to sell and her memory continued to fascinate. Like the spinster romantic novelist, the Scottish nationalists of this period worked to improve the Union for the benefit of Scotland and of Britain. This was consistent with a preferred constitutional solution which did not add to the remit of central government, be it at Westminster or a devolved body at Edinburgh, but instead made the locality, and local government, the guarantor of those freedoms. The solution of the NAVSR was not to add another layer of centralised government – which a Scottish parliament would do – but to strengthen the independence of local government, in both town and country. This explains the involvement of Scotland's town councillors, sustaining the politicisation of the national tale against independent nation-statehood: good legislation was only possible from local action and local appointments.[18] This element of the argument was carried through the 1880s into the first two decades of the twentieth century with support for municipal trading and, on occasion, municipal socialism. The local politician was a force to be reckoned with, and embodied the spirit of respectability and civic duty, as Tom Johnston observes:

In the homely burghs of Scotland we may find the first spring of that public spirit, the voice of the people, which in the worst of times, when the Crown and the law were powerless and feudal aristocracy altogether selfish in its views, supported the patriot leaders, Wallace and Bruce, in their desperate struggle, and sent down that tide of native feeling which animated Burns and Scott, and which is not yet dead . . . Whatever of thought, of enterprise, of public feeling, appears in our poor history took rise in our burghs and among the burgess class.[19]

The end of the NAVSR coincided with the events in Crimea. Momentum had clearly been lost and the war provided the excuse for standing down while the patriotic flag still flew.[20] For those who continued to explore the national tale and follow in the footsteps of Wallace, there endured good reason to celebrate British victories in Prussia.[21] The mid-century fashioning of the Wallace tale made plain that Britain's military exploits were to be honoured:

> The writer of these pages has a great respect for English people, and does much business with many of them; but he cannot see how a judicious history of our hero should give them any offence, for they have enjoyed all the benefits resulting from his achievements as much as we [the Scots] have done.[22]

Quoting a 'living English historian', Hutchison's political comment from 1859 stands contrary to Paton's plea for improved English understanding of cross-border historical events (pp. 7–8): 'The Englishman who now reads of the deeds of Wallace or of Bruce, or hears the stirring words of one of the noblest lyrics, feels that the call to "lay the proud usurpers low", is one which stirs the blood as much as that of the Scotsman.'[23] More than being pro-Union on the Scottish side, Wallace's biography was now offered as a means for the English to conceive of Britain's strength. Wallace was to be shared, Scotland and England were now blessed by a Union of equals, and each nation had the right to have their respective blood stirred by the warrior-patriot.[24]

Meeting in 1859 to set out its plans, the National Wallace Monument Movement was joined by the remnants of the NAVSR. There was then a hiatus in the organisational history of Scottish nationalism until the Scottish Home Rule Association was formed in 1886. Of its active leadership, only John Romans bridged the thirty-year gap. The analysis of these nationalists was still Unionist, but the argument for federalism, mobilised through the Liberal party, was a new departure. Still, their administrative rationale was based on the evils of centralisation at Westminster, the inequalities of the Exchequer and the lack of parliamentary time for discussion of Scottish legislation.[25] Introducing his study of Hary in 1888,

Moir claimed that Scottish Home Rule would have taken a different path had it not been for the success of Wallace:

> Had the result of Edward's wars in Scotland been to make him his lord, we might have had today a Scottish Home Rule Question as difficult to settle as the Irish one. The aggression of Edward only helped to consolidate Scotland and make the country not a geographical expression, but a nation. Dr Arnold of Rugby points out that the battles of Bannockburn and Orleans, in both of which the English were defeated, were really blessings for England. The one secured the independence of Scotland, the other put an end to the English pretensions to a continental sovereignty. The conquest of Ireland, on the other hand, was complete, with the result that the Irish have always been dissatisfied with their position, whereas the Scots can look back to the War of Independence with pride, and can feel that when the Union took place it was between equals, and not between a conquered and a conquering nation.[26]

When offering their own interpretation of Wallace and the national tale, the contemporary Home Rulers were explicit on history's bearing upon Scotland's current plight. Linking Wallace in this way, J. Morrison Davidson quotes approvingly Goldwin Smith, Regius Professor of Modern History at the University of Oxford:

> Nothing contributed more than the distinct national character (entirely Wallace's work), and the distinct national religion of the Scots to save Britain from being entirely subjugated by the absolutism of Stratford and the Anglicanisation of Laud.[27]

Charles Waddie, William Mitchell, G. B. Clark and John Stuart Blackie made up the remainder of the SHRA's leadership, and all penned pamphlets and submitted letters to the newspaper to further their cause. Failure to persuade Gladstone to place Scotland's claims alongside those of Ireland, despite his fleeting support during his first Midlothian campaign, a commitment he then tried assiduously to avoid on subsequent visits, was a constant sore.[28] Nor could the SHRA persuade Rosebery that the creation of the Scottish Office was no substitute for a federal structure.[29] Despite his belief in Imperial Federation, Rosebery was remarkably lukewarm to such reform at home.[30] Both failures confirmed the SHRA as being on the margins of Scottish and British politics,[31] but this did not stop an immensely active propaganda campaign in the regional press, polticising national identity although still not of itself influencing party politics.[32] The Irish situation was to became the SHRA's nemesis, as Ireland, not the Scots, received cross-party discussion.[33] Writing in the newspapers in 1896, Charles Waddie recalled a trip to Dublin, made in an effort to join the claims of the two Celtic countries into the All Round principle. While applauding the hospitality he received, Waddie was clearly marginalised by his hosts.[34] A decade after its formation, the SHRA was convinced of the harm Irish home rule was causing to its own claims: 'Let our Liberal leaders drop "Ireland first" and patriotically and logically include their own country as well as Ireland. This will make the case a stronger one, and England (with Scotland, Ireland and Wales demanding Home Rule) will not long continue opposing their combined demand.'[35] This first phase of the Scottish Home Rule Association stuttered into the late 1890s because of this political failure. Then the response to these difficulties was to develop the cultural roots of Scottishness, in the hope that it would arouse the voters from apathy. William Mitchell wrote a short history of Bannockburn for the *Stirling Observer* in 1893, which was then picked up in pamphlet form by the publishers of the Scottish Home Rule Association.[36] Complaining that the Scots were intractably indifferent to their political subjugation, the Melbourne-born Scottish nationalist Theodore Napier, secretary of the Wallace Robroyston Memorial committee, conjured up the memory of Wallace to chide them:

> They are more interested in a football or a golf match than in the political welfare and freedom of their country. Was it for this our great hero-patriot Wallace struggled for so long and lost his life? Was it not for the object of delivering Scotland from English aggression and predominance? Do we not hail Bruce as the successful champion of our independence from English thraldom? And yet we have basely surrendered our political freedom to England. For a country that does not govern itself cannot be regarded as free.[37]

Developing the theme, as the 600th anniversary of the battle of Stirling Bridge approached, the *Montrose Review* placed Wallace's contribution as a never-ending inspiration, helped by Burns and completed by Bruce:

> Shades o' the immortal Wallace,
> Bruce an' Burns tae duty call us,
> Shail we let oor foes enthrall us,
> Merit thy eternal scorn;

Shall thy monuments revile us,
Base degenerate cowards style us,
Frae thy bluid-bocht gift exile us,
Freedom gained at Bannockburn?[38]

In the same week, with another piece of verse sent in by an unnamed supporter of the Home Rule cause, the *Patriot Scot* celebrated Wallace's noble martyrdom, but reserved the epithet 'The nation's saviour' to Bruce:

Hoo noble Wallace in the strife,
For independence lost his life,
A martyr tae the headsman's knife,
An' despot's ire,
Whilk nocht but bribes and traiters rife,
Cud e'er acquire?

[. . .]

An' hoo the Bruce, wi royal micht,
Avenged that deed as dark as nicht,
An saved intact oor country's right,
A nation's place,
An' left her bairns wi honour bricht
A fee born race.[39]

This transition to Bruce has been shown to be most dominant in the twentieth century in the pre-*Braveheart* decades (pp. 162–3). Even as the national tale was evolving in the last phase of the nineteenth century, it was Bannockburn that focused valorisation of the life of Wallace. In July 1896, at the Bannockburn field, the Scottish Home Rule Association marked the famous victory with the conclusion that it was Bruce who avenged the death of Wallace, and it was Bruce who completed his work:

Departed heroes! Whose great presence now
We feel around us on this hallowed spot!
No eloquence is needed to tell how
Your noble deeds shall never be forgot!
Scotland had fallen – lay bleeding on the ground,
And basely trampled on by southron foes,
And Wallace wight was dead, her martyred chief;
And everywhere around
Was dark and stormy when Bruce arose
And with his valient comrades brought relief.

[. . .]

And friendly voices speak across the Tweed,
And we are brethren now, no longer foes;
Each helps the other in the hour of need,
And mutual love with every season grows.
We are both loyal to one common crown,
But claim to have our Parliament restored.
Scotland shall never leave the task undone
Till she gets back her own,
Her name and nationhood; nor cease to guard
The sacred freedom which her heroes won.[40]

The use of text in newspapers and pamphlets to promote the nationalist cause was a consequence of the movement's lack of party infrastructure, but it had the effect of broadening the textual basis of the national tale. When the anniversary of the battle of Stirling Bridge in 1897 was marked, patriotic verse appeared in a range of Scottish newspapers and in over forty newspapers in the USA, each suggestive of the continued contemporary relevance of the patriots in the minds of editors and readers alike: 'Where'er our eyes we turn/Twas here that glorious Wallace fought –/There, Bruce at Bannockburn.'[41] In 1899 Charles Waddie staged a series of historical plays in an attempt to stimulate Scottish patriotism, including 'Wallace' and 'The Bruce',[42] and overall there was a marked promotion of Bruce as the key patriot. John Romans, for example, mentions Bruce and the Declaration of Arbroath, not Wallace, when introducing his case for Home Rule, wishing to 'celebrate the glorious day of freedom on 24 June', Bannockburn day (although he did then exhort the Scottish people to educate all children over the age of ten in the words of 'Scots Wha Hae'[43]). Two years later, Theodore Napier focused solely on king Robert in his verse: 'Land of the Bruce, awake, reply/Assert your rights, avenge or die!/Break now your chain, be free, ye brave,/Nor live degraded – England's Slave!'[44] And, again with some attempt at balance, Napier wrote to the *Stirling Observer* to remind the people of Stirling of the approaching anniversary of Wallace's execution, clearly worried that amnesia had set in; but, if anything, it stimulated interest in Bruce rather then Wallace.[45]

Other events could be brought into the equation, too. Davidson used Wallace in his analysis of the Boer War, arguing that 'William

Wallace, the stainless knight of Elderslie, was the Scottish Kruger and Steyn, Botha, de la Rey and De Wit rolled into one'.[46] Mitchell celebrated the inauguration of the cross at Kinghorn for Alexander III, which marked the most quoted point of origin for any explanation of Wallace's rise to prominence.[47] When the SHRA's Rev. David Macrae, from Gilfillan Memorial Church in Dundee, begun his history of Wallace for the Scottish Patriotic Association, he did so with two quotations from inspirational radicals, one from Burns and the other from Garibaldi, which declared: 'William Wallace sheds as bright a glory upon his valorous nation as ever was shed upon their country by the greatest men of Greece or Rome.'[48] When the Scottish Home Rule Association froze its activities in 1900, the mantle was taken up by the Young Scots Society (YSS) which formed in that year. The Society was very much a Liberal Party organisation, becoming particularly active in the issue of free trade, temperance, education and working-class poverty.[49] Only after 1909 did the YSS focus all its attentions on Scotland's governance, whereupon it achieved some electoral success up until 1914.[50] The society published greatly and produced leaflets in the thousands.[51] Among politicians of the Empire, it was argued that home rule in Britain was the question that 'most excites the dominions' – although this was qualified with the considered conclusion that Scotland would be content with land reform and some vague promise of home rule all round following legislation for Ireland.[52] This intransigence blocked any headway for the nationalist movement despite the innovative elicitation of the Wallacian national tale. Others sought to play the patriotic British card when seeking to place Wallace's fight for independence within current events. Lewis Spence, soon to form the Scots National Movement from the disaffected in the Scots National League in 1926, tied his biography of Wallace to the Great War:

> But in older days men did not stop to discover whether their cause was right or wrong. It was enough for them to know that their country was at war. The land in which they lived was sacred to them, and to defend it was part of their religion. Their patriotism and their faith was as one.[53]

Spence built up his personal nationalism as one borne out of profound belief – a life's purpose – projected through a warrior whose patriotism was 'a religion, deep, passionate, intense'.[54] Here, the national tale was used as a resource to politicise and mobilise social democracy: 'We cannot all be Wallaces, but we can all serve the land that gave us birth as our strength or abilities permit.'[55] Deploying Wallace as an international cry for freedom, Spence ignores any intellectual contradiction that might be raised from melding Bannockburn's national independence and a nationality embedded in the federal structures of home rule. At the Elderslie commemoration of Wallace in 1921, the Rev. James Barr proclaimed the patriot the only prominent Scot not to have changed sides during the Wars of Independence, and a man whose simplistic loyalty to the people was contrasted with the sophisticated (and therefore mendacious) actions of Bruce. Resurrecting the radical sentiment around betrayal, bribery and English gold, he proclaimed that, rather than together in Union, Scottish and British matters were best handled separately. Daring to embellish Burns' verse identifying the threat to eighteenth-century Britain of a potential French invasion, Barr projects the poet's focus onto Scotland's twentieth-century ills:

Be Britain still to Britain true,
Amang ourselves united;
For never but by British hands
Maun British wrangs be righted!

Be Scotsmen still to Scotsmen true
Amang ourselves united;
For never but by Scottish hands
Maun Scottish wrongs be righted![56]

Barr's failure to guide the Bill on Home Rule through Parliament in 1927 was a setback that blocked the momentum of the Scots National League and the Scottish Home Rule Association during its second phase.[57] And when the political path proved rocky, cultural events continued to find a role for Wallace that spoke to contemporary needs. At the Scottish Historical Pageant held at Craigmillar Castle in 1927, in front of 50,000 ticket holders, some 'hardy Scots' enacted the traditions of Wallace and Bruce in order that they might 'bear arms for their native land, should the need arise'.[58] Yet few could hope for such numbers to gather in support of the nationalist cause. When the National Party of Scotland took up the slack, its President Roland Muirhead regarded the 'fully 1000 people' who attended as evidence 'of the gradual awakening of the spirit of Scottish nationalism'.[59] It was only a modest repoliticisation of the national tale, although in 1931 R. B. Cunninghame Graham could feel the 'demand for home rule in the air all over the world' because 'since the war many states have risen into being, and if these states were worthy of independence, surely it was a strange thing if Scotland, the best educated of all, should be the one State without it'.[60] Quickening military expansion made the inter-war years a period of evolution in the relationship of state and nation, and so also the political space that could contain the national tale: central government increasingly dominated a more streamlined local government following its reform in the Local Government (Scotland) Act of 1929.

Other bodies were formed to structure Scotland's governance and civil society at this time, moving the debate from the locality towards the national and quasi-non-governmental organisations. The National Trust for Scotland (1931), the Saltire Society (1936) and the Gilmour Report (1937), which precipitated the move of the Scottish Office from London to Edinburgh, are rightly identified as marking a change in perceptions of how the state should intervene in society.[61] The move north of the Scottish Office and the slow expansion of its staff, and the growing seniority of its leadership, comprised the ideological shift in the superiority of central over local government.[62] This move also signalled a more corporatist approach to government, one that the Scottish nationalists reflected in their deployment of a national memory of Wallace. The Wallace Commemoration Day in 1933 took place against the backdrop of the final moves towards creating the Scottish National Party out from various tensions and nationalist structures. The event was chaired by the veteran Roland Muirhead, with another doyen of the past, Cunninghame Graham, giving the lead address, framing Wallace's life-history against the pressures then facing the Scottish economy:

> We must imitate him and take in hand our bread and butter questions. Look at the Clyde, as silent and as shipless as the Orinoco. Whilst Liberals, Socialists, and Tories fight their mimic wars at Westminster and Scottish questions are postponed or neglected. We call on Scotsmen, and above all Scotswomen – the hand that rocks the cradle shapes the man – to join the National Party, and not allow the martyrdom of Wallace to be lost.[63]

A decade later, the ongoing war did not stop the commemoration of Wallace at Elderslie, an occasion dominated by polymath and

Figure 4   *Postcard of William Wallace Statue, Lanark Lanimer Day 1932. © Newsquest (Herald & Times). Licensor www.scran.ac.uk*

Figure 5 *Wallace Statue being installed at Bellahouston Park for the British Empire Exhibition of 1938. © Scottish Life Archive. Licensor www.scran.ac.uk*

nationalist Douglas Young's railing, on Wallace's behalf, against conscription to 'defend far-flung tracts of the London profiteer's empire'. Being fearful of the radio, cinema, the press and the Kirk being used 'to spread propaganda', he argued for the legacy of the national tale to empower Scots to challenge the legality of conscription under that 1707 Treaty.[64] Even without some of Young's emotive rhetoric, in the Scots Secretariat's pamphlet on Wallace produced in 1955, the war is remembered not for its *esprit de corps*, but for its denudation of the young.[65] The pamphlet *How Scots Opposed the Peacetime Call-up* was a corrective to the party's motives during Young's leadership, justifying its lack of British patriotism and concluding with a 'Buy Scottish' campaign to counter the 'Buy British' rhetoric of John Bull.[66]

In the years of the 1950s, the chosen evocation of the national tale was widespread and unfocused, appearing in cultural and political manifestations of various degrees of coherence. Politically, the National Covenant Movement was the major challenge to the state, garnering 2 million signatures in favour of Home Rule (a number boosted by more than one 'William Wallace', and a 'Mickey Mouse' or two too). When the anniversary of R. B. Cunninghame Graham's birth was marked by the Young Scots National League in 1952, in a gathering at the Lake of Menteith, the event closed with the singing of 'Scots Wha Hae'.[67] And in the celebration of Wallace Day on 22 August 1953, the procession to the Elderslie monument was presented with an 'exact replica' of the Wallace sword to be carried in a procession comprising representatives from all branches of the Young Scots and of Fianna Na h-Alba, an event followed by the annual Celtic Congress of that year.[68] This growing strength of the nationalist movement, aided by a developing Celtic agenda, resulted in the Wallacian national tale being deployed to shape a much stronger element of anti-Union analysis. The representation of Wallace by the Scots Secretariat, produced to commemorate the 650th anniversary of the patriot's death, was directly political, taking the opportunity to belittle the efforts of the 'English-controlled' political parties to satisfy the demand for Home Rule. The Conservative and Unionist Party was painted as having never made Home Rule part of its platform, and was accused of following a policy of increased centralisation of government. Equally, despite the heritage of Keir Hardie to the formation of the Labour Party, it was claimed that this unwelcome policy is also lost amongst the 'witch-hunting gang of power-greedy wire-pullers who now dictate the policies of the Labour Party'. The name of the patriot was called to remedy this neglect: 'The story of William Wallace is an inspiration to the modern Scot in the struggle he is called upon to pursue.'[69]

A survey of the pamphlet and campaign literature of the SNP in the decades which followed suggests there was less and less appeal to the memory of Wallace or to Bruce.[70] The explanatory power of the Wallacian national tale for contemporary politics was lost as instrumental conceptions of the nation won out over existential constructions, typified most by the evidence of administrative neglect gathered by the Kilbrandon Commission and the neo-nationalism formed in the wake of the discovery of North Sea oil. Renowned for his role in the removal of the Stone of Destiny from Westminster Abbey in 1950, Ian Hamilton now argued for practical not emotional issues to come to the fore.[71] The 1950s had been a decade of direct cultural protest, including the firebombing of postboxes displaying E[II]R (there never was an Elizabeth I in Scotland), and later Wendy Wood's ink-filled egg-bombing of the offending royal shield on a lamp-post on Edinburgh's North Bridge (on the morning of King Olaf's visit in 1962).[72] With her left-wing credentials, Wood was enamoured more than were most of her contemporaries with the politics of the fourteenth-century martyr. She perceived 'Freedom as [being] of the same content down the ages', and so connected Scotland's medieval Wars of Independence to the conflict of present-day Czechoslovakia.[73] But when the SNP launched an appeal for funds in 1962 it chose to call upon the spirit of St Andrew rather than Wallace or Bruce.[74] Nor was Wallace trumpeted as the inspiration when the SNP made its modern political breakthrough with Winnie Ewing's by-election victory in Hamilton in 1968. Bureaucratic governance took over from democratic deficit most clearly following the publication of the Kilbrandon Report in 1973 – a document strong on administration, but short on inspiration from a chivalric past.[75] The Report identified a series of contradictory pressures destabilising the constitution. Most notable was the existence of a national feeling that made London rule unpopular in Scotland, yet, in apparent contradiction, it was also perceived that the powers of the Scottish Office were too great and without sufficient democratic accountability.[76] The Commissioners rejected the argument that independence for Scotland or Wales would be economically advantageous to those countries, even with the likely revenues flowing from oil exploration in the North Sea.[77] Neither was federalism a popular option in the evidence presented to the Commissions; they concluded it was a system 'designed and . . . appropriate for states coming together to form a single unit, and not for a state breaking up into smaller units'.[78] Having rejected those positions, and that of the status quo, and despite no agreement on the form it would take, devolved assemblies were proposed for Scotland and Wales.[79] With constitutional change so high up the agenda, the Scottish National Party achieved its highest-ever share of the vote at the 1974 (October) general election, gaining eleven MPs. The minority Labour administration, requiring nationalist support to say in power, published its White Paper *Our Changing Democracy: Devolution to Scotland and Wales* (1975) in response.[80] Through the White Paper, the Government agreed with Kilbrandon's recommendations to reject federalism or independence for any part of the UK,[81] yet stated that 'something more is needed – the creation of elected as well as administrative institutions distinctive to Scotland and Wales'.[82] The administrative tone of governance put forward in both documents was no different from the 1980s' Constitutional Convention and its *Claim of Right*, although the latter embodied the power of the people's will in some stirring rhetoric. In response, the Conservative administration's 'Taking Stock' programme, *Scotland and the Union: A Partnership for Good*, brought further rhetoric to define Scotland's history as successful through Union.[83] Throughout these legislative proposals, the Wallacian national tale was sidelined in favour of instrumental and constitutional concerns, where political representation and management of resources came to shape the devolutionary debate.

The demise of the national tale under the pressure to manage the nation's resources more effectively and to better advance democratic accountability came to an abrupt halt with the release of *Braveheart* in 1995. The then-current incarnation of political nationalism was not royal or federal or unionist Scotland hoarding the rhetoric; instead it was the language and structures of independence. The film's release led the leader of the SNP to declare unequivocally: 'So that we can say with Wallace – head and heart – the one word which encapsulates all our hopes – Freedom, Freedom, Freedom.'[84] Yet the national tale has defied long-term capture by Gibson's film. When nearly two decades later those hopes were entrusted to a referendum on Scottish independence, the SNP counselled its campaign team to drop reference to freedom and other 'Braveheart-esque rhetoric' and instead deploy 'positive language and phrases'; advice that came not by way of Hary or Porter but a sports psychologist.[85] No prediction can be made, but it would appear that fracture lines, once again, can be identified in the tale's twenty-first-century construction.

NOTES

1. http://www.braveheart.co.uk/macbrave (accessed 12 January 2001); http://www.highlanderweb.co.uk/wallace/index.html (accessed 12 January 2001).
2. *The Scotsman*, 1 September 1995.
3. http://www.snp.org.uk (11 August 1995).

4. Morton, *Unionist-Nationalism*, pp. 198–9.
5. *The Scotsman*, 31 October 1996.
6. *The Scotsman*, 12 September 1995, T. Edensor, 'Reading Braveheart: representing and contesting Scottish identity', *Scottish Affairs*, 21 (1997), p. 144.
7. D. Petrie, *Screening Scotland* (London: BFI Publishing, 2000), p. 220 for the 1995 figure; the latter is cited in C. McArthur, 'Scotland and the *Braveheart* effect', *Journal for the Study of British Cultures*, 5, 1 (1998), p. 36.
8. D. Hesse, 'Finding Neverland: Homecoming Scotland and the "Affinity Scots"', in M. Varricchio (ed.), *Back to Caledonia: Scottish Homecomings from the Seventeenth Century to the Present* (Edinburgh: John Donald, 2012), pp. 228–9.
9. *BBC News*, 23 August 2005.
10. For an extended analysis of this movement, see Morton, 'Returning Nationalists, Returning Scotland' and G. Morton, 'Scottish rights and "centralisation" in the mid-nineteenth century', *Nations and Nationalism*, 2, 2, 1996.
11. See *Memorial of the Council of the National Association, to the Right Honorable the Lords Commissioners of her Majesty's Treasury*, 27 September 1854.
12. See a list of the provosts attending the Eglinton Banquet, along with many other notables, in *Banquet in Honour of the Right Honourable the Earl of Eglinton & Winton, K.T., President of the National Association for the Vindication of Scottish Rights, to be held in the City Hall, Glasgow, 4 Oct. 1854*. The Convention of Royal Burghs and twenty-four Town Councils signed an appeal to the Queen, *May it Please your Majesty. The Petition of the undersigned, your Majesty's loyal subjects, inhabiting that part of your Majesty's United Kingdom called Scotland* (c.1854).
13. I. Anstruther, *The Knight and the Umbrella: An Account of the Eglinton Tournament 1839*, 2nd edn (Gloucester: Alan Sutton, 1986).
14. *Justice to Scotland. Report of the Great Public Meeting of the National Association for the Vindication of Scottish Rights, held in the City Hall, Glasgow, December 15 1853* (n.p., 1853), p. 8.
15. Red Lion, *Scotland and 'The Times'. To the editors of the 'Edinburgh Evening Post' and the 'Scottish Record'* (n.p., 1853).
16. 'One Behind the Scenes', *Red-Tapism*, 2nd edn (London: Ridgeway, 1855).
17. *A National Memorial of the War of Independence under Wallace and Bruce and its Results in the Union of England and Scotland to be Erected in the Metropolis in Scotland* (Edinburgh, c.1859).

18   A Scotchman, *Scottish Rights and Grievances*, pp. 12–13.
19. Johnston, *The History of the Working Classes in Scotland*, p. 122, quoting from *Ancient Laws and Customs of the Burghs of Scotland* (Burgh Records Society), Preface, p. xlix.
20. 'Without forgoing their claims as Scotsmen', stated William Burns in 1855: 'Association for the Vindication of Scottish Rights'.
21. P. R. Sawers, *Footsteps of Sir William Wallace, Battle of Stirling: Or, Wallace on the Forth* (Glasgow, 1856).
22. A. Brunton, *A New Work in Answer to the Pamphlet, 'Wallace on the Forth', proving the stratagem at Stirling Bridge and that the Bridge was at Kildean, etc. Also the history of the famous battle of Stirling Bridge, to which is added two letters written by Sir William Wallace himself, and Wallace's charter to Scrymgeour of Dundee* (Dunfermline: W. Clark, 1841, Stirling: R. S. Shearer, 1861), p. 4.
23. Hutchison, *Life of Sir William Wallace; or Scotland Five Hundred Years Ago* (Glasgow, Thomas Murray & Son, 1858), p. viii. A verbatim copy of this statement was made in C. G. Glass, *Stray Leaves from Scotch and English History, with the Life of Sir William Wallace, Scotland's Patriot, hero, and Political Martyr* (Montreal: A. and A. Stevenson, c.1873), pp. 8–9; Paton, *The Claim of Scotland*, pp. 24, 42–3.
24. The English attraction to Wallace is examined in C. Kidd, 'The English Cult of Wallace and the Blending of Nineteenth-Century Britain', in E. J. Cowan, *The Wallace Book* (Edinburgh: John Donald, 2007), pp. 136–50.
25. The continuities and discontinuities between the National Association for the Vindication of Scottish Rights and first Scottish Home Rule Association are discussed in. G. Morton, 'The First Home Rule Movement in Scotland, 1886 to 1918', in H. Dickinson and M. Lynch (eds), *Sovereignty and Devolution* (East Linton: Tuckwell Press, 2000).
26. J. Moir, *Sir William Wallace: a critical study of his biographer Blind Harry* (Aberdeen, 1888), pp. 60–1.
27. J. M. Davidson, *Scotia Rediva: Home Rule for Scotland with the Lives of Sir William Wallace, George Buchanan, Fletcher of Saltoun, and Thomas Spence* (London: William Reeves, 1888, 1893), p. 112.
28. *Midlothian Campaign. Political Speeches delivered in November and December 1879 and March and April 1880 by the Right Hon. W. E. Gladstone, MP* (Edinburgh, 1880), p. 44.
29. S. J. Brown, '"Echoes of Midlothian": Scottish liberalism and the South African War, 1899–1902', *Scottish Historical Review*, 71, 1, 2: 191/2 (1992), p. 58. Indeed, Rosebery complained that he was fed up being always censured by the SHRA, see further comment in W.

Mitchell, *Lord Rosebery and Home Rule for Scotland: A Challenge* (Edinburgh: Scottish Home Rule Association, c.1894), pp. 5–6.

30. R. J. Akroyd, 'Lord Rosebery and Scottish Nationalism, 1868–1896', unpublished Ph.D. thesis, University of Edinburgh (1996), p. 280.
31. M. Fry, *Patronage and Principle: A Political History of Modern Scotland* (Aberdeen: Aberdeen University Press, 1987), pp. 105–7; I. G. C. Hutchison, *A Political History of Scotland 1832–1924. Parties, Elections and Issues* (Edinburgh: John Donald, 1986), pp. 172–3.
32. Morton, 'First Home Rule Movement'.
33. This was explored in *Scottish versus Irish Grievances* (Edinburgh: Scottish Home Rule Association, c.1890).
34. *Methodist Times*, 28 May 1896.
35. *Scottish Highlander*, 21 May 1896.
36. W. Mitchell, *Bannockburn: A Short Sketch of Scottish History* (Edinburgh: Scottish Home Rule Association, c.1894).
37. W. T. Pike (ed.), 'Contemporary Biographies', in *Edinburgh and the Lothians at the opening of the twentieth century by A Eddinton* (Edinburgh: Pike & Co., 1904), p. 128; *Scottish Highlander*, 11 June 1896.
38. Verse five of seven, the *Montrose Review*, 22 May 1896.
39. Verses three and four of nine, and appeared in various newspapers in May 1896.
40. First and last verse of seven, *Scottish Highlander*, 23 July 1896.
41. Scottish Home Rule Association, 10 September 1897.
42. Mitchell, *Strategies for Self-Government*, p. 26.
43. J. Romans, *Home Rule for Scotland* (Edinburgh: Scottish Home Rule Association, c.1894), pp. 6, 28.
44. Theodore Napier writing in the *Scottish Highlander*, 21 May 1896.
45. T. Napier, 'Honouring Sir William Wallace', *Stirling Observer*, 17 August 1896.
46. Quoted in Fraser, *Scottish Popular Politics*, p. 145.
47. W. Mitchell, *Home Rule for Scotland and Imperial Federation* (Edinburgh: Scottish Home Rule Association, 1892), p. 11.
48. D. Macrae, *The Story of William Wallace, Scotland's National Hero* (Scottish Patriotic Association, 1905), p. 3.
49. R. J. Finlay, 'Continuity and Change: Scottish Politics, 1900–45', in T. M. Devine and R. J. Finlay, eds, *Scotland in the Twentieth Century* (Edinburgh: Edinburgh University Press, 1996), pp. 66–7; Finlay, *Partnership for Good?*, pp. 52–3; Mitchell, *Strategies for Self-Government*, p. 72.
50. Hutchison, *Political History*, p. 241.
51. Finlay, *Partnership for Good?*, p. 59.

52. *The Round Table. A Quarterly Review of the Politics of the British Empire*, Vol. 5, December (1911–12), pp., 12, 15.
53. Spence, *Story of William Wallace*, p. 3.
54. Ibid., p. 4.
55. Ibid.
56. *Scotland Yet! An Address Delivered by the Rev. James Barr, B.D., at the Wallace Monument, at Elderslie, on 27th August, 1921; and now re-printed from the 'Forward' of 3rd September, 1921* (Glasgow: Scottish Home Rule Association, 1921), pp. 12, 16; taken from Burns' 'Does Haughty Gaul Invasion Threat?', a song written during 1795 when fears of French invasion were high.
57. Finlay, *Independent and Free*, pp. 55–9.
58. *Scottish Historical Pageant to be held at Craigmillar Castle (13–16 July 1927), in aid of the Queen Victoria Jubilee Institute for Nurses (Scottish Branch), Official Souvenir Programme*, pp. 99, 156.
59. The 624th anniversary of Wallace's death, held at Elderslie, *The Scotsman*, 26 August 1929.
60. *The Scotsman*, 24 August 1931.
61. C. Harvie, *Scotland and Nationalism: Scottish Society and Politics, 1707–1994* (London: Routledge, 1994), pp. 28–9.
62. D. McCrone, 'The Unstable Union: Scotland since the 1920s', in M Lynch, ed., *Scotland, 1850–1979: Society, Politics and the Union* (London: The Historical Association for Scotland, 1993), pp. 44–5; I. Levitt, 'Scottish Sentiment, Administrative Devolution and Westminster, 1885–1964', in Lynch (ed.), *Scotland, 1850–1979*, pp. 35–7.
63. *Wallace Commemoration Day, Saturday, 26th August, 1933, Held at Wallace Monument, Elderslie. Official Souvenir Programme*.
64. Young, *William Wallace and this War*, pp. 3, 8. Young was twice imprisoned for his refusal to be conscripted, Young, *A Clear Voice*, p. 17.
65. *William Wallace: National hero of Scotland, Special Commemorative Publication to Mark the 650th Anniversary of his Martyrdom* (Glasgow: Scots Secretariat, 1955), p. 3.
66. A. Lamont, *How Scots Opposed the Peace Time Call-up* (Penicuik: Scots Secretariat, 1976); M. Taylor, 'John Bull and the iconography of public opinion in England, c.1712–1929', *Past and Present*, 134 (1992).
67. 'Anniversary Gathering, R. B. Cunninghame Graham's birth' (1952). NLS: P.med.3505 (1928–66).
68. *Scottish Newsletter*, 20, September 1953.
69. *William Wallace: National hero of Scotland, Special Commemorative*

Publication to Mark the 650th Anniversary of his Martyrdom (Glasgow: Scots Secretariat, 1955), pp. 1–2.

70. A good selection can be found deposited in the National Library of Scotland: P.med.3505 (1928–66); P.la.7030 (1967–93); P.el.680 (Others).

71. Mitchell, *Strategies for Self-Government*, p. 272.

72. A pictorial account of the events if this period is found in A. Clements, K. Farquarson and K. Wark, *Restless Nation* (Edinburgh: Mainstream, 1996), p. 28; Wood, *Yours Sincerely for Scotland*, pp. 121–2.

73. Wood, *Yours Sincerely for Scotland*, p. 259.

74. 'Miscellaneous pamphlets and leaflets', Scottish National Party. NLS: P.med.3505 (1928–66).

75. Lord Willie Ross was Heath's Scottish Secretary, who continued to remind his party of its manifesto commitment to a Scottish Assembly, *The Scotsman* , 11 June 1988, describing the constitutional debate of the 1970s. A wider analysis of these matters, upon which the present discussion draws, is found in Morton, 'The moral foundations of constitutional change', pp. 98–103.

76. *Royal Commission on the Constitution, 1969–1973* , Vol. 1, Report (Cmnd 5460) (Chairmen, Lord Crowther, Lord Kilbrandon) (London: HMSO, 1973) [*Kilbrandon Report*], pp. 107–8, 112–14.

77. *Kilbrandon Report*, pp. 140, 146.

78. Their plan to have around 125 members, directly elected, who would sit in Edinburgh for about 40 days each year to scrutinise Scottish legislation was deemed inadequate. Ibid., p. 157.

79. 'Eight of us favour a scheme of legislative devolution for Scotland. Of those, all but two favour legislative devolution for Wales also. Those two favour for Wales an assembly with deliberative and advisory functions. One of us favours assemblies with deliberative and advisory functions for both Scotland and Wales, with the addition in the case of the Scottish assembly of some powers in relation to Parliamentary legislation. Two of us, who support the principle of uniformity, favour schemes of executive devolution for both Scotland and Wales (and for the regions of England).' Ibid., pp. 336–7.

80. 'Our Changing Democracy: Devolution to Scotland and Wales', Cmnd 6348 (HMSO, November 1975).

81. Ibid., p. 4.

82. 'Our Changing Democracy', pp. 4, 9.

83. These discussions are discussed in greater depth in G. Morton, 'The moral foundations of constitutional change in Canada and Scotland at the end of the twentieth century', *International Review of Scottish Studies*, 33 (2008), pp. 87–122.

84. A. Salmond, 'Winning with Wallace', Address to the 61st Annual National Conference of the Scottish National Party, 22 September 1995 (Perth City Halls).
85. *Herald Scotland*, 8 January 2012.

Chapter 12

Moving Image

The national tale is not singular in its manifestation, but a single life has been at its heart. William Wallace, a short-lived late medieval patriot, has been the thread that has bound Scots to their national identity throughout centuries of change, and through evolving ideologies of political nationalism. Formed around oft-repeated episodes, Wallace's tale has gathered up many stories which overlap and borrow content, style and substance from one another. National identity may be a category on a form, but it flows from a state of mind. The very idea of the imagined community, that eloquent phrase coined by Benedict Anderson, stresses national identity through recollection and understanding, among people who have never met. A sense of nationhood comes to like-minded inhabitants of a demarcated territory, usually one that has its own state, or makes the demand for one.[1] The Wallace story is part of Scotland's imagined community, but we have seen how disparate groups have used the story for their own ends. As the state of mind changes, so does the Wallace story.

This fluidity within the many versions of Wallace's life and legacy which make up the national tale reached new extremes in the twenty-first century. The *Braveheart* effect from 1995, coupled to the expansion of internet access, and Web publishing, has transformed the narrative. At time of writing, there are more people who have joined the social media behemoth Facebook than lived on planet Earth when Jane Porter published *The Scottish Chiefs*.[2] The proliferation of new media should remind us that how we tell stories is as important as the story itself. From the sixteenth until the eighteenth century, reprints of a single text (by Hary) were the story. From the end of the eighteenth century and throughout the nineteenth, and again into the twentieth century, it was still the written text which ruled the transmission of the Wallace narrative, and it was added to by song, poetry, monument building and sites of commemoration associated with the patriot. The scope of the myth could expand and permeate the national conscience from a number of different directions. And while the market for novels remained a middle-class preserve for most of the nineteenth century, newspapers, magazines and the all-encompassing chapbook literature ensured the printed text would spread down the social order.[3]

Technological change has had an immense and well-documented impact on story-telling. The information city has taken over from the manufacturing city in the rank order of urban size.[4] One of the most useful aids to organising the revolutionary movements which split the USSR was the humble photocopier. The ability to cheaply and rapidly reproduce and then distribute *samizdat* literature was a key component in organising resistance against the state from within civil society.[5] Communication knits the associations of civil society, and identity formation flows through every available channel of communication. What is important to understand is how individuals, groups or leaders dominate the cultural frame of reference. From Charles Tilly's work on revolutions and uprisings in the nineteenth-century to Alberto Melucci's studies of new social movements in the late twentieth century, including most especially Castells on the networked society, emphasis falls on the constraints and the opportunities available to mobilise information by organisations and political leaders.[6] The phrase offered by Melucci is 'resource mobilisation' and the expansion of printing and publishing have been the key resources which have been mobilised to transmit the Wallace tale.[7] The photocopier has done much to free the reproduction of materials, and now it is the Internet. In many ways, the reduction in the cost of accessing the Web and sending and receiving emails and texts is analogous to the removal of the Stamp Tax in 1855: the barrier to access was dismantled. It became easier to pass on and to circulate information. Examples of just how the Internet has transformed the reproduction of the Wallace myth will be turned to in a moment. But this is more than just cheap reproduction; it is more than just presenting text, pictures, sound and video clips through the Internet as direct replication of older forms of media (text, engraving, canvass, video tape). The Internet has had a profound influence on how its content is read, viewed and listened to. The media itself has changed how the story is consumed, and with these processes has changed the relationship between author, text and reader, shattering any sense of coherence to the narrative. In effect, the Wallace story has become organic, where all of us (if we so wish) are equally consumers and producers.

The concept of globalisation is behind explanations of these changed relationships, but it has been utilised in so many different settings that confidence in its precision has wavered. At the core, globalisation is more than increased levels of economic and political interaction, it is the creation of a single 'international society'.[8] 'McDonaldisation' and 'Disneyisation' are terms coined to mirror this society. More controversially, too, the tracking of browser data and the Wikileaks insight into government monitoring of digital communications show how interconnected we have become.[9] But doubts persists about how complete this transition has been, and even if it is really new. That the world is increasingly interrelated in matters of trade, commerce and communication has been a feature since the sixteenth century, if not before. This is certainly not a phenomenon of our age alone, a point made by a number of authors in their critique of the globalisation thesis.[10] Nor is it clear that an international society has replaced the political and cultural power of the nation-state. Emigration policies have tightened within the European Union despite moves to free up and harmonise employment legislation within its boundaries. Moreover, the nation and the nation-state have retained remarkable resilience in the face of political, military and economic transnational organisations, such as the United Nations, NATO and the G7, as well the large multinational business and financial speculators who wield immense power over credit flows and interest rates.[11] Added to these specific criticisms, Hirst and Thompson have been among the most explicit opponents of the very concept itself, suggesting that nothing but ongoing change is being witnessed. They conclude that the current fashion for this concept is unwarranted and superfluous.[12]

Still, theoretical weight acknowledges that the *pace* of change has quickened, even if the relative amount of change has not, and rather than us finding the homogenisation of culture dominant from the late twentieth century, new momentum has imbued peripheral cultures. What currency globalisation has gained has been boosted by the internet revolution, which has impacted most greatly on personal communication, e-commerce and social media. From the telephone call to the text message, new technology has transformed national cultures. Opportunities afforded by the Internet have produced a level of cultural consumption and information transfer to a degree never seen before. Exploiting our ability to digitise text and images and to present that manipulation in a number of different guises has decimated the one-time coherence of national cultures, creating a mosaic, comprising many elements rather than being dominated by a small number of core institutions, literatures or debates.[13] Coincidentally or not, *Mosaic* was the name given to the world's first popular graphic Web browser in 1993. But the point of this analogy is to state that although the Internet – and the process of globalisation – contributes to the standardisation of economic and cultural processes, it also has an almost illogical counter-effect. It affords the opportunity for the particular and the specific to be emphasised on a global scale. As Appadurai has argued, despite being its impelling force, 'the globalisation of culture is not the same as its homogenisation'[14] – a comment germane to analysing Scotland's national tale through the prism of the Internet. Through this prism, Wallace's patriotism has secured a niche market for Scottish culture.[15] This is why, despite doubts about how new or complete the globalisation process can be said to be, there is an important new level of interaction between those who present and those who consume the Wallace narrative. Globalisation has blurred the divide between core and peripheral cultures, allowing individuals to move easily between the two. What we have now are 'global cultures in the plural'.[16] National culture can now be projected around the world even more easily than the Irish and American presses reprinted copies of *The Scottish Chiefs* copyright-free in the nineteenth century. The break between author, text and reader – and between nation and transnationalism – is complete. All can be the author *and* the reader, and the national tale has evolved within this interaction.

* * *

The coincidence of ongoing technological change, the Oscar-winning success of *Braveheart* (1995) and the 700th anniversary of Wallace's exploits (1997) were opportune, and continue to impress. The Internet has taken over as the dominant media in the Wallace tale, purporting to offer both historical record ('the truth') and interactive discussion. The coming together of fan(atic)s around admiration for *Braveheart* is at the root of much of this. The MacBraveHeart website gives an indication of this phenomenon through its many-viewings list,[17] with people anywhere in the world who choose to contribute detailing the number of screenings people have seen of *Braveheart*. Taking 2001 as a census date, over eighty people claimed to have seen the film between thirty and 500 times (although only one person goes beyond 100, and of course there is some rounding up and exaggeration going on here). Around seventy people fit the category of 15–29 viewings, and over thirty claim to have sat through 11–15 viewings, with similar numbers for the 8–10 and 2–7 bands. Being top of the list brought excitement:

> My name is Betty Austin and I've seen Braveheart 500 times. I love it. I want it. I want some more of it. It's the first movie I've ever seen that an actor has actually become the character in the movie. There are parts where it seems he actually isn't Mel anymore and actually is William Wallace. I am 46 years old, and it's the best movie I've ever seen in my entire life!!!!! I want to get some statues, and visit Scotland and . . . I could go on and on. I love it!!!![18]

As well as having multiple repeats on satellite and terrestrial TV, *Braveheart* has been the focus of two major fan conventions organised through the MacBraveHeart website established by John Anderson and Linda Anderson.[19] The first Braveheart Convention was held on 12–14 September 1997, opening the day after the referendum vote in favour of a Scottish parliament with tax-varying powers was held. The star attractions of the occasion were Randall Wallace, who wrote the screenplay for *Braveheart*, and Seoras Wallace, head of the Wallace Clan and re-creator of historical battles for screen and festival. A key objective of the Convention was to present 'someone to thank' for the movie, and the organisers were 'delighted' with the turn-out. The second gathering, 'Braveheart 2000', took place in Stirling, Falkirk and Airth Castle on 18–20 August 2000.[20] The festivities included 'Stirling Day', with a 'Braveheart Banquet' in the King's Chambers in Stirling Castle; 'Wallace Day', with the planned re-enactment of the storming of Airth Castle; and 'Braveheart Day', with exhibitions and public talks, including a fifth-anniversary screening of the film in the company of some of its stars.[21] The Convention was arranged by email and online booking, its website having attracted 220,348 visitors, albeit that claim included 'visits' dating back to

1314! Further showing the continued influence of the movie five years after its release, the Convention attracted the interest of the media and comment from both the organisers and academics. Appearing on Scottish Television's cultural magazine programme *Seven Days*, John Anderson revelled in the 'confidence in Scotland' which the film created. He highlighted the support he had received from English fans, many of whom had come to the Convention, and many of whom had declared their wish 'to be Scottish'. He recounted the anecdote from his first viewing of the film, waiting a week for a ticket, and seeing a women punch the air and shout 'Yes!' upon the film's conclusion, prompting the audience to give a standing ovation to the screen. His interview was interspersed with comment from Professor Bill Scott, who likened the film to a kitsch cartoon which was badly made, as well as being grossly anti-English for its characterisation of the English as vicious upper-class fascists and/or pampered pansies; whereas, in contrast, the Scots were presented as boisterous and democratic individuals able to achieve success through teamwork.[22]

Anderson had picked up on the pride and political confidence which the film inspired by following the known trope of peripheral culture turned into a self-assured (and therefore somehow more real) culture able to stand in distinction to a core and previously dominant culture. By contrast, Scott's critique focused on the film's perpetuation of narratives which are themselves myth-histories: that the Scots are more democratic than the English, and that they are, if need be, unproblematically anti-English. These dualities, while powerful, are simplistic.[23] Similarly, opinion-poll and other data disprove assertions that following the Scottish football team as a member of the Tartan Army is the single clearest indicator of Scottish national identity.[24] Yet naive them-and-us narrations are often perpetuated in national tales, and it is no surprise that analysis of the film has been framed in such terms. Indeed, belief that the film is quintessentially Scottish in its 'us and them' constructions is added to by the film career which subsequently opened up for members of the Wallace Clan. Seoras Wallace and his colleagues have been able to make a living from what was a hobby – of battle re-enactments – since working with Mel Gibson, taking on roles in *Rob Roy* (1995) and Ridley Scott's epic *Gladiator* (2000). In the rhetoric of Seoras Wallace: 'Ridley said that our reputation in Hollywood was second to none because they couldn't buy our experience.'[25] Part of the legitimacy of the Wallace Clan Trust comes from the support it received from Randall Wallace. They worked together when filming *Braveheart* and engaged in statements of mutual admiration at the first Braveheart Convention in 1997. The Wallace Clan Trust pages on the MacBraveHeart website quote Randall Wallace, declaring: 'The spirit of Braveheart is the spirit of the Clan Wallace.'[26]

This version of the *Braveheart* narrative, then, had become one of circularity. Randall Wallace's book produced the screenplay, then the *Braveheart* film, the Wallace Clan Trust were hired for the battle scenes, the film is followed by two Braveheart Conventions, more film roles come for the Wallace Clan Trust, and continuing statements of approbation confirm how essential each is to the new *Braveheart Geist*. And if we extend this analysis into the post *Braveheart* years, the Wallace Clan Trust was attempting to both attract film money into Scotland and to focus the world's attention on the 'Clan Lands', an activity that was receiving 150 enquiries a week in 1997. Because of this, the Trust claims its politics were focused upon supporting 'indigenous peoples' rather than nation-states, attempting to deploy this internationalisation of the Wallace narrative in order to secure investment in Scotland.[27] Indeed, and as a mark of how an acceptable history can be shaped and mobilised, Forth Valley Enterprise, Stirling Council and the European Regional Development fund put together resources, co-ordinated by the Council's 'Battle of Stirling Bridge office', to mark the event's 700th anniversary.[28]

A further outcome of globalising the tale in these ways is that the *Braveheart* version has been taken for granted, and the debate between fiction and historical sources which so marked the nineteenth century has been forgotten. Yahoo Answers and ScottishHistory.com do continue to offer reflection on the film's veracity, and Ewan's valuable scholarly assessment remains much-cited.[29] Yet among the wider populace the absent sources, and the mythical inventions on Wallace's life that each century has propagated, are taken out of the loop. Instead, the uncritical and uncomplicated acceptance of historical doubt fuels the fiction to the extent that the fiction now becomes the primary source. This, for example, was the view taken by Randall Wallace in defence of his screenplay:

> Historians agree on only a few facts about Wallace's life, and yet they cannot dispute that his life was epic. There were times when I tried

myself to be a fair historian, but life is not all about balance, it's about passion, and this story raised my passions. I had to see through the eyes of a poet.[30]

With a similar dependence on passion over historical actuality, Tammy MacLaren Saari's brief history of the Wallace story produced for *Clannada na Gadelica* (in 1998) used the discredited biographer James Mackay as one of its two cited sources.[31] *Highlander Web* magazine also used Mackay – 'from which most of this information is gathered' – before positioning *Braveheart* as its empirical comparator.[32] This was not just to add to the popular genuflection to all things Wallace, but 'These pages have been constructed and written with the truth at heart'.[33] *Braveheart* has been marketed as the 'only fact-based story from the High Middle Ages to have won a Best Picture Oscar', and 'In spite of its inaccuracies, the film manages to convey an impressive sense of 13th-century Britain'.[34] To be fair, a number of the websites have based their work on firmer foundations, such as *Highlander Web* magazine's use of Andrew Fisher on the simplenet.com site,[35] and scotsmart. com's use of Fisher and Hamilton of Gilbertfield's Hary.[36] But their bibliographies rarely go beyond that, with no mention, for example, of McDiarmid's standard introduction to Hary's *Wallace*, let alone the chronicles, or the work of historians such as Cowan, Duncan and Watson.[37] Others have not made their sources plain: and the stories feed on each other. Rather than debate the veracity of fact and fiction, the Web-based narratives look for self-corroboration or rely on the fictions of Mackay and Tranter:

> There are many books about William Wallace and interpretations of his life. Since it happened so long ago and no substantial written records exist, no one knows for certain what happened. It is good to look at all viewpoints since no one knows the truth. In all the books I have read about William Wallace Nigel Tranter's 'The Wallace' shows the most what the man must have been like. From its opening pages we meet William Wallace, a man, like us, with human emotions of pain, weakness, joy and courage. [. . .] If you want to know more about what William Wallace, a person, might have been like then this book is a 'must' for you. It is because . . . it happened so long ago and no substantial written records exist, no one knows for certain what happened, that we should turn to a book like Tranter's which shows the most what the man must have been like.[38]

When I first picked up WILLIAM WALLACE: BRAVE HEART, I

was bogged down with who-beget-whom, but once past that, the book took off. So much so, that I began to doubt its accuracy. Therefore, I did what any skeptical reader does in this case – checked the Internet. Apparently, James Mackay's book is one of the most thorough books on William Wallace on the market. His research centers around the epic poem of William Wallace by Blind Henry, as well as surviving documents and historical and archaeological references.[39]

*   *   *

The Braveheart effect has not only invigorated the afterlife of fictional accounts of Wallace's life, it has broadened out the scope for consuming the national tale in a new line of souvenirs and mementos. Even at the start of the twenty-first century it was possible to deliver the material culture of Wallace through e-commerce, a trend that has developed over the following two decades. Many examples could be offered, such as Dr Celt's Celtic Treasure, which has produced a four-inch-tall pewter figurine on a mahogany base depicting Sir William Wallace, presented as 'One of Scotland's greatest warriors', and 'featured in the movie Braveheart'.[40] Similarly, Clan Crafts offers hand-painted lead figures that include William Wallace, Robert the Bruce, Bonnie Prince Charlie and Highland Clansmen (and is it symbolic that the price of Wallace was £50 greater than that of Bruce?).[41] With the rise of roots tourism since the mid-1990s, interest has focused around the Clan name, with requests for information on the Wallaces in West Virginia during the Civil War, the Wallaces of Tennessee, and other attempts to find the genealogical history of the clan name.[42]

This capture of Scotland's national tale through the medium of Gibson's film is further evidenced in how the descriptor, Braveheart-eque' is deployed. The term has come to define a genre of movies that mix patriotic sentiment with historical events.[43] In both Scotland and the USA, a rousing team talk is described in such terms;[44] the rap song 'One Lonely Owl' depicts the narrator raising a Braveheart-eque banner to the moon;[45] more disturbingly, a riot during a football match in Egypt is described as Braveheart-eque for its 'atmosphere of terror',[46] as was a 'huge battle' between American accountants.[47] Here the national tale is tied into an interlocking Web-based story where the Gibson-shaped sentiment of Wallace comes to the fore, and 'truth' is presented as the product of simple repetition or fictional corroboration. This has also turned

Wallace – as cultural product – into an even more intricate mosaic. As his story spread for a digital generation of consumers, so the national tale fragmented further.

Braveheart was crowned top Scots movie of all time in 2008, yet the previous chapter ended with the instruction by the SNP to its activists to avoid Braveheart-esque language in the lead-up to the referendum vote in 2014.[48] Nor was a proposed 'blockbuster' mini-series on the life of Wallace to be ready to air in time for the 700th anniversary of Bannockburn, a consequence of uncertain finance and creative differences.[49] The centrality of Wallace to the national tale of the twenty-first century is far from over, but there is increasingly a perceptible weakness in its moorings. A news feature offering journalistic insight into Scottish national identity in the months prior to the 2014 referendum did not mention Wallace or *Braveheart* by name, although the picture editor still used two related images: one of a street entertainer, his face painted blue, dressed as the Mel Gibson incarnation of the patriot; the other of a tattoo, declaring 'Freedom', drawn against a background of the Scottish saltire and thistle.[50] Notably, and of psephological interest to future scholarly studies, the referendum is the first in the UK to allow sixteen-year-olds the vote – a group born after *Braveheart* was released and after the 700th anniversary of the battle of Stirling Bridge. Their consciousness of Scotland's representation on film is much more likely to come from *Brave* (2012), an Oscar-winning Disneyfication of Scottish historical themes loosely based on the Wallace tale. The name, of course, speaks to the international resonance of Scotland in the world, at least as far as the movie-going public is concerned. The narrative is set in a medieval world of castles, sword fights and chivalric honour, with a strong component of Porter-esque domestic intrigue to the fore.[51] Here, the commodification of the tale is extensive, with toys, books, clothes and downloads available.[52] The world premiere of *Brave* was designated a 'major set-piece event' for the Scottish government in order that ministers might engage with the diaspora and others in the USA. In June 2012, VisitScotland launched what it determined was a unique partnership with Disney-Pixar to market Scotland through TV and the Internet, taking the connection out into non-tourism sectors.[53] Members of VisitScotland regularly attended board meetings at Disney, and a partnership with American Airlines was developed with the aim of encouraging the parents of those children who saw the movie to then 'Discover Scotland – the land that inspired Disney-Pixar's Brave'.[54]

Whether it be *Brave* or *Braveheart*, in the examples presented in this chapter the Wallace narrative has been globalised. The digital age has allowed the commodification of Wallace to grow beyond the National Wallace Monument and its 1920s Tea Garden and Wallace sword brooch. The tale does retain a radical age, despite the fun and games that have lightened the story for an internet age. During a high-profile European football match against AC Milan in November 2013, supporters of Celtic used cards to depict Wallace alongside the hunger striker Bobby Sands. Their intention was to show up the hypocrisy of the football authorities' ban on them singing songs in support of the Irish freedom fighter, but not to halt any commemoration by the crowd of Wallace. Alongside the depictions of each man, banners were displayed which read:

> The terrorist or the dreamer? The savage or the brave? Depends whose vote you are trying to catch or whose face you are trying to save.[55]

There is little doubt that the national tale will continue to play a political role in the nation's development and will continue to evolve. Wallace's history and afterlife will still be called upon to open up Janusian pathways for the present and for expectations of future improvement. These changes will gather pace within the constitutional arrangements post-2014, and will shape Scotland's relationship with the rest of the UK. In all the ways in which Wallace's biography and his commemoration have sustained the national tale – forever episodic, readily mobilised, and sufficiently malleable within tenets laid down before the age of nationalism – the narrative fulfils the expectations of personal nationalism, sustaining a reading of history that fits contemporary lives. R. B. Cunninghame Graham, for one, was convinced:

> Wallace made Scotland, he is Scotland; he is the symbol of that which is best and purest and truest and most heroic in our national life. You cannot figure to yourself Scotland without Wallace. He prepared the way, and is preparing the way, with your assistance for a National Legislature in Scotland. He is a man whose memory can never die. So long as grass grows green, or water runs, or whilst mist curls through the corries of the hills, the name of Wallace will live.[56]

To conclude, I offer one final example of the national tale framed within personal nationalism. On viewing the *Brave Art* exhibition at the Stirling Smith Art Gallery and Museum in 1996 I was presented with a picture of Mel Gibson as Wallace, accompanied on the canvas by depictions of the actor Gary Cooper dressed as a cowboy, and of a soldier, Sgt George Morton.[57] The artwork tells of a Scottish soldier who fought for his country during World War I and is badly injured, with the consequence that he is late to return home once hostilities had ceased. His family thought he was dead, his wife married another man. He fought for his nation, survived, and returned to rejection. The artist James W. Hardie is asking us to choose the real hero from these three heroes. That sergeant was my paternal grandfather. And this, an artistic evocation of the national tale, captures the one yet many of national lives. Wallace is Scotland's national tale because he is our national tale.

NOTES

1. Anderson, *Imagined Communities*, pp. 6–7.
2. UberFacts: https://twitter.com/UberFacts/status/2937693059029688 33 (accessed 3 January 2014).
3. See S. Nenadic, 'Middle-rank consumers and domestic culture in Edinburgh and Glasgow, 1720–1840', *Past and Present*, 145 (1994); E. J. Cowan, 'William Wallace: "The Choice of the Estates"', in E. J. Cowan (ed.), *The Wallace Book* (Edinburgh: John Donald, 2007), p. 14.
4. D. Harvey, *Money, Time, Space, And The City* (Cambridge: Granta, c.1985); D. Sudjic, *The 100 Mile City* (London: André Deutsch, 1992); M. Moss, 'Telecommunications, world cities and urban policy', *Urban Studies*, 24 (1987); K. Fujita, 'A world city and flexible specialisation', *International Journal of Urban and Regional Research*, 15, 2, June 1991; A. Coupland, 'Docklands: dream or disaster', in A. Thornley (ed.), *The Crisis of London* (London: Routledge, 1992).
5. J. A. Hall, 'After the fall: an analysis of post-communism', *British Journal of Sociology*, 45, 4, December 1994, pp. 525, 538.
6. M. Castells, *The Rise of the Networked Society: The Information Age: Economy, society and culture* (Oxford: Wiley-Blackwell, 2000).
7. C. Tilly, L. Tilly and R. Tilly, *The Rebellious Century 1830–1930* (London: J. M. Dent & Sons, 1975); A. Melucci, *Nomads of the*

Present: Social Movements and Individual Needs in Contemporary Society (London: Radius, 1989).

8. J. Boli and G. M. Thomas, 'World culture in the world polity: a century of international non-governmental organization', *American Sociological Review*, 62, April 1997, p. 171.

9. http://wikileaks.org (accessed 14 January 2014); the extent of the global surveillance undertaken by the US National Security Agency (NSA) and the UK's CGHQ was revealed by ex NSA director Edward Snowden in 2013, http://en.wikipedia.org/wiki/Global_surveillance_disclosures_(2013–present) (accessed 14 January 2014); G. Ritzer, *The McDonaldization of Society*, rev. edn (Thousand Oaks: Pine Forge Press, 1996); A. Bryman, 'The Disneyization of Society', *Sociological Review*, 47, 1 (1999).

10. I. Wallerstein, *The Modern World System* (New York: Academic Press, 1989); M. Mann 'Nation-states in Europe and Other Countries: Diversifying, Developing, Not Dying', in G. Balakrishnan (ed.), *Mapping the Nation* (London: Verso, 1996), p. 298.

11. Mann, 'Nation-states', in Balakrishnan (ed.), *Mapping the Nation*, p. 298.

12. P. Hirst and G. Thompson, *Globalization in Question* (Cambridge: Polity, 1996).

13. J.-G. Lacroix and G. Tremblay, 'The emergence of cultural industries into the foreground of industrialization and commodification: elements of context', trans. R. Ashby, *Current Sociology*, 45, 4, October 1997, p. 36.

14. A. Appadurai, 'Disjuncture and difference in the global cultural economy, *Theory, Culture and Society*, 7, 2–3, June 1990, p. 307.

15. Hesse, 'Finding neverland: homecoming Scotland and the "affinity Scots"'.

16. M. Featherstone, 'Global culture: an introduction', *Theory, Culture and Society*, 7, 2–3, June 1990, p. 10.

17. This site is no longer active, but can be accessed through the 'Way Back Machine' facility of the Internet Archive (web.archive.org; accessed 14 January 2014). http://www.macbraveheart.freeserve.co.uk/html/messages/bhtimes.htm

18. http://www.macbraveheart.freeserve.co.uk/html/messages/bhtim-01.htm 'Way Back Machine' facility of the Internet Archive (web.archive.org; accessed 14 January 2014).

19. http://www.macbraveheart.freeserve.co.uk/ 'Way Back Machine' facility of the Internet Archive (web.archive.org; accessed 14 January 2014).

20. http://www.braveheart.co.uk (15 February 2014).

21. Ibid.

22. *Seven Days*, broadcast by Scottish Television, 13.10–14.10 hrs, 20 August 2000.
23. There are strong academic investigations into these tropes. Social mobility and egalitarianism in Scotland are examined in McCrone, *Understanding Scotland*, pp. 88–120, while the main focus of the debate has been on the social openness of Scottish education: A. McPherson, 'An Angle on the Geist: Persistence and Change in the Scottish Educational Tradition', in W. Humes and H. Paterson (eds), *Scottish Culture and Scottish Education, 1800–1980* (Edinburgh: Edinburgh University Press, 1983); R. D. Anderson, *Education and Opportunity in Victorian Scotland* (Oxford: Clarendon Press, 1983); H. Corr, 'Where is the Lass o' Pairts? Gender, Identity and Education in Victorian Scotland', in D. Broun, R. Finlay and M. Lynch (eds), *Image and Identity: The Making and Remaking of Scotland through the Ages* (Edinburgh: John Donald, 1998). All these works offer a response to the renowned G. E. Davie, *The Democratic Intellect: Scotland and her Universities in the Nineteenth Century* (Edinburgh: Edinburgh University Press, 1964). Davie later followed up some of his early statements in G. E. Davie, *The Crisis of the Democratic Intellect: The Problem of Generalism and Specialisation in Twentieth-century Scotland* (Edinburgh: Polygon, 1986).
24. This research by Joseph Bradley into football and national identity has been reported in the press: *Metro*, 26 September 2000; *The Scotsman*, 26 September 2000.
25. *Daily Record*, 16 May 2000; http://www.macbraveheart.freeserve. co.uk/html/organisations/wallace_clan_trust/index.htm (accessed 12 January 2001).
26. http://www.macbraveheart.freeserve.co.uk/html/organisations/wallace _clan_trust/index.htm (accessed 12 January 2001).
27. A representative speaking on behalf of Ian Cree, 'Braveheart and the Work of the Wallace Clan Trust', One Day Wallace Conference, 17 May 1997, Smith Art Gallery and Museum, Stirling. The relationships between Highland Scots and North American and Maori indigenes are explored, respectively, in C. Calloway, *White People, Indians and Highlanders: Tribal Peoples and Colonial Encounters in Scotland and America* (Oxford: Oxford University Press, 2008); B. Patterson, '"It is curious how keenly allied in character are the Scotch Highlander and the Maori": encounters in a New Zealand colonial settlement', *Journal of Irish and Scottish Studies* 4, 1, Autumn 2010, pp. 163–84.
28. *Stirling Initiative Update*, May 1997, pp. 1, 3.
29. Ewan, 'Braveheart', 1,219–21; http://uk.answers.yahoo.com/question/index?qid=20060704051951AA1GiG8 (accessed 15 February

2014); http://uk.answers.yahoo.com/question/index?qid=200809071 35030AAiwfc4 (accessed 15 February 2014); http://www.scottish history.com/articles/independence/braveheart.html (accessed 15 February 2014).

30. Wallace, *Braveheart*, pp. ix–x.
31. http://www.clannada.org/docs/wallace.htm (accessed 10 January 2001).
32. http://www.highlanderweb.co.uk/wallace/index2.html (12 January 2001). An advert for Mackay's book followed the history. Highlanderweb's text is replicated and linked to by http://ctc.sim plenet.com/braveheart/ (accessed 12 February 2014).
33. http://www.highlanderweb.co.uk/wallace/index2.html (accessed 12 January 2001).
34. http://historymedren.about.com/homework/historymedren/library/ movies/blmvbrave.htm?iam=dpile&terms=Wallace+William+History (accessed 12 January 2001).
35. http://ctc.simplenet.com/braveheart/ (accessed 12 January 2001).
36. http://www.scotsmart.com/info/histfigures/wallace.html (accessed 17 February 2014).
37. McDiarmid, *Hary's Wallace*.
38. http://www.scottishradiance.com/wallrev.htm (accessed 12 January 2001).
39. http://www.silcom.com/~manatee/mackay_wallace.html accessed 12 January 2001).
40. http://www.drcelt.com/celtictreasure/sirwilwal.html (accessed 12 January 2001).
41. http://www.braveheart.co.uk/clann/ (accessed 17 February 2014).
42. http://www.macbraveheart.freeserve.co.uk/ (accessed 12 January 2001).
43. http://www.pinterest.com/pin/29203097554071487/ (accessed 17 February 2014); http://madstalk.libsyn.com/film-pigeons-episode-13 7-michael-collins-missing-top-4-braveheartesque-films (accessed 17 February 2014).
44. http://www.youtube.com/watch?v=9_joJIo507g; http://bleacherrep ort.com/articles/1484255-video-nc-state-fan-gives-braveheart-esque-pregame-speech (accessed 29 January 2014).
45. http://rapgenius.com/Milo-one-lonely-owl-lyrics#lyric (accessed 29 January 2014).
46. http://www.topdrawersoccer.com/the91stminute/2012/02/13128/ (accessed 29 January 2014).
47. http://goingconcern.com/2009/10/if-there-was-a-huge-braveheart-esq ue-battle-between-accounting-firms-in-chicago-our-money-would-be -on-deloitte (accessed 29 January 2014).

48. *The Scotsman*, 23 June 2008; *Herald Scotland*, 8 January 2012.
49. *Herald Scotland*, 3 January 2014.
50. Stuart Cosgrove, 'In a year of big decisions, what does it mean to be Scottish?', *BBC News*: http://www.bbc.co.uk/news/uk-scotland-scotland-politics-25966146 (accessed 4 February 2014).
51. http://www.imdb.com/title/tt1217209/plotsummary (accessed 31 January 2014).
52. http://www.disney.co.uk/brave/ (accessed 31 January 2014).
53. *Scottish Government's Plan For Engagement in The USA* – 2nd *Annual Progress Report* (July 2012), pp. 1–2.
54. Presentation by EventScotland and VisitScotland at the 10th Annual Scottish–North American Leadership Conference, Troy, Michigan (27 October 2012); http://www.visitscotland.com/brave/ (accessed 31 January 2014).
55. http://www.huffingtonpost.co.uk/2013/11/29/celtic-green-brigade-bobby-sands_n_4359685.html (accessed 31 January 2014). Celtic were fined *c.*£42,000 by Uefa for displaying the banner under regulations prohibiting messages with a political or ideological nature being displayed, http://www.bbc.co.uk/sport/0/football/25373147 (accessed 4 February 2014).
56. R. B. Cunninghame Graham, 'Wallace Day Commemoration, 1920'; reprinted in *Self-Government for Scotland* (Glasgow, 1920), p. 6; J. Walker, 'Culture and politics: the work of R. B. Cunninghame Graham and Scottish Nationalism', *Scottish Tradition*, 17 (1992), pp. 51–70.
57. *Brave Art. An exhibition of contemporary art celebrating the 699th Anniversary of the Battle of Stirling Bridge, 11 September – 8 December 1996*, Smith Art Gallery and Museum.

Bibliography

ARCHIVAL HOLDINGS

BRO: Bristol Record Office
DULA: Durham University Library Archives
EPL: Edinburgh Public Library
EUL: Edinburgh University Library
IU: Indiana University Lilly Library Manuscript Collection.
NLS: National Library of Scotland
RUL: Reading University Library
SCA: Stirling Council Archive
UCA: University of California Archives
UVL: University of Virginia Library

MANUSCRIPT SOURCES

'Anniversary Gathering, R. B. Cunninghame Graham's birth' (1952). NLS: P.med.3505 (1928–66).
'Copies of contracts with Messrs. Longman by Jane Porter and Anna Maria Porter', Porter Family Correspondence. DULA: MSS GB-0033-POR, E, 45–6.
'Correspondence of the Custodians of the National Wallace Monument, 1936-1938', 29 January 1837, 2 April, 1937. SCA: SB10/1/1-SB10/4/1.
'Description of Wallace State, Aberdeen; Lord Provost's Greeting (December 1951)'. NLS: Pt.sm.1.(7).
'Draft Letter to Miss Porter', 17 May 1825. RUL: MS 1393, Longman I, 10, No. 507B.
'Letter from Mr Owen Rees', 29 April 1833. RUL: MS 1393, Longman I, 102, No. 195H

'Miscellaneous pamphlets and leaflets', Scottish National Party, NLS: P.med.3505 (1928–66).

'National Wallace Monument Stirling: Minute Book kept by William Burns. Minutes of the meeting held at Glasgow 1 May 1856'. SCA.

'Political Squibs, Edinburgh 1820–21'. EPL: YJN1213.820, A106X.

Jane Porter [spurious?] to Walter Scott, 12 December 1820. NLS MS 23118, fos 22–3.

Jane Porter to Eliza Vanderhorst [1837], thanking her for 'the images of Kościuszko and his kind friend', Bristol Record Office [BRO], Acc 5097, Ref 8032/88.

Jane Porter to Eliza Vanderhorst, 1837. BRO: Ref 8032/98.

Jane Porter to Henry Robinson, 29 November 1840. UVL: Papers of Jane Porter, Acc. No 1625-A, Box No. Wf1588-a.

Jane Porter to T. C. Vanderhorst, 4 April 1845, BRO: Acc 5097, Ref 8032/98.

Jane Porter to Walter Scott, 10 September 1825. NLS: MS 3901 fo. 118–19.

Jane Porter to Walter Scott, 31 May 1823. NLS: MS 3896 fo. 183–4.

Jane Porter to Walter Scott, 5 October 1831. NLS: MS 5317 fo. 185–6.

Jane Porter to Walter Scott, 8 April 1828. NLS: MS 3906 fo. 196–7.

Jane Porter, 'Porter mss., 1799–1850'. IU: Lilly Library Manuscript Collection.

John Porter to Miss Jane Porter, 14 May 1806. DULA: MSS GB-0033-POR, MS A.

Katherine Grimston, Countess Clarendon, Letter: 1843 July 1, Grosvenor Crescent [London] to Agnes Strickland. EUL: Gen. 1070 fos 278–9.

Longman & Co to Miss Porter (at Mrs Gills, Carisbrook, Isle of Wight): RUL: MS 1393

Longman & Co. to Mr Barclay, Liverpool, 12 August 1824. RUL: MS 1393, Longman I, 101, No. 459B.

Longman Group Collection. RUL: MS 1393, Longman I, 101, No. 14.

Longman, Rees & Co. to Mrs Opie, 7 April 1831. RUL MS 1393, Longman I, 102, No. 166A.

Owen Rees to Jane Porter, 29 March 1831. RUL: MS 1393, Longman I, 102, No. 165D.

Owen Rees to Miss A. M. Porter, 24 December 1825. RUL MS 1393, Longman I, 101, No. 520C.

Owen Rees to Miss Porter, 10 December 1824. RUL MS 1393 Longman I, 101, No. 519B.

Owen Rees to Miss Porter, 17 December 1824. RUL: MS 1393, Longman I, 101, No. 480.

Owen Rees to Miss Porter, 26 May 1821. RUL: MS 1393: MS 1393, Longman I, 99, No. 229.

Owen Rees to Miss Porter, 31 May 1816. RUL: MS 1393: MS 1393, Longman I, 101, No. 421.

Porter Family Correspondence. DULA, MSS GB-0033-POR, A, 63–6.

Porter Family Correspondence. DULA: MSS GB-0033-POR, B, 49–5.

Porter Family Correspondence. DULA: Porter Correspondence B [1831]: 'A note on the binding of presentation copies of Sir Edward Seaward's narrative'.

Porter, Jane, 'Correspondence', BRO: Acc 5097, Ref 8032/88.

Porter, Jane, 'Diary', 1832 RUL: Jane Porter Papers, No. 715, Box 1.

Porter, Jane, 'Expenditure Record and Note Book for the years 1830–1839'. UCA: Collection No. 715, Box 1, Folder 3.

Subscription Schedule for the National Monument of Sir William Wallace on the Abbey Craig, Near Stirling (n.p., n.d.). SCA.

W. O. Porter to Miss [Jane] Porter at Ditton, Kingston, Surrey, from Bristol, 7 March 1817. DULA: MSS GB-0033-POR, MS A.

W. O. Porter to Miss [Jane] Porter at Ditton, Kingston, Surrey, from Bristol, 31 May 1820. DULA: MSS GB-0033-POR, MS A.

W. O. Porter to Miss A. M. Porter [on paper with watermark date of 1830, with notes on payments relating to Miss Jane Porter dated 7 July 1826 on two small scraps of paper attached]: DULA: MSS GB-0033-POR, MS B.

W. O. Porter to Miss Jane Porter at Esher, Surrey, 12 April 1829. DULA: MSS GB-0033-POR, MS A.

W. O. Porter to Miss Porter at Ditton, Kingston, Surrey, from Bristol, 12 July 1822. DULA: MSS GB-0033-POR, MS A.

W. O. Porter to Miss Porter at Ditton, Kingston, Surrey, from Bristol, 30 August 1822. DULA: MSS GB-0033-POR, MS A.

W. O. Porter to Miss Porter from Bristol, 5 April 1830. DULA: MSS GB-0033-POR, MS A.

W. O. Porter to Mrs. Jane [Blenkinsop] Porter at Ditton, Kingston, Surrey, from Bristol, 20 May 1824. DULA: MSS GB-0033-POR, MS A.

PRINTED PRIMARY SOURCES

700th Anniversary Guide to Events: Easter to Autumn, 1997.

'A former Subscriber for a Wallace Monument' [Patrick Yule], *Traditions, etc., Respecting Sir William Wallace; Collected chiefly from Publications of Recent Date* (Edinburgh, 1856).

'A Scotchman', *Scottish Rights and Grievances* (n.p., n.d.).

'Colossal Statue of Sir William Wallace', *Gentleman's Magazine*, Vol. lxxxvii (1817).

'Index to the Inventory of Monuments maintained by the District', *Edinburgh District Council, Department of Architecture.*

'Letters from Miss Porter during this trip to her friends back in England', transcribed by *The Public Ledger*, 19 April 1842, 4.

'Miss Jane Porter', in *National Portrait Gallery of Illustrious and Eminent Personages of the Nineteenth Century; with Memoirs*, Vol. V (London, 1834).

'Mr. Robert Ker Porter', in *Public Characters* (Dublin: J. Moore, 1801).

'One Behind the Scenes', *Red-Tapism*, 2nd edn (London: Ridgeway, 1855).

'Order of the Procession' (Edinburgh: Grand Procession and National Jubilee, n.d., c.1832).

'Our Changing Democracy: Devolution to Scotland and Wales', Cmnd 6348 (HMSO November 1975).

'*Scheme of the Acting Committee*', *National Monument to Sir William Wallace on the Abbey Craig near Stirling* (n.p., 1856).

'The Sword of Wallace' found within *Wallace, or, the Vale of Ellerslie.*

'Wallace Statue Appeal by the Saltire Society, Edinburgh', designed and published by Clydesdale District Council (c.1992).

Alexander, G., *Sir William Wallace: the Hero of Scotland. A historical Romance* (London, 1903).

Ancient Laws and Customs of the Burghs of Scotland (Burgh Records Society).

Anon (J. C.), *Life of Sir William Wallace*, 3rd edn (London: Griffen & Co., 1849).

Anon (L. G. M. G.), *Authentic Life of Sir William Wallace; with chapter on Traditional Wallace. Compiled from the best authorities* (Dundee: George Montgomery, 1877).

Anon [Red Lion], *Scotland and 'The Times'. To the editors of the 'Edinburgh Evening Post' and the 'Scottish Record'* (1853).

Anon [Reginald Heber], 'Art. V. *Travelling Sketches in Russia and Sweden, during the Years 1805, 1806, 1807, 1808. By Robert Ker Porter*, 2 vols. pp. 600. London. Phillips. 1809', *Quarterly Review* II, 4 (1809).

Anon [William Maginn], 'Gallery of Literary Characters. No. *59*: Miss Jane Porter', *Fraser's Magazine* 11 (1835).

Anon, 'Death of Sir Robert Ker Porter, K.C.II', *Scotsman*, 1 June 1842.

Anon, 'Memoirs of Miss Porter (with a Portrait)', *The Monthly Mirror* (December 1810).

Anon, 'Miss Jane Porter', *Gentleman's Magazine* XXIV July–December (1850)

Anon, 'Miss Jane Porter', *Museum of Foreign Literature and Science* XXVII (1835).

Anon, *Guide to the National Wallace Monument* (n.d.), SPL, Box 19, LC/SAL, 6/64, 16

Anon, *History of Sir William Wallace: The renowned Scottish Champion* (Glasgow, Printed for the Booksellers, c.1840).

Anon, *Illustrated Souvenir of the National Wallace Monument, Stirling* (Stirling, R. S. Shearer & Son, 1896).

Anon, *Queen Victoria: Story of Her Life and Reign, 1819–1901* (n.d., n.p.).

Anon, *The Scottish socialists: A gallery of contemporary portraits* (London: Faber & Faber, 1931).

Anon, *The Sir William Wallace Album. Wallace Monument Stirling, Bridge of Allan, Dunblane, Doune, Callander, The Trossachs, and Loch Katrine* (Stirling, 1904?).

Anon, *William Wallace: National Hero of Scotland, Special Commemorative Publication to Mark the 650th Anniversary of his Martyrdom* (Glasgow: Scots Secretariat, 1955).

Arnold, M., *On the Study of Celtic Literature* (London, 1867).

Bain, Rev. J. and Paterson, J., *The Surroundings of the Wallace Monument as seen from the top* (5th edn, 19—).

Bannatyne Miscellany, Containing Papers and Tracts Cheifly Relating to the History and Litterature of Scotland, ed. T. Thomson, Bannatyne Club No. 19, 1823(?) (reprinted from the 1855 edn, New York: Ams Press, 1973).

Barr, J., *Scotland Yet! An Address Delivered by the Rev. James Barr, B.D., at the Wallace Monument, at Elderslie, on 27th August, 1921; and now re-printed from the 'Forward' of 3rd September, 1921* (Glasgow: Scottish Home Rule Association, 1921).

Begg, J., *Scotland's Dream of Electoral Justice or the Forty Shilling Freehold Questions Explained. With Answers to Objections* (Edinburgh: James Nichol, 1857).

Brave Art. An exhibition of contemporary art celebrating the 699th Anniversary of the Battle of Stirling Bridge, 11 September – 8 December 1996, Smith Art Gallery and Museum.

Brunton, A., *A New Edition of the Life and Heroic Actions of Sir William Wallace, Knight of Elderslie: in three parts* (Glasgow, Stirling, Dunfermline, Newburgh, Edinburgh, Inverkeithing: Porteous Brothers, R. S. Shearer, W. Clark & Son; J. Wood, J. Stillie, W. Pringle, 1881).

Brunton, A., *A New Work in Answer to the Pamphlet, 'Wallace on the Forth', proving the stratagem at Stirling Bridge and that the Bridge was at Kildean, etc. Also the history of the famous battle of Stirling Bridge, to which is added two letters written by Sir William Wallace himself, and Wallace's charter to Scrymgeour of Dundee* (Dunfermline: W. Clark, 1841, Stirling, R. S. Shearer, 1861).

Buchan, Earl, *Copy of Earl of Buchan's Letter to General Washington, President of the United States of America, send enclosed in the box of Wallace's oak, June 28th, 1791; contained in The Earl of Buchan's Address to the Americas at Edinburgh on Washington's Birth-day, February 22nd* (1811).

Buchanan, R., *Wallace: A Tragedy in Five Acts* (Glasgow: Griffen & Co., 1856).

Burns, W., 'Association for the Vindication of Scottish Rights' (n.p., 1855).

Bury, Lady Charlotte, *The Diary of a Lady-in-Waiting*, ed. A. F. Stuart, 2 vols (London, 1908).

Carlyle, T., 'Miss Baillie's Metrical Legends', *New Edinburgh Review* I (1821).

Carnegie, A., *Autobiography of Andrew Carnegie* (Boston and New York: The Riverside Press, 1920).

Carrick, J. D., *Life of Sir William Wallace of Elderslie* (London: London: Whittaker & Co., 1840).

Carrick, J. D., *Life of Sir William Wallace, Knight of Ellerslie and Guardian of Scotland*, 2nd edn (Glasgow: Griffen & Co., 1827).

Carruth, J. A., *Heroic Wallace and Bruce* (Norwich: Jarrold Colour Publications, 1986).

Chairing of the Lord Advocate and the Honourable Mr. Abercrombie (Edinburgh, c.1832).

Chronicle of Lanercost, 1272–1346, trans. H. E. Maxwell (Glasgow: MacLehose, 1913).

Complaynt of Scotland (1549), With an appendix of contemporary English tracts, ed. J. A. Murray (London: Early English Text Society, 1872).

Conditions Relative to Proposed Public Competition for the Wallace and Bruce Memorial, Captain Reid's Bequest, City of Edinburgh (1882).

Cunninghame Graham, R. B., 'Wallace Day Commemoration, 1920'; reprinted in *Self-Government for Scotland* (Glasgow, 1920).

Davidson, J. M., *Leaves from the Book of Scots, The Story of William Wallace, Robert the Bruce, Fletcher of Saltoun and Other Patriots, first Published by the Civic Press, Glasgow, 1914* (Penicuik: Scots Secretariat, 1971).

Davidson, J. M., *Scotia Rediva: Home Rule for Scotland with the Lives of Sir William Wallace, George Buchanan, Fletcher of Saltoun, and Thomas Spence* (London: William Reeves, 1888, 1893).

Donaldson, P., *The Life of Sir William Wallace, the Governor General of Scotland and Hero of the Scottish Chiefs. Containing his parentage, adventures, heroic achievements, imprisonment and death; drawn from authentic materials of Scottish History* (Hartford: Silus Andrus, 1825).

Eyre-Todd, G. (ed.), *Ancient Scots Ballads, with their traditional airs to which they were wont to be sung* (Glasgow, n.d.).

Fergusson, J., *William Wallace: Guardian of Scotland* (London: Alexander MacLehose & Co., 1938).

Finlay, J., *Wallace, or the Vale of Ellerslie, with other poems*, 2nd edn (Glasgow: R. Chapman, 1804).

Fletcher, Mrs, 'Lines Written After Reading *Sir Edward Seaward's Narrative*', *Athenaeum*, 1 December 1832.

Four new songs, and a prophecy: I. A song for joy of or ancient race of Stewarts. II. The battle of Preston, that was fought by his Royal Highness Prince Charles, the 21st of September 1745. III. On an honorable achievement of Sir William Wallace, near Falkirk. IV. A song, call'd, The rebellious crew. V. A prophecy by Mr. Beakenhead, Song III (Edinburgh?, 1750?) [NLS: Ry.1.2.85(21).

Fraser's Magazine, Vol. 11, No. LXCIX (April 1835).

Fyfe, W. T., *Wallace, the Hero of Scotland* (Edinburgh: Anderson, 1920).

Gentleman's Magazine XXIII January–June (1845). DULA: MSS GB-0033-POR, B, 295–6.

Gladstone, W. E., *Midlothian Campaign. Political Speeches delivered in November and December 1879 and March and April 1880 by the Right Hon. W. E. Gladstone, MP* (Edinburgh, 1880).

Glass, C. G., *Stray Leaves from Scotch and English History, with the Life of Sir William Wallace, Scotland's Patriot, hero, and Political Martyr* (Montreal: A. & A. Stevenson, c.1873).

Gloucestershire notes and queries, ed. Rev. B. H. Blacker (London: Wm Ken & Co., 1887).

Guide to the National Wallace Monument. Situated on the Abbey Craig near Stirling containing the Great Sword of Sir William Wallace. The Finest View in Scotland (Stirling?: R. W. Salmond, c.1964).

Hall, S. C., 'Memories of Jane Porter', *Harper's Magazine*, 1 (1850).

Harlowe, G., 'Miss Jane Porter', in W. Jerden (ed.), *National Portrait Gallery of Illustrious and Eminent Personages of the Nineteenth Century; with Memoirs*, 5 vols (London, 1834).

Holford, M., *Wallace; or, the Fight of Falkirk; a Metrical Romance* (London, 1809).

Hutchison, *Life of Sir William Wallace; or Scotland Five Hundred Years Ago* (Glasgow: Thomas Murray & Son, 1858).

International Magazine of Literature, Art, and Science, Vol. 1, Issue 1 (1 July 1850).

Justice to Scotland. Report of the Great Public Meeting of the National Association for the Vindication of Scottish Rights, held in the City Hall (Glasgow, 15 December 1853).

Keith, A., *Several Incidents in the Life of Sir William Wallace, with an account of Lanark, the theatre of his exploits, and a description of the romantic scenery in the neighbourhood* (Lanark, 1844).

Lamont, A., *How Scots Opposed the Peace Time Call-up* (Penicuik: Scots Secretariat, 1976).

Les chefs écossais mélodrame héroïque en trois actes et en prose by R.-C. Guilbert de Pixerecourt; Alexandre Piccinni; Theatre de la Porte-Saint-Martin (Paris, 1819).

Leypoldt, H. A and G. Ile (eds), *List of books for girls and women and their clubs: with descriptive and critical notes and a list of periodicals and hints for girls' and women's clubs* (Boston, 1895).

Look at Ayr (Doncaster: Bessacarr Prints, 1985).

Mackay, J., *William Wallace: Brave Heart* (Edinburgh: Mainstream, 1995).

Macrae, D., *The Story of William Wallace, Scotland's National Hero* (Scottish Patriotic Association, 1905).

Mair, J., *A History of Greater Britain as well England as Scotland compiled from the ancient authorities by John Major* (1521), ed. and trans. A Constable (Edinburgh: Publications of the Scottish History Society, Vol. X, 1892).

Mair, J., *A History of Greater Britain, As Well as England and Scotland* (Edinburgh: T. & A. Constable, 1892).

May it Please your Majesty. The Petition of the undersigned, your Majesty's loyal subjects, inhabiting that part of your Majesty's United Kingdom called Scotland (c.1854).

McKerlie, P. H., *Sir William Wallace: the Hero of Scotland. Contains Fresh Information about the Traitorous Opposition he had to encounter in his struggle for Scottish Independence* (Glasgow: Morrison Brothers, 1900).

Memorial of the Council of the National Association, to the Right Honourable the Lords Commissioners of her Majesty's Treasury, 27 September 1854.

Miller, J. F. 'Some additions to the Bibliography of Blind Harry's Wallace' (read 19 March 1917), *Records of the Glasgow Bibliographical Society*, Vol. VI (Glasgow, 1920).

Miller, J. F., 'Editions of Blind Harry's "The Wallace"' (1912, read 13 December 1913), Prepared for the Glasgow Bibliographical Society [NLS: LC.3351(16)].

Mitchell, W., *Bannockburn: A Short Sketch of Scottish History* (Edinburgh: Scottish Home Rule Association, c.1893).

Mitchell, W., *Home Rule for Scotland and Imperial Federation* (Edinburgh: Scottish Home Rule Association, 1892).

Mitchell, W., *Lord Rosebery and Home Rule for Scotland: A Challenge* (Edinburgh: Scottish Home Rule Association, c.1894).

Moir, J., *Sir William Wallace: a critical study of his biographer Blind Harry* (Aberdeen, 1888).

Morgan, Lady, 'Personal reflections of Lady Morgan', *New York Times*, 26 July 1874.

Murison, A. F., *Sir William Wallace* (Edinburgh: Oliphant, Anderson & Ferrier, 1898).

Museum of Foreign Literature and Science, XXVII (1835).

Napier, T., 'Honouring Sir William Wallace', *Stirling Observer*, c.19 August 1896.

Napier, T., 'Untitled', *Scottish Highlander*, 21 May 1896.

Patterson, J., *Memoir of Joseph Train, F.S.A. Scot., the antiquarian correspondent of Sir Walter Scott* (Glasgow, 1857).

Peach, L. Du Garde, *Robert Bruce: An Adventure from History*, Ladybird Series 561 (Loughborough: Wills & Hepworth, 1964).

Pixérécourt, R.-C. Guilbert de, *Les chefs écossais mélodrame héroïque en trois actes et en prose* (Paris, 1819).

Porter, J., 'The Youth of Sir Philip Sidney', in *The Iris: A religious and literary offering*, ed. Rev. T. Dale (London and Philadelphia: Sampson Low, Hurst, Chance & Co., Thomas Wardle, 1831).

Porter, R. K., *Letters from Portugal and Spain written during march of British Troops* (London, 1809).

Porter, R. K., *Travels in Georgia, Persia, Armenia, ancient Babylonia, &c. &c.* (London: Longman, Hurst, Rees, Orme & Brown, 1821).

Prospects of the Scottish Home Rule Association (Edinburgh: Scottish Home Rule Association, 1892).

Robinson, M. to S. J. Pratt, 31 Aug. 1800, cited in K. N. Cameron (ed.), *Shelley and His Circle 1773–1822* (Cambridge, 1961).

Rogers, C., *The Book of Wallace in Two Volumes* (Edinburgh: Printed for the Grampian Club 1889).

Romans, J., *Home Rule for Scotland* (Edinburgh: Scottish Home Rule Association, c.1894).

Rosebery, Lord, *In Memory of Sir William Wallace: Address by Lord Rosebery* (Stirling, Eneas Mackay, 1897).

Rosebery, Lord, *Wallace, Burns, Stevenson: Appreciations by Lord Rosebery* (Stirling, Eneas Mackay, 1905).

Ross, D. R., *In Wallace's Footsteps: A Guide to Places Associated with the Life of William Wallace* (Glasgow: The Society of William Wallace, n.d.).

Royal Commission on the Constitution, 1969–1973, Vol. 1, Report (Cmnd 5460) (Chairmen, Lord Crowther, Lord Kilbrandon) (London: HMSO, 1973).

Russell French, G., *The Ancestry of Her Majesty Victoria, and of His Royal Highness Prince Albert* (London: William Pickering, 1841).

Sadler, T. (ed.), *Diary, Reminiscences, and Correspondence of Henry Crabb Robinson*, 3 vols (London, 1872 edn).

Sawers, P. R., *Footsteps of Sir William Wallace. Battle of Stirling: Or, Wallace on the Forth* (Glasgow: Thomas Murray & Son, 1856).

Scotichronicon by Walter Bower (ed.), D. E. R. Watt (Aberdeen: Aberdeen University Press, 1998), Vols 1–9.

Scotichronicon, Johannis de Fordun Chronica gentis Scotorum, ed. W. F. Skene (Edinburgh: Edmonston & Douglas).

Scott, W., Letter of Sir Walter Scott to T. Scott, July 20 1808 and letter of Sir Walter Scott to J. Baillie, September 18 1808, *The Letters of Sir Walter Scott*, ed. H. J. C. Grierson (London: Constable, 1932–7), Vol. II.

Scott, W., Sir Walter Scott to J. Baillie, February 20, 1810; Sir Walter Scott to Lord Montagu, November 13th, *The Letters of Sir Walter Scott* (ed.), H. J. C. Grierson (London: Constable, 1932–7), Vol. VI.

Scott, W., *The Journal of Sir Walter Scott. From the Original manuscript at Abbotsford*, Vol. 1 (New York, 1970 [1890]), 10 December 1825.

Scott, W., *The Letters of Sir Walter Scott*, ed. H. J. C. Grierson (London: Constable, 1932–7).

Scottish Government's Plan For Engagement in the USA – 2nd Annual Progress Report (Edinburgh, 2012).

Scottish Historical Pageant to be held at Craigmillar Castle, 13–16 July 1927, in aid of the Queen Victoria Jubilee Institute for Nurses (Scottish Branch), Official Souvenir Programme (n.p., c.1927).

Scottish versus Irish Grievances (Edinburgh: Scottish Home Rule Association, c.1890).

Shearer's Illustrated Souvenir of the National Wallace Monument, Stirling (Stirling, 1896).

Six Hundredth Anniversary of the Granting of the Bruce Charter (City and Royal Burgh of Edinburgh, 1929).

Some Records of the Origin and Progress of the National Wallace Monument Movement, initiated at Glasgow in March 1856 (printed for private circulation, 1880).

Steill, J., *Scottish Independence: Letter on the Necessity of Dissolving the Union Between England and Scotland, and on Restoring Scotland to Her Ancient Supremacy as an Entire and Distinct Nation* (Edinburgh, 1844).

Stirling of Keir, W., 'The Designs for the Wallace Monument: a letter to the Lord-Advocate of Scotland, convenor of the committee of the Wallace Monument', *Stirling Journal* 28 January 1859 (printed at the *Journal and Advertiser* Office, Stirling, 1859).

The Life of Sir William Wallace, the Scots Patriot (Edinburgh: Oliver & Boyd, 1810).

The Only True and Correct Copy. Order of the Procession (August 1832). [NLS: RB.1.54(17)].

The Shade of Wallace: A poem (Glasgow: D. Mackenzie, 1807).

The Tragedy of the Valiant Knight Sir William Wallace to which is prefixed a brief Historical Account of the Knight, and his Exploits for the Delivery of Scotland, and added a more particular Account of the way which he was betrayed into the hands of the English (Glasgow: Hutchison & Co., 1815?).

To His Grace, James, Duke of Perth, &c. Lieutenant General of His Majesty's army, under the command of His Royal Highness Charles, Prince of Wales, &c. (n.p., c.1745?) NLS: Mf.SP.159(14)].

Tranter, N., *The Wallace* (London: Hodder & Stoughton, 1975).

Traquair, P., *Freedom's Sword* (London: HarperCollins, 1998).

Veitch, J., *The Feeling for Nature in Scottish Poetry*, Vol. I (Edinburgh: William Blackwood, 1887).

Victoria, *Leaves from the Journal of Our Life in the Highlands from 1848 to 1861* (London: Smith Elder, 1868), ed. A. Helps.

Victoria, *More Leaves from the Journal of a Life in the Highlands, from 1862 to 1882* (London: Smith Elder, 1884), ed. A. Helps.

Wallace and Bruce, a poem (n.p., 1825?).

Wallace Commemoration Day, Saturday 26th August 1933. Held at Wallace Monument, Elderslie, Official Souvenir Programme.

Wallace Monument. Official Papers and Newspaper Extracts relating to the Wallace Monument Movement kept by Wm. Burns.

Wallace, or, the Vale of Ellerslie with Other Poems (Glasgow: Chapman & Lang, 1802).

Wallace, the Hero of Scotland, a drama, in three Acts: Adapted to Hodgeson's Theatrical Characters and Scenes in the Same (London: Hodgeson & Co., 1822), pp. 8–10.

Wallace, the Hero of Scotland; or Battle of Dumbarton, A historical Romance in which the love of liberty and Conjugal Affections are exemplified in the characters of Sir William Wallace and Lady Wallace, with the unparalleled Bravery of the former against a band of Ruffians in the rescue of the Earl of Mar, and his revenge on the governor of Lanark for the Murder of Lady Wallace (London: Thomas Redruffe, 1825?).

Wallace's Women, a play in two acts by Margaret McSeveney and Elizabeth Roberts, 31 October–2 November 1997, Smith Art Gallery and Museum, Stirling.

Watson, J. S., *Sir William Wallace, the Scottish Hero: A narrative of his Life and Actions, chiefly as recorded in the Metrical History of Henry the Minstrel on the authority of John Blair, Wallace's*

Chaplain, and Thomas Gray, Priest of Liberton (London: Saunders, Otley & Co., 1861).

William Wallace: National hero of Scotland, Special Commemorative Publication to Mark the 650th Anniversary of his Martyrdom (Glasgow: Scots Secretariat, 1955).

Wyntoun, A., *The Orygynale Cronykil of Scotland by Andrew of Wyntoun* (ed.), David Laing (Edinburgh: Edmonston & Douglas, 1872), Vol. II.

Young, Alexr from Sir Walter Scott [November 1821], in H. J. C. Grierson et al. (eds), *The Letters of Sir Walter Scott*, Vol. 7 (London, 1932–7).

Young, D. C. C., *William Wallace and this War*, speech at the Eldeslie Commemoration (Glasgow: Scots Secretariat, 1943).

ONLINE DATABASES

'Anecdotal Records' for Jane Porter's *The Scottish Chiefs* (1810), Database of British Fiction [DBF] 18100A070.

'Contemporary Libraries' for Jane Porter's *The Scottish Chiefs* (1810), *DBF*: 1810A070.

Boase, G. C., 'Bury, Lady Charlotte Susan Maria (1775–1861)', rev. Pam Perkins, *Oxford Dictionary of National Biography*, Oxford University Press, 2004, http://www.oxforddnb.com/view/article/4147 (accessed 17 July 2012).

Brown, S., Clements, P., and Grundy, I. (eds), 'Jane Porter' within *Orlando: Women's Writing in the British Isles from the Beginnings to the Present* (Cambridge, 2006), http://orlando.cambridge.org/ (accessed 16 August 2010).

Canmore, Royal Commission on the Ancient and Historical Monuments of Scotland (RCAHMS).

Dean, D., 'Morgan , Sydney, Lady Morgan (*bap.* 1783, *d.* 1859)', *Oxford Dictionary of National Biography*, Oxford University Press, 2004; online edn, January 2008, http://www.oxforddnb.com/view/article/19234 (accessed 17 July 2012).

Deas, M., 'Powles, John Diston (1787/8–1867)', in *Oxford Dictionary of National Biography*, ed. L. Goldman (Oxford: Oxford University Press, 2004).

Longman Impression Book No. 4, fo. 31, fo. 107, and *No. 6*, fo. 11; *Longman Impression Book No. 6*, fo. 11; *Longman Impression Book No. 7*, fo. 39v; *Longman Impression Book No. 8*, fo.

69v, cited in 'Publishing Papers' for Jane Porter's *The Scottish Chiefs* (1810), *Database of British Fiction, 1800–1829* [DBF]: 1810A070.

McMillan, D., 'Porter, Jane (*bap.* 1776, *d.* 1850)', *Oxford Dictionary of National Biography*, Oxford University Press, 2004; online edn, May 2008, http://www.oxforddnb.com/view/article/22571 (accessed 17 July 2012).

Morriss, R., 'Smith, Sir (William) Sidney (1764–1840)', *Oxford Dictionary of National Biography*, Oxford University Press, 2004; online edn, May 2009, http://www.oxforddnb.com/view/article/25940 (accessed 17 July 2012).

Polasky, J. L., 'Leopold I (1790–1865)', *Oxford Dictionary of National Biography* (Oxford, 2004), http://www.oxforddnb.com.subzero.lib.uoguelph.ca/view/article/41227 (accessed 10 February 2010).

Woudhuysen, H. R., Sidney, Sir Philip (1554–1586)', in *Oxford Dictionary of National Biography*, Oxford University Press, 2005.

Quayle, E., 'Porter, Anna Maria (1778–1832)', *Oxford Dictionary of National Biography*, Oxford University Press, 2004, http://www.oxforddnb.com/view/article/22559 (accessed 17 July 2012).

Seccombe, T., 'Porter, Sir Robert Ker (1777–1842)', rev. R. Lister, *Oxford Dictionary of National Biography*, ed. H. C. G. Matthew and B. Harrison (Oxford: Oxford University Press, 2004).

Taylor, C. L., 'Knox, Robert (1791–1862)', *Oxford Dictionary of National Biography* (Oxford, 2004), http://www.oxforddnb.com/view/article/15787 (accessed 25 February 2010).

FILM/TV

Brave (2012).
Braveheart (1995).
Rob Roy (1995).
Seven Days, Scottish Television, 20 August 2000.
History of Britain, BBC Television, 18 October 2000.

THESES

Akroyd, R. J., 'Lord Rosebery and Scottish Nationalism, 1868–1896', unpublished Ph.D. thesis (University of Edinburgh, 1996).
Forrest, M., 'The Wallace Monument and the Scottish National

Identity', unpublished BA dissertation (University of Stirling, 1993).

Tate Irvine Jr, R., 'The Life of Jane Porter', unpublished MA thesis (University of Virginia, 1942).

Watson, C., 'How Useful is Blind Hary's 'The Wallace' as a Source for the Study of Chivalry in Late Medieval Scotland?', unpublished M.Sc. dissertation (University of Edinburgh, 2010).

WEB RESOURCES

http://battleofbannockburn.com/the-project/about-the-centre/
http://ctc.simplenet.com/braveheart/
http://digital.nls.uk/printing/texts-titles.cfm.
http://digital.nls.uk/printing/towns.cfm
http://en.wikipedia.org/wiki/Global_surveillance_disclosures_(2013–present)
http://historymedren.about.com/homework/historymedren/library/movies/blmvbrave.htm?iam=dpile&terms=Wallace+William+History
http://mccoist.hypermart.net/wallace.html
http://wikileaks.org
http://world-interactive.com/armory/Indexes/scottish_sword_index.htm
http://www.500yearsofprinting.org/printing.php.
http://www.braveheart.co.uk/clann/
http://www.clannada.org/docs/wallace.htm
http://www.clydesdalewallaceday.info/index.html
http://www.drcelt.com/celtictreasure/sirwilwal.html
http://www.educationscotland.gov.uk/scotlandshistory/warsofindependence/executionofwallace/index.asp
http://www.highlanderweb.co.uk/wallace/sword.htm
http://www.impressions.uk.com/castles/castle_8.html
http://www.macbraveheart.freeserve.co.uk/
http://www.nas.gov.uk/documents/WilliamWallaceWorkingGroupTNAmeeting5August2010.pdf
http://www.nationalwallacemonument.com/downloads/laying-foundation-stone.pdf
http://www.scotland.gov.uk/Topics/Business-Industry/Tourism
http://www.scotsmart.com/info/histfigures/wallace.html
http://www.scottish.parliament.uk/parliamentarybusiness/CurrentCommittees/40047.aspx
http://www.scottishradiance.com/wallrev.htm

http://www.silcom.com/~manatee/mackay_wallace.html
http://www.snp.org.uk
http://www.thefreelibrary.com/william+wallet+wanted+to+buy+brave
heart+statue.-a0110838928
https://twitter.com/UberFacts/status/293769305902968833

NEWSPAPERS

Ayrshire Post; Belfast News-Letter; Bruce Herald; Caledonian Mercury; Daily Record; Daily Southern Cross; Glasgow Evening News; Glasgow Herald; Methodist Times; Metro; Montrose Review; Nelson Examiner and New Zealand Chronicle; New York Times; New Zealand Gazette and Wellington Spectator; New Zealand Tablet; New Zealander; Newcastle Courant; Otago Witness; Pall Mall Gazette; Record and Mail; Scientific American; Scotland on Sunday; Scottish Highlander; Star; Stirling News; Sunday Herald; Supplement to the Hampshire Telegraph and Sussex Chronicle; Supplement to the Western Mail; The Aberdeen Journal; The Atlantic Monthly; The Bristol Mercury; The Bristol Mercury and Western Counties Advertiser; The Builder; The Courier; The Era; The Examiner; The Freeman's Journal; The Glasgow Herald and Mail; The Graphic; The Herald; The Hull Packet and East Riding Times; The Illustrated London News; The Leeds Mercury; The Leeds Mercury and Weekly Supplement; The Liberal; The Liverpool Mercury; The London Literary Gazette; The Manchester Examiner and Times; The Manchester Times; The North American Review; The Preston Chronicle; The Scotsman; The Stirling Antiquary; The Sydney Gazette and New South Wales Advertiser; The Times.

EDITIONS OF HARY'S *WALLACE*

Craig, W., *The Acts and Deeds of Stir William Wallace, 1570* (Edinburgh: Scottish Text Society, 3rd series, 1938).

Hamilton of Gilbertfield, *A New Edition of the Life and Heroick Actions of the Renoun'd Sir William Wallace, General and Governour of Scotland. Wherein the Old obsolete Words are rendered more Intelligible; and adapted to the understanding of such who have not the leisure to study the Meaning, and Import of such, Phrases without the help of a Glossary* (Glasgow: William Duncan, 1722).

Hamilton of Gilbertfield, *Blind Harry's Wallace, William Hamilton of Gilberfield,* ed. and introd. E. King (Edinburgh: Luath Press, 1998).
Jamieson, J. (ed.), *Wallace; or the life and acts of Sir William Wallace, of Ellerslie. By Henry the Minstrel. Published from a manuscript dated M.CCCLXXXVIII,* new edn (Glasgow, 1820, 1869).
McDiarmid, M. P., *Hary's Wallace (Vita Nobilissimi Defensoris Scotie Wilelmi Wallace Milits)* (Edinburgh: Scottish Text Society, 1968).
Moir, J. (ed.), *The Actis and Deidis of the Illustere And Vailzeand Campioun Schir William Wallace, Knight of Ellerslie by Henry the Minstrel, commonly known as Blind Harry* (Edinburgh: Scottish Text Society, 1889).
The Metrical History of Sir William Wallace, Knight of Ellerslie, by Henry, commonly called Blind Harry: carefully transcribed from the ms. copy of that work in the Advocates' Library, under the eye of the Earl of Buchan. And now printed for the first time, according to the ancient and true orthography. With Notes and Dissertations. In Three Volumes (Perth: Morrison & Son, 1790).

EDITIONS OF JANE PORTER'S *THE SCOTTISH CHIEFS*

Porter, J., *The Scottish Chiefs, a Romance. In Five Volumes* (London: Longman, Hurst, Rees, and Orne, Paternoster-Row, 1810).
Porter, J., *The Scottish Chiefs: A Romance in Two Volumes* (Edinburgh and Dublin: Bell & Bradfute; London: Colburn, 1831).
Porter, J., *The Scottish Chiefs . . . Revised, corrected and illustrated with a new retrospective introduction, notes, &c., by the author. [With plates, including a portrait.]* (London: J. S. Virtue, 1840).
Porter, J., *The Scottish Chiefs* (London: J. S. Virtue, 1841).
Porter, J., *The Scottish chiefs by Jane Porter*; adapted by John H. O'Rourke; illustrated by Alex A. Blum (Sydney, 19—).
Porter, J., *The Scottish Chiefs* (New York: T. Y. Crowell & Co. 1903?).
Porter, J., *The Scottish Chiefs,* ed. and introd. G. Kelly (London: Pickering & Chatto, 2002).
Porter, J., *The Scottish Chiefs: A Romance,* ed. and introd. F. Price (Plymouth: Broadview Press, 2007).

PUBLIC TALKS

Ainsworth, G., 'Repairing Wallace Monuments', One Day Wallace Conference, 17 May 1997, Smith Art Gallery and Museum, Stirling.

Cree, I., 'Braveheart and the Work of the Wallace Clan Trust', One Day Wallace Conference, 17 May 1997, Smith Art Gallery and Museum, Stirling.

Page, R., 'The Archeology of Stirling Bridge', *One Day Wallace Conference*, 17 May 1997, Smith Art Gallery and Museum, Stirling.

Salmond, A., 'Winning with Wallace', Address to the 61st Annual National Conference of the Scottish National Party, 22 September 1995, Perth City Halls.

VisitScotland and EventScotland presentation at the 10th Annual Scottish–North American Leadership Conference, 27 October 2012, Troy, Michigan, USA.

BOOKS AND ARTICLES

Allanson, P. and M. Whitby, *The Rural Economy and the British Countryside* (London: Earthscan, 1996).

Almeida, H. de and G. H. Gilpin, *Indian Renaissance: British Romantic Art and the Prospect of India* (Aldershot: Ashgate, 2005).

Anderson, B., *Imagined Communities: Reflections on the Origin and Spread of Nationalism*, rev. edn (London: Verso, 1996; 2nd edn 2006).

Anderson, R. D., *Education and Opportunity in Victorian Scotland* (Oxford: Clarendon Press, 1983).

Anstruther, I., *The Knight and the Umbrella: An Account of the Eglinton Tournament 1839*, 2nd edn (Gloucester: Alan Sutton, 1986).

Appadurai, A., 'Disjuncture and difference in the global cultural economy', *Theory, Culture and Society*, 7, 2–3 (June 1990).

Armitage, D., 'Greater Britain: a useful category of historical analysis?', *America Historical Review*, 104, 2 (1999).

Armstrong, J. A., *Nations before Nationalism* (Chapel Hill: University of North Carolina Press, 1982).

Ascherson, N., *Games With Shadows* (London: Radius, 1988).

Ash, M., 'William Wallace and Robert the Bruce', in R. Samuel and P. Thompson (eds), *The Myths We Live By* (London: Routledge, 1990).

Ashplant, T. G., G. Dawson and M. Roper (eds), *The Politics of War Memory and Commemoration* (London: Routledge, 2000).

Assman, J., *Cultural Memory and Early Civilization: Writing, Remembrance and Political Imagination* (Cambridge: Cambridge University Press, 2011).

Baines, D., *Migration in a Mature Economy: Emigration and Internal Migration in England and Wales, 1861–1900* (Cambridge: Cambridge University Press, 1985).

Balaban, J., 'Blind Harry and *The Wallace*', *The Chaucer Review*, 8 (1974).

Bannerman, J., 'MacDuff of Fife', in A. Grant and K. J. Stringer (eds), *Medieval Scotland: Crown, Lordship and Community. Essays presented to G. W. S. Barrow* (Edinburgh: Edinburgh University Press, 1993).

Barrow, G. W. S., *Robert Bruce and the Community of the Realm of Scotland*, 2nd edn (Edinburgh: Edinburgh University Press, 1976).

Beasley, P., 'Georgiana Molloy, Jane Porter and the significance of exploration narratives for new beginnings in a strange land', *Victorian Network*, 1, 1 (2009).

Behrendt, S. C., *British Women Poets and the Romantic Writing Community* (Baltimore: Johns Hopkins University Press, 2009).

Bell, D. D. A., 'Mythscapes, mythology and national identity', *British Journal of Sociology* 54 (2003).

Bellamy, J. G., *The Law of Treason in England in the Later Middle Ages* (Cambridge: Cambridge University Press, 1970).

Berglund, S., 'Mercantile credit and financing in Venezuela, 1830–1870', *Journal of Latin American Studies*, 17, 2 (November 1985).

Bhabha, H., 'Narrating the Nation', in Homi Bhabha (ed.), *Nation and Narration* (London: Routledge, 1990).

Billig, M., *Banal Nationalism* (London: Sage, 1995).

Blaikie, A., 'Imagining the face of a nation: Scotland, modernity and the places of memory', *Memory Studies* 4 (2011), pp. 416–31.

Blaikie, A., *The Scots Imagination and Modern Memory* (Edinburgh: Edinburgh University Press, 2010).

Boli, J. and G. Thomas, 'World culture in the world polity: a century of international non-governmental organization', *American Sociological Review*, 62 (April 1997).

Brand, J., *The National Movement in Scotland* (London: Routledge & Kegan Paul, 1978).

Breitenbach, E. and L. Abrams, 'Gender and Scottish Identity', in L. Abrams, E. Gordon, D. Simonton and E. J. Yeo (eds), *Gender in Scottish History since 1700* (Edinburgh: Edinburgh University Press, 2006).

Breuilly, J., 'Dating the Nation: How Old Is an Old Nation?', in

I., Atsuko and U. Gordana (eds), *When Is the Nation? Towards an Understanding of Theories of Nationalism* (London: Routledge 2003), pp. 15–39.

Breuilly, J., *Nationalism and the State* (Manchester: Manchester University Press, 1982).

Broadie, A., 'John Duns Scotus and the Idea of Independence', in E. J. Duncan (ed.), *The Wallace Book* (Edinburgh: John Donald, 2007).

Brockmann, S., *Literature and German Reunification* (Cambridge: Cambridge University Press, 1999).

Brown, I., T. O. Clancy, S. Manning and M. G. H. Pittock (eds), *The Edinburgh History of Scottish Literature. Volume Two: Enlightenment, Britain and Empire* (1707–1918) (Edinburgh: Edinburgh University Press, 2007).

Brown, J. T. T., 'The Wallace and The Bruce Restudied', in *Bonner Beiträge zur Anglistik* (Bonn: P. Hansteins Verlag, 1900).

Brown, P. H., *History of Scotland to the Present Time* (Cambridge: Cambridge University Press, 1911), Vol. I.

Brown, S. J., '"Echoes of Midlothian": Scottish liberalism and the South African War, 1899–1902', *Scottish Historical Review*, 71, 1, 2: nos 191/2 (1992).

Brunsden, G. M., 'Aspects of Scotland's Social, Political and Cultural Scene in the Late 17th and Early 18th Centuries, as Mirrored in the Wallace and Bruce Traditions', in E. J. Cowan and D. Gifford (eds), *The Polar Twins* (Edinburgh: John Donald, 1999).

Bryce, G., 'Jane Porter', *Notes and Queries*, 3rd Series, 30 April 1864.

Bryman, A., 'The Disneyization of Society', *Sociological Review*, 47, 1 (1999).

Bueltmann, T., A. Hinson, A. and G. Morton, *The Scottish Diaspora* (Edinburgh: Edinburgh University Press, 2013).

Burton, J. H., *The History Of Scotland; From Agricola's Invasion To The Extinction of The Last Jacobite Insurrection*, 4 vols, new edn (Edinburgh: Blackwood & Sons [1873], 1897).

Burton, J. H., *The History of Scotland* (Edinburgh: William Blackwood, new edn, 1897), Vol. II.

Calder, A., *Revolving Cultures: Notes from the Scottish Republic* (London: I. B. Tauris, 1994).

Caldwell, D. H., 'The Wallace Sword', in E. J. Cowan (ed.), *The Wallace Book* (Edinburgh: John Donald, 2007).

Calendar of Documents Relating to Scotland, ed. J. Bain (Edinburgh, 1887).

Calloway, C., *White People, Indians and Highlanders: Tribal Peoples and Colonial Encounters in Scotland and America* (Oxford: Oxford University Press, 2008).

Cant, R. G., 'David Steuart Erskine, 11th Earl of Buchan: Founder of the Society of Antiquaries of Scotland', in A. S. Bell (ed.), *The Scottish Antiquarian Tradition: Essays to Mark the Bicentenary of the Society of Antiquaries of Scotland, 1780–1980* (Edinburgh: John Donald, 1981).

Carlyle, T., 'The Amoral Scott', *London and Westminster Review* (January 1838).

Castells, M., *The Rise of the Networked Society*, 2nd edn. Vol. 1: *The Information Age: Economy, Society and Culture* (Oxford: Blackwell, 1996, 2000).

Cattell, M. G. and J. J. Climo, 'Meaning in Social Memory and History: Anthropological Perspectives', in Jacob J. Climo and Maria G. Cattell (eds), *Social Memory and History: Anthropological Perspectives* (Oxford: Rowman & Littlefield, 2002).

Chambers, R., *Traditions of Edinburgh*, 2 vols (Edinburgh: Chambers & Co., 1825).

Child, F. C., *English and Scottish Ballads* (Boston: Little, Brown, 1859), Vol. VI.

Clark, T. and T. Dickson, 'The Birth of Class?', in T. M. Devine and R. Mitchison (eds), *People and Society in Scotland, Vol. 1, 1760–1830* (Edinburgh: John Donald, 1988).

Clayton, A., 'Enunciating difference: Sydney Owenson's (extra-) national tale', *The Journal of Irish and Scottish Studies*, 1, 2 (March 2008).

Cohen, A. P., 'Peripheral Vision: Nationalism, National Identity and the Objective Correlative in Scotland', in A. P. Cohen (ed.), *Signifying Identities: Anthropological Perspectives on Boundaries and Contest Values* (London: Routledge, 2000).

Cohen, A. P., 'Personal nationalism: a Scottish view of some rites, rights, and wrongs', *American Ethnologist*, 23, 4 (1996).

Coleman, J., 'Unionist-Nationalism in Stone? The National Wallace Monument and the Hazards of Commemoration in Victorian Scotland', in E. J. Cowan (ed.), *The Wallace Book* (Edinburgh: John Donald, 2007).

Colley, L., 'The apotheosis of George III: loyalty, royalty and the British nation 1760–1820', *Past and Present*, 102 (1984).

Conversi, D., 'Ernest Gellner as critic of social thought: nationalism, closed systems and the Central European tradition', *Nations and Nationalism*, 5, 4 (1999).

Corr, H., 'Where Is the Lass o' Pairts? Gender, Identity and Education in Victorian Scotland', in D. Broun, R. Finlay and M. Lynch (eds), *Image and Identity: The Making and Re-making of Scotland through the Ages* (Edinburgh: John Donald, 1998).

Coupland, A., 'Docklands: dream or disaster', in A. Thornley (ed.), *The Crisis of London* (London: Routledge, 1992).

Cowan, E. J., 'Identity, Freedom and the Declaration of Arbroath', in D. Broun, R. Finlay and M. Lynch (eds), *Image and Identity: The Making and Re-making of Scotland through the Ages* (Edinburgh: John Donald, 1998).

Cowan, E. J., 'The Wallace Factor in Scottish History', in R. Jackson and S. Wood (eds), *Images of Scotland*, in *The Journal of Scottish Education*, Occasional Paper, No. 1 (Dundee: The Northern College, 1997).

Cowan, E. J. (ed.), *The Wallace Book* (Edinburgh: John Donald, 2007).

Cowan, E. J., 'The Political Ideas of a Covenanting Leader: Archibald Campbell, Marquis of Argyll 1607–1661', in R. A. Mason (ed.), *Scots and Britons: Scottish Political Thought and the Union of 1603* (Cambridge: Cambridge University Press, 1994).

Cowan, E. J., 'William Wallace: "The Choice of the Estates"', in E. J. Cowan (ed.), *The Wallace Book* (Edinburgh: John Donald, 2007).

Craig, C., *Intending Scotland: Explorations in Scottish Culture since the Enlightenment* (Edinburgh: Edinburgh University Press, 2009).

Craig, C., *Out of History: Narrative Paradigms in Scottish and British Culture* (Edinburgh: Edinburgh University Press, 1996).

Craig, F. W. S., *British Parliamentary Elections 1885–1918*, 2nd edn (Aldershot: Parliamentary Research Services, 1989).

Craik, G. L., *A Compendious History of English Literature and the English Language from the Norman Conquest* (London: Griffen, Bohn & Co., 1861), Vol. 1.

Crang, M., 'On the heritage trail: maps of and journeys to olde Englande', *Environment and Planning D: Society and Space*, 13 (1994).

Crawford, R., *The Bard: Robert Burns, A Biography* (Princeton: Princeton University Press, 2009).

Criagie, W. A., 'Barbour and Blind Harry as literature', *The Scottish Review*, 22 (July 1893).

Dalrymple, D., of Hailes, *Annals of Scotland: From the accession of Malcome III to the Accession of the House of Stewart* 3rd edn (1776–9) (Edinburgh: A. Constable, 1819).

Daniels, S., 'Mapping National Identities: The Culture of Cartography with Particular Reference to the Ordnance Survey', in G. Cubitt (ed.), *Imagining Nations* (Manchester: Manchester University Press, 1998).

Davidson, R., *Dangerous Liaisons: A Social History of Venereal Disease in Twentieth-Century Scotland* (Amsterdam: Rodopi, 2000).

Davidson, R., '"The sexual state": sexuality and Scottish governance, 1950–1980', *Journal of the History of Sexuality*, 13, 4 (October 2004).

Davie, G. E., *The Crisis of the Democratic Intellect: The Problem of Generalism and Specialisation in Twentieth-century Scotland* (Edinburgh: Polygon, 1986).

Davie, G. E., *The Democratic Intellect: Scotland and her Universities in the Nineteenth Century* (Edinburgh: Edinburgh University Press, 1964).

Dennis, I., *Nationalism and Desire in Early Historical Fiction* (Basingstoke: Palgrave Macmillan, 1997).

Devine, T. M., *Scotland's Empire: 1600–1815* (London: Allen Lane, 2003).

Devine, T. M., *To the Ends of the Earth: Scotland Global Diaspora, 1750–2010* (London: Allen Lane, 2011).

Dîaz-Andreu, M., 'The Past in the Present: The Search for Roots in Cultural Nationalism. The Spanish Case', in J. G. Beramendi, R. Máiz and X. M. Núñez (eds), *Nationalism in Europe: Past and Present, Volume I* (Santiago de Compostela: University Press of Santiago de Compostela, 1994).

Donachie, I. and C. A. Whatley (eds), *The Manufacture of Scottish History* (Edinburgh: Polygon, 1992).

Donaldson, G., *The Scots Overseas* (London: Robert Hale, 1966).

Donaldson, G. and R. S. Morpeth, *A Dictionary of Scottish History* (Edinburgh: John Donald, 1977).

Dunbar, A. H., *Scottish Kings: A Revised Chronology of Scottish History, 1000–1625* (Edinburgh: David Douglas, 1906).

Duncan, A. A. M., 'The Process of Norham, 1291', in P Cross and S. Lloyd (eds), *Thirteenth Century England*, No. 5 (Woodbridge: Boydell, 1995).

Duncan, A. A. M., 'William, Son of Alan Wallace: The Documents', in E. J. Cowan (ed.), *The Wallace Book* (Edinburgh; John Donald, 2007).

Duncan, I., *Modern Romance and the Transformation of the Novel, The Gothic, Scott, Dickens* (Cambridge: Cambridge University Press, 1992).

Durie, A., 'Tourism in Victorian Scotland: the case of Abbotsford', *Scottish Economic and Social History*, Vol. 12 (1992).

Early Popular Poetry in Scotland and the Northern Border, ed. D. Laing in 1822/26, rearranged and revised with additions and glossary by W. Carrew-Hazlitt, 2 Vols (London: Reeves & Turner, 1895), Vol. II.

Edensor, T., 'National identity and the politics of memory: remembering Bruce and Wallace in symbolic space', *Environment and Planning D: Space and Society*, 15, 2 (1997).

Edensor, T., 'Reading Braveheart: representing and contesting Scottish identity', *Scottish Affairs*, 21 (1997).

Edmunds, J., 'Generations, Women and National Consciousness', in J. Edmunds and B. S. Turner (eds), *Generational Consciousness, Narrative and Politics* (Boston: Rowman & Littlefield, 2002).

Edwards, O. D., *Macaulay* (London: Weidenfeld & Nicolson, 1988).

Ellis, J. S., 'The prince and the dragon: Welsh national identity and the 1911 investiture of the Prince of Wales', *The Welsh History Review*, 18 (1996).

Ellis, P. B. and MacA'Ghobhainn, S., *The Scottish Insurrection of 1820* (London: Gollancz, 1970)

Evans, N., 'Introduction: Identity and Integration in the British Isles', in N. Evans (ed.), *National Identity in the British Isles* (Harlech: Coleg Harlech Occasional Papers in Welsh Studies, No. 3, 1989).

Ewan, E., 'Braveheart', *The America historical Review*, Vol. 100, No. 4 (October 1995).

Featherstone, M., 'Global culture: an introduction', *Theory, Culture and Society*, 7, 2–3 (June 1990).

Ferris, I., 'Melancholy, Memory, and the "Narrative Situation" of History in Post-Enlightenment Scotland', in L. Davis, I. Duncan and J. Sorenson (eds), *Scotland and the Borders of Romanticism* (Cambridge: Cambridge University Press, 2004).

Ferris, I., *The Achievement of Literary Authority* (Ithaca: Cornell University Press, 1991).

Ferris, I., *The Romantic National Tale and the Question of Ireland* (Cambridge: Cambridge University Press 2002).

Fielding, P., 'Genre, geography and the question of the national tale: D. P. Campbell's Harley Radington', *European Romantic Review*, 23, 5 (2012).

Fielding, P., *Scotland and the Fictions of Geography: North Britain, 1760–1830* (Cambridge: Cambridge University Press, 2008).

Finlay, R. J., *A Partnership for Good?*: *Scottish Politics and the Union since 1800* (Edinburgh: John Donald, 1997).

Finlay, R. J., 'Continuity and Change: Scottish Politics, 1900–45', in T. M. Devine and R. J. Finlay (eds), *Scotland in the Twentieth Century* (Edinburgh: Edinburgh University Press, 1996),

Finlay, R. J., 'Controlling the past: Scottish historiography and Scottish identity in the 19th and 20th centuries', *Scottish Affairs*, 9 (Autumn 1994).

Finlay, R. J., *Independent and Free: Scottish Politics and the Origins of the Scottish National Party, 1918–1945* (Edinburgh: John Donald, 1994).

Fisher, A., *William Wallace* (Edinburgh: John Donald, 1986).

Foster, R., 'Storylines: narratives and nationality in nineteenth-century Ireland', in G. Cubitt (ed.), *Imagining Nations* (Manchester: Manchester University Press, 1998).

Fraser, W. H., *Scottish Popular Politics: From Radicalism to Labour* (Edinburgh: Polygon, 2000).

Fraser, W. H., 'The Scottish Context of Chartism', in T. Brotherstone (ed.), *Covenant, Charter and Party: Traditions of Revolt and Protest in Modern Scottish History* (Aberdeen: Aberdeen University Press, 1989).

Fry, M., *Patronage and Principle: A Political History of Modern Scotland* (Aberdeen: Aberdeen University Press, 1987).

Fujita, K., 'A world city and flexible specialisation', *International Journal of Urban and Regional Research*, 15, 2 (June 1991).

Fussel, P., *The Great War and Modern Memory* (Oxford: Oxford University Press, 2000).

Gans, H. J., 'Symbolic ethnicity: the future of ethnic groups and cultures in America', *Ethnic and Racial Studies* 2, 1 (January 1979).

Garside, P., 'The English Novel in the Romantic Era', in Peter Garside and Rainer Schöwerling, *The English Novel 1770–1829. A Bibliographical Survey of Prose Fiction Published in the British Isles, II, 1800–1829* (Oxford: Oxford University Press, 2000).

Geddie, W. (ed.), *A Bibliography of Middle Scots Poets: with an introduction on the history of their reputations*, Scottish Text Society Vol. 61 (Edinburgh: Blackwood & Sons, 1912).

Geisler, M. E., 'National Symbols', in G. H. Herb and D. H. Kaplan (eds), *Nations and Nationalism: A Global Historical Overview, Vol. 1, 1770 to 1880* (Santa Barbara and Oxford: ABC Clio, 2008).

Gellner, E., *Nations and Nationalism* (Oxford: Blackwell, 1983).

Gellner, E., 'Reply: do nations have navels?' *Nations and Nationalism*, 2, 3 (1996).

Gellner E., *Thought and Change* (London: Weidenfeld & Nicolson, 1964).

Gerth, H. H. and C. Wright Mills (trans. and ed.), *From Max Weber: Essays in Sociology* (London: Routledge, 1948).

Giles, J. and T. Middleton, *Writing Englishness, 1900–1995* (London: Routledge, 1995).

Goldstein, R. J., *The Matter of Scotland: Historical Narrative in Medieval Scotland* (Lincoln, NE and London: University of Nebraska Press, 1993).

Grant, A., 'Bravehearts and Coronets: Images of William Wallace and the Scottish Nobility', in E. J. Cowan (ed.), *The Wallace Book* (Edinburgh: John Donald, 2007).

Grant, A. and K. Stringer, 'Introduction: the enigma of British History', in A. Grant and K. Stringer (eds), *Uniting the Kingdom? The Making of British History* (London and New York: Routledge, 1995).

Gray, A., *Independence: An Argument for Home Rule* (Edinburgh: Canongate Books, 2014).

Gray, D. J., *William Wallace: The King's Enemy* (London: Robert Hale, 1991).

Greenfeld, L. *Nationalism: Five Roads to modernity* (Cambridge, MA: Harvard University Press, 1992).

Grosby, S., 'The chosen people of ancient Israel and the Occident: why does nationality exist and survive?', *Nations and Nationalism*, 5, 3 (1999).

Guibernau, M., *Nationalisms: The Nation-State and Nationalism in the Twentieth Century* (Cambridge: Polity Press, 1996).

Gurney, G., *The Childhood of Queen Victoria by Mrs Gerald Gurney (Dorothy Frances Blomfeld)* (London: Nisbet & Co., 1901).

Habermas, J., *The Structural Transformation of the Public Sphere. An Inquiry into a Category of Bourgeois Society*, trans. Thomas Burger (Cambridge: Polity Press, 1989).

Halbwachs, M., *On Collective Memory*, ed. and trans. Lewis A. Coser (Chicago: University of Chicago Press, 1992).

Hall, J. A., 'After the fall: an analysis of post-communism', *British Journal of Sociology*, 45, 4 (December 1994).

Hall, S., 'The question of cultural identity', in S. Hall, D. Held and A. McGrew (eds), *Modernity and Its Futures* (Cambridge: Polity Press, 1992).

Harvey, D., *Money, Time, Space, and The City* (Cambridge: Granta, c.1985).

Harvie, C., *Scotland and Nationalism: Scottish Society and Politics, 1707–1994* (London: Routledge, 1994).

Hastings, A., 'Special peoples', *Nations and Nationalism*, 5, 3 (1999).

Hearn, J., *Claiming Scotland: National Identity and Liberal Culture* (Edinburgh: Polygon, 2000).

Hearn, J., 'National identity: banal, personal and embedded', *Nations and Nationalism*, 13, 4 (2007).

Hechter, M., 'Internal colonialism revisited', *Cencrastus*, 10 (1982).

Henderson, A., *Hierarchies of Belonging: National Identity and Political Culture in Scotland and Quebec* (Montreal and Kingston: McGill-Queen's University Press, 2007).

Henderson, T. F., *Scottish Vernacular Literature: A Succinct History* (London: David Nutt, 1898).

Hendrick, B. J., *The Life of Andrew Carnegie* (New York: Doubleday, Doran & Co., 1932), Vol. 1.

Herr, R. S., 'The possibility of nationalist feminism', *Hypatia*, 18 (2003).

Heuer, J., 'Gender and Nationalism', in G. H. Herb and D. H. Kaplan (eds), *Nations and Nationalism: A Global Historical Overview*, Vol. 1 (Santa Barbara: ABC-Clio, 2008).

Hewer, C. J., and R. Roberts, 'History, culture and cognition: towards a dynamic model of social memory, *Culture & Psychology* 18 (2012).

Hewison, R., *The Heritage Industry: Britain in a Climate of Decline* (London: Methuen, 1987).

Hill, R. J., *Picturing Scotland through the Waverley Novels. Walter Scott and the Origins of the Illustrated Novel* (Aldershot: Ashgate, 2010).

Hirst, P. and G. Thompson, *Globalization in Question* (Cambridge: Polity, 1996).

Hobsbawm, E. J. and T. Ranger (eds), *The Invention of Tradition* (Cambridge: Cambridge University Press, [1983] 1994).

Hogg, J., *Domestic Manners of Sir Walter Scott* (Stirling, 1909)

Holt, J. C., *Robin Hood* (London: Thames & Hudson, 1983).

Hook, A. D., 'Jane Porter, Sir Walter Scott, and the historical novel', *Clio 5*, 2 (1976).

Hume, D., *An Enquiry Concerning Human Understanding* (New York: Harvard Classics, 1910 [1748]).

Hutchings, K., '"Teller of Tales": John Buchan, First Baron Tweedsmuir of Elsfield, and Canada's Aboriginal Peoples', in G. Morton and D. A. Wilson (eds), *Irish and Scottish Encounters with Indigenous Peoples: Canada, the United States, Australia and New Zealand* (Montreal and Kingston: McGill-Queen's University Press, 2013).

Hutchison, I. G. C., *A Political History of Scotland 1832–1924. Parties, Elections and Issues* (Edinburgh: John Donald, 1986).

Hutchison, *Life of Sir William Wallace; or Scotland Five Hundred Years Ago* (Glasgow: Thomas Murray & Son, 1858).

Ichijo, A., *Scottish Nationalism and the Idea of Europe* (London: Routledge, 2004).

Johnson, N. C., 'Framing the past: time, space and the politics of heritage tourism in Ireland', *Political Geography*, 18, 2 (1999).

Johnston, T., *The History of the Working Classes in Scotland* (Glasgow: Forward Publishing, 1920, 1929).

Jones, D., *A Wee Guide to William Wallace* (Edinburgh: Goblinshead, 1997).

Keane, J. (ed.), *Civil Society and the State: New European perspectives* (London: Verso, 1988).

Kearney, H., *The British Isles: A History of Four Nations* (Cambridge: Cambridge University Press).

Keen, M., *The Outlaws of Medieval Legend* (London: Routledge & Kegan Paul, 1961).

Kennedy, J., *Liberal Nationalism: Empire, State and Civil Society in Scotland and Quebec* (Montreal and Kingston: McGill-Queen's University Press, 2013).

Kidd, C., 'Sentiment, Race and Revival: Scottish Identities in the Aftermath of Enlightenment', in L. Brockliss and D. Eastwood (eds), *A Union of Multiple Identities. The British Isles, c.1750–c.1850* (Manchester: Manchester University Press, 1997).

Kidd, C., *Subverting Scotland's Past. Scottish Whig Historians and the*

Creation of an Anglo-British Identity, 1689–c.1830 (Cambridge: Cambridge University Press, 1993).

Kidd, C., 'The English Cult of Wallace and the Blending of Nineteenth-Century Britain', in E. J. Cowan, *The Wallace Book* (Edinburgh: John Donald, 2007).

King, A., 'Englishmen, Scots and marchers: national and local identities in Thomas Gray's *Scalacronica*', *Northern History*, 36, 2 (2000).

King, B., *The New English Literatures: Cultural Nationalism in a Changing World* (London: Macmillan, 1980).

King, E., *Introducing William Wallace: The Life and Legacy of Scotland's Liberator* (Fort William: Firtree, 1997).

King, E., 'The Material Culture of William Wallace', in E. J. Cowan (ed.), *The Wallace Book* (Edinburgh: John Donald, 2007).

Knightley, C., *Folk Heroes of Britain* (London: Thames & Hudson, 1982).

Knox, W., 'The Red Clydesiders and the Scottish Political Tradition', in T. Brotherstone (ed.), *Covenant, Charter and Party* (Aberdeen: Aberdeen University Press).

Kohl, P. L. and C. Fawcett, 'Archaeology in the Service of the State: Theoretical Considerations', in P. L. Kohl and C. Fawcett (eds), *Nationalism, Politics and the Practice of Archaeology* (Cambridge: Cambridge University Press, 1995).

Kumar, K., 'Civil society: an inquiry into the usefulness of a historical term', *British Journal of Sociology*, 44, 3 (September 1993).

Kuper, A., *Incest and Influence: The Private Life of Bourgeois England* (Cambridge, MA: Harvard University Press, 2009).

Lacroix, J.-G. and G. Tremblay, 'The emergence of cultural industries into the foreground of industrialization and commodification: elements of context', trans. R. Ashby, *Current Sociology*, 45, 4 (October 1997).

Landsman, N. C., 'Nation, migration, and the province in the first British Empire: Scotland and the Americas, 1600–1800', *America historical Review*, 104, 2 (1999).

Leneman, L, *A Guid Cause: The Women's Suffrage Movement in Scotland* (Edinburgh: Mercat Press, 1991, 1995).

Leneman, L., *Alienated Affections: The Scottish Experience of Divorce and Separation, 1684–1830* (Edinburgh: Edinburgh University Press, 1998).

Leneman, L., *Martyrs in Our Midst: Dundee, Perth and the Forcible*

Feeding of Suffragettes (Dundee: Abertay Historical Society, Publication No. 33, 1993).

Levitt, I., 'Scottish Sentiment, Administrative Devolution and Westminster, 1885–1964', in M. Lynch (ed.), *Scotland, 1850–1979: Society, Politics and the Union* (London: Historical Association, 1993).

Lindsay, M., *History of Scottish Literature* (London: Robert Hale, 1977).

Lockhart, J. G., *Memoirs of the Life of Sir Walter Scott, Bart* (Edinburgh, 1844).

Lockhart, J. G., *The Life of Sir Walter Scott* (London, 1906).

Looser, D., 'The great man and women's historical fiction: Jane Porter and Sir Sidney Smith', *Women's Writing*, 19 (2012).

Looser, D., *Women Writers and Old Age in Great Britain, 1750–1850* (Baltimore: Johns Hopkins University Press, 2008).

Lowenthal, D., *The Past is a Foreign Country* (Cambridge: Cambridge University Press, 1985)

Lukács, G., *The Historical Novel* (London: Merlin Press, 1963).

Lynch, M., 'A Nation Born Again? Scottish Identity in the Sixteenth and Seventeenth Centuries', in D. Broun, R. Finlay and M. Lynch (eds), *Image and Identity: The Making and Re-making of Scotland through the Ages* (Edinburgh: John Donald, 1998).

Lynch, M., *Scotland: A New History* (London: Century, 1991).

Macdonagh, O., *States of Mind: A Study of Anglo-Irish Conflict, 1780–1980* (London: Allen & Unwin, 1983).

Macdonald, C. M. M., *The Radical Thread: Political Change in Scotland. Paisley Politics, 1885–1924* (East Linton: Tuckwell Press, 2000).

Macdonald, M., 'Scottish literature and visual art: A Caledonian synergy', *International Review of Scottish Studies*, 38 (2013).

Macdougall, N. A. T., 'The Sources: A Reappraisal of the Legend', in J. M. Brown (ed.), *Scottish Society in the Fifteenth Century* (London: Edward Arnold, 1977).

Mackenzie, A. M., *Robert Bruce: King of Scots* (London: Alexander MacLehose, 1936).

Mackenzie, A. M. (ed.), *Scottish Pageant*, 2nd edn (Edinburgh: Oliver & Boyd for the Saltire Society, 1952).

MacKenzie, J. M., 'Empire and national identities: the case of Scotland', *Transactions of the Royal Historical Society* 6th series, 8 (1998).

Maclean, J., *In the Rapids of Revolution. Essays, Articles and Letters 1902–23*, ed. with introduction by N. Milton (London: Allison & Busby, 1978).

Macleod, D., *Gloomy Memories in the Highlands of Scotland: Versus Mrs. Harriet Beecher Stowe's Sunny Memories* (Toronto, 1857).

MacQueen, J., 'The Literature of Fifteenth-century Scotland', in J. M. Brown (ed.), *Scottish Society in the Fifteenth Century* (London: Edward Arnold, 1977).

Magnusson, M., *Scotland: The Story of a Nation* (London: HarperCollins, 2000).

Mann, M., 'A Political Theory of Nationalism and its Excesses', in S. Periwal (ed.), *Notions of Nationalism* (Budapest: Central European Press, 1995).

Mann, M., 'Nation-states in Europe and Other Countries: Diversifying, Developing, not Dying', in G. Balakrishnan (ed.), *Mapping the Nation* (London: Verso, 1996),

Martin, M. M., *The Mighty Scot: Nation, Gender, and the Nineteenth-Century Mystique of Scottish Masculinity* (Albany, NY: State University of New York Press, 2009).

Maxwell, H. E., *The Chronicle of Lanercost, 1272–1346: Translated, with notes.* (London: J. MacLehose & Son, 1903).

Maxwell, H. E., *The Early Chronicles Relating to Scotland* (Glasgow: MacLehose, 1912).

Mayer, T., 'Gender Ironies of Nationalism', in T. Mayer (ed.), *Gender Ironies of Nationalisms; Sexing the Nation* (London: Routledge, 2000).

McArthur, C., '*Braveheart* and the Scottish Aesthetic Dementia', in T. Barta (ed.), *Screening the Past: Film and Representation of History* (Westport: Praeger, 1998).

McArthur, C., 'Culloden: a pre-emptive strike', *Scottish Affairs*, 9 (1994).

McArthur, C., 'Scotland and the *Braveheart* effect', *Journal for the Study of British Cultures*, 5, 1 (1998).

McClintock, A., 'Family feuds: gender, nationalism and the family', *Feminist Review*, 44 (Summer 1993).

McCrone, D., 'The Unstable Union: Scotland since the 1920s', in M. Lynch (ed.), *Scotland, 1850–1979: Society, Politics and the Union* (London: The Historical Association for Scotland, 1993).

McCrone, D., *The Sociology of Nationalism: Tomorrow's Ancestors* (London: Routledge, 1998).

McCrone, D., *Understanding Scotland – The Sociology of a Nation*, 2nd edn (London: Routledge, 2001).

McCrone, D., *Understanding Scotland: The Sociology of a Stateless Nation* (London: Routledge, 1992).

McCrone, D., A. Morris and R. Kiely, *Scotland – the Brand: the Making of Scottish Heritage* (Edinburgh: Edinburgh University Press, 1995).

McDiarmid, M. P., 'The date of the *Wallace*', *Scottish Historical Review*, 24 (1955).

McFarland, E. W., 'Commemoration of the South African War in Scotland', *The Scottish Historical Review*, 89, 2 (October 2010).

McKay, K., *Mel Gibson* (London: Sidgwick & Jackson, 1988).

McKinlay, A. and R. J. Morris (eds), *The ILP on Clydeside 1893–1932: From Foundation to Disintegration* (Manchester: Manchester University Press, 1991).

McKinlay, R., 'Barbour's *Bruce*', *Records of the Glasgow Bibliographical Society*, Vol. VI (Glasgow, 1920).

McLean, T., 'Jane Porter's portrait of Benjamin West', *Huntington Library Quarterly*, 66 (2003).

McLean, T., 'Nobody's argument: Jane Porter and the historical novel', *The Journal for Early Modern Cultural Studies*, 7, 2 (Fall/Winter 2007).

McMaster, R. D., *Thackeray's Cultural Frame of Reference* (Montreal and Kingston: McGill-Queen's University Press, 1991).

McNie, A., *Clan Wallace* (Jedburgh: Cascade Publishing, 1986).

McPherson, A., 'An Angle on the Geist: Persistence and Change in the Scottish Educational Tradition', in W. Humes and H. Paterson (eds), *Scottish Culture and Scottish Education, 1800–1980* (Edinburgh: Edinburgh University Press, 1983).

Mellor, A. K., *Romanticism and Gender* (London: Routledge, 1993).

Melucci, A., *Nomads of the Present: Social Movements and Individual Needs in Contemporary Society* (London: Radius, 1989).

Mitchell, J., 'Conservatism in Twentieth Century Scotland: Society, Ideology and the Union', in M. Lynch (ed.), *Scotland, 1850–1979: Society, Politics and the Union* (London: Historical Association for Scotland, 1993).

Mitchell, J., *Strategies for Self-government: The Campaigns for a Scottish parliament* (Edinburgh: Polygon, 1996).

Molloy, M., 'Imagining (the) difference: gender, ethnicity and metaphors of nation', *Feminist Review*, 51 (Autumn 1995).

Monnickendam, A., 'The Scottish National Tale', in M. G. H. Pittock (ed.), *The Edinburgh Companion to Scottish Romanticism* (Edinburgh: Edinburgh University Press, 2011).

Morris, A. and Morton, G., *Locality, Community and Nation* (London: Hodder & Stoughton, 1998).

Morris, L., 'Globalization, migration and the nation-state: the path to post-national Europe?', *British Journal of Sociology*, 48, 2 (June 1997).

Morris, R. J., 'Scotland, 1830–1914: The Making of a Nation within a Nation', in W. H. Fraser and R. J. Morris (eds), *People and Society in Scotland, Volume II, 1830–1914* (Edinburgh: John Donald, 1990).

Morton, G., *Ourselves and Others: Scotland, 1832–1914* (Edinburgh: Edinburgh University Press, 2012).

Morton, G., 'Returning Nationalists, Returning Scotland: James Grant and Theodore Napier', in M. Varricchio (ed.), *Back to Caledonia: Scottish Homecomings from the Seventeenth Century to the Present* (Edinburgh: John Donald, 2012).

Morton, G., 'Review: Sir William Wallace and other tall stories (unlikely mostly)', *Scottish Affairs*, 14 (Spring 1996).

Morton, G., 'Scotland is Britain: the Union and Unionist-Nationalism, 1807–1907', *Journal of Irish and Scottish Studies*, 1, 1 (2008).

Morton, G., 'Scottish Rights and "centralisation" in the mid-nineteenth century', *Nations and Nationalism*, 2, 2 (1996).

Morton, G., 'The First Home Rule Movement in Scotland, 1886 to 1918', in H. Dickinson and M. Lynch (eds), *Sovereignty and Devolution* (East Linton: Tuckwell Press, 2000).

Morton, G., 'The moral foundations of constitutional change in Canada and Scotland at the end of the twentieth century', *International Review of Scottish Studies*, 33 (2008).

Morton, G., 'The most efficacious patriot: the heritage of William Wallace in nineteenth-century Scotland', *The Scottish Historical Review*, 77, 2, No. 204 (October 1998).

Morton, G., *Unionist Nationalism: Governing Urban Scotland, 1830–1860* (East Linton: Tuckwell Press, 1999).

Morton, G., 'What If? The Significance of Scotland's "Missing Nationalism" in the Nineteenth Century', in D. Broun, R. Finlay and M. Lynch (eds), *Image and Identity: The Making and Re-making of Scotland through the Ages* (Edinburgh: John Donald, 1998).

Morton, G. and T. Griffiths, 'Closing the door on modern Scotland's gilded cage', *The Scottish Historical Review*, 92, Supplement, No. 234, April 2013.

Morton, G. and R. J. Morris, 'Civil Society, Governance and Nation: Scotland, 1832–1914', in W. W. J. Knox and R. A. Houston (eds), *The Penguin History of Scotland* (Harmondsworth: Penguin, 2001).

Moss, M., 'Telecommunications, world cities and urban policy', *Urban Studies*, 24 (1987).

Murray, C. J. (ed.), *Encyclopaedia of the Romantic Era, 1760–1850, Vol. 1 A–K* (New York: Taylor & Francis, 2004).

Nairn, T., *Faces of Nationalism: Janus revisited* (London: Verso, 1997).

Nairn, T., 'Internationalism and the second coming', *Daedalus*, 122, 3 (1993).

Nairn, T., *The Break-Up of Britain*, 2nd edn (London: Verso, 1981).

Nash, A., 'The Kailyard: Problem of Illusion?', in I. Brown, T. O. Clancy, S. Manning and M. Pittock (eds), *The Edinburgh History of Scottish Literature. Volume 2: Enlightenment, Britain and Empire (1707–1918)* (Edinburgh: Edinburgh University Press, 2007).

Neilson, G., *John Barbour: Poet and Translator* (London: Kegan Paul, 1900).

Neilson, G., 'On Blind Harry's "Wallace"', *Essays and Studies*, Vol. I (Oxford: Clarendon Press, 1910).

Nenadic, S., 'Middle-rank consumers and domestic culture in Edinburgh and Glasgow, 1720–1840', *Past and Present*, 145 (1994).

Nicholson, R., *Scotland: The Later Middle Ages* (Edinburgh: Oliver & Boyd, 1974).

Page, R., 'The ancient bridge at Stirling: investigations, 1988–2000, *Scottish Archaeological Journal*, 23 (2001).

Palmer McCulloch, M., *Scottish Modernism and its Contexts 1918–1959: Literature, National Identity and Cultural Exchange* (Edinburgh: Edinburgh University Press, 2009).

Paterson, J., *Wallace and His Times* (Edinburgh: William Paterson, 1858).

Paterson, L., 'Civil Society and Democratic Renewal', in S. Baron, J. Field and T. Schüller (eds), *Social Capital: Social Theory and the Third Way* (Oxford: Oxford University Press, 2001).

Paterson, L., *The Autonomy of Modern Scotland* (Edinburgh: Edinburgh University Press, 1994).

Paton, H. J. , *The Claim of Scotland* (London: George Allen & Unwin, 1968).

Patterson, B., '"It is curious how keenly allied in character are the Scotch Highlander and the Maori": Encounters in a New Zealand colonial settlement', *Journal of Irish and Scottish Studies* 4, 1 (Autumn 2010).

Pears, I., 'The Gentleman and the Hero: Wellington and Napoleon in the Nineteenth Century, in R. Porter (ed.), *Myths of the English* (Cambridge, Polity, 1993).

Peiss, K., 'Crime without punishment', *London Review of Books* (November 1998).

Pendreight, B., 'History in the faking', *The Scotsman*, 12 June 1995.

Penman, M., 'Robert Bruce's bones: reputations, politics and identities in nineteenth-century Scotland', *International Review of Scottish Studies*, 34 (2009).

Petrie, D., *Screening Scotland* (London: BFI Publishing, 2000).

Pike, W. T. (ed.), 'Contemporary Biographies', in *Edinburgh and the Lothians at the opening of the twentieth century by A Eddinton* (Edinburgh: Pike & Co., 1904).

Pittock, M. G. H., *Celtic Identity and the British Image* (Manchester: Manchester University Press, 1999).

Pittock, M. G. H., 'The Complaint of Caledonia: Scotland and the Female Voice', in Philip Schwyzer and Simon Mealor (eds), *Archipelagic Identities: Literature and Identity in the Atlantic Archipelago, 1550–1800* (Aldershot: Ashgate, 2004).

Pittock, M. G. H., *The Myth of the Jacobite Clans* (Edinburgh: Edinburgh Univeristy Press, 1995).

Pittock, M. G. H., *The Road to Independence: Scotland since the 1960s*, 2nd edn (Edinburgh: Edinburgh University Press, 2014).

Plunkett, J., *Queen Victoria: First Media Monarch* (Oxford: Oxford University Press, 2003).

Pocock, J. G. A., 'Conclusion: Contingency, Identity, Sovereignty', in A. Grant and Stringer (eds), *Uniting the Kingdom? The Making of British History* (London: Routledge, 1995).

Pocock, J. G. A., 'The limits and divisions of British history: in search of an unknown subject', *America historical Review*, 87, 2 (1982).

Pocock, J. G. A., 'The new British history in Atlantic perspective: An Antipodean commentary' *America Historical Review*, 10, 2 (1999).

Pope-Hennessy, U., *Agnes Strickland: Biographer of the Queens of England* (London, 1940).

Prestwich, M., 'The Battle of Stirling Bridge: An English Perspective', in E. J. Cowan (ed.), *The Wallace Book* (Edinburgh: John Donald, 2007).

Prestwich, M., *The Three Edwards: War and State in England 1272–1377* (London: Weidenfeld & Nicolson, 1980).

Prestwich, M., *War, Politics and Finance under Edward I* (London: Faber & Faber, 1972).

Price, F., 'Jane Porter and the authorship of *Sir Edward Seaward's Narrative*: previously unpublished correspondence', *Notes and Queries* (March 2002).

Price, F., 'Resisting "the spirit of innovation": the other historical novel and Jane Porter', *Modern Language Review*, 101 (2006).

Pryke, S., 'Nationalism and sexuality: what are the issues?', *Nations and Nationalism*, 4, 4 (October 1998).

Raeburn, A., *The Militant Suffragettes* (London: Michael Joseph, 1973).

Rauser, A., 'Death or liberty: British political prints and the struggle for symbols in the American Revolution', *Oxford Art Journal*, 21, 2 (1998).

Read, D., *The English Provinces, c.1760–1960: A Study in Influence* (London: Arnold, 1964).

Reid, H. H., 'Alexander III: The Historiography of a Myth', in N. H. Reid (ed.), *Scotland in the Reign of Alexander III 1249–1286* (Edinburgh: John Donald, 1990).

Renan, E. 'What Is a Nation?', in G. Eley and R. G. Suny (eds), *Becoming National: A Reader* (Oxford: Oxford University Press, 1996).

Renan, E., 'What Is a Nation?' [1882], in H. K. Bhabha (ed.), *Nation and Narration* (London: Routledge, 1990).

Rendall, J., 'Tacitus Engendered: "Gothic Feminism" and British Histories, c.1750–1800', in G. Cubitt (ed.), *Imagining Nations* (Manchester, Manchester University Press, 1998).

Ritzer, G., *The McDonaldization of Society*, rev. edn (Thousand Oaks: Pine Forge Press, 1996).

Robertson, D., M. Wood and F. C. Mearns, *Edinburgh 1329–1929* (Edinburgh: Oliver & Boyd, 1929).

Robertson, J. (ed.), *Lives of the Scottish Poets in Three Volumes* (Edinburgh: The Society of Ancient Scots, 1821).

Rogers, A., 'A Planned Countryside', in G. Mingay (ed.), *The Rural Idyll* (London: Routledge, 1989).

Samuel, R., *Theatres of Memory, Vol. 1: Past and Present in Contemporary Culture* (London: Verso, 1994).

Schlicke, P. (ed.), *The Oxford Companion to Charles Dickens: Anniversary Edition* (Oxford: Oxford University Press, 2011).

Schofield, W. H., *Mythical Bards and the Life of Sir William Wallace* (Cambridge, MA: Harvard University Press, 1920).

Scholes, P. A., *God Save the Queen! The History and Romance of the World's First National Anthem* (Oxford: Oxford University Press, 1954).

Seal, G., *The Outlaw Legend: A Cultural Tradition in Britain, America and Australia* (Cambridge: Cambridge University Press, 1996).

Shields, J., 'Family roots to the routes of Empire: national tales and the domestication of the Scottish Highlands', *English Literary History*, 72 (2005).

Shields, J., *Sentimental Literature and Anglo-Scottish Identity, 1745–1820* (Cambridge: Cambridge University Press, 2010).

Sibbald, J., *Chronicle of Scottish Poetry from the thirteenth century to the Union of the Crowns, to which is added a glossary*, 4 Vols (London: Longman & Rees, 1802).

Smith, A. D. 'Memory and modernity: reflections on Ernest Gellner's theory of nationalism', *Nations and Nationalism*, 2, 3 (1996).

Smith, A. D., *The Cultural Foundations of Nations: Hierarchy, Covenant, and Republic* (Oxford: Blackwell, 2008).

Smith, A. D., *The Ethnic Origin of Nations* (Oxford: Basil Blackwell, 1986).

Smith, A. D , 'The myth of the 'Modern Nation' and the myths of nation', *Ethnic and Racial Studies*, 11, 1 (1988).

Smith, A. D., *The Nation in History: Historiographical Debates about Ethnicity and Nationalism* (Cambridge: Polity Press, 2000).

Smith, J., 'Textual Afterlives: Barbour's Bruce and Hary's Wallace', in John M. Kirk and Iseabail Macleod (eds), *Scots: Studies in its Literature and Language* (Amsterdam/New York: Rodopi, 2013).

Smout, T. C., *A Century of the Scottish People, 1830–1950* (London: Collins, 1986).

Smout, T. C., 'The core and periphery in history', *Journal of Common Market Studies*, 18, 3 (1980).

Spence, L., *Story of William Wallace: Little Stories of Great Lives* (London: Humphrey Milford, 1919)

Stapleton, J., *Englishness and the Study of Politics: The Social and Political Thought of Ernest Barker* (Cambridge: Cambridge University Press, 1994).

Stevenson, J. (ed.), *Documents Illustrative of Sir William Wallace, his life and times*, Maitland Club 54 (Edinburgh: Maitland Club, 1841).

Stevenson, K., *Chivalry and Knighthood in Scotland, 1424–1513* (Woodbridge: Boydell Press, 2006).

Stirling, K., *Bella Caledonia: Women, Nation, Text* (Amsterdam: Rodopi, 2008).

Stones, E. L. G., 'The submission of Robert Bruce to Edward I, c.1301–2', *The Scottish Historical Review*, 34, 118 (October 1955).

Strickland, A., *Letters of Mary, Queen of Scots, and documents connected with her personal history. Now first published with an introd.* (London: Henry Colburn, 1842).

Sudjic, D., *The 100 Mile City* (London: André Deutsch, 1992).

Szechi, D., *The Jacobites: Britain and Europe, 1699–1788* (Manchester: Manchester University Press, 1994).

Taylor, M., 'John Bull and the iconography of public opinion in England, c.1712–1929', *Past and Present*, 134 (1992).

Terry, C. S., *A Catalogue of the Publications of Scottish Historical and Kindred Clubs and* Societies, 1780–1908 (Glasgow: MacLehose, 1909).

The Round Table. A Quarterly Review of the Politics of the British Empire, Vol. 5, December (1911–12).

Thompson, E. P., 'Time, work-discipline, and industrial capitalism', *Past and Present*, 38 (1967).

Thompson, W., *The Good Old Cause: British Communism, 1920–1991* (London: Pluto Press, 1992).

Tilly, C., L. Tilly and R. Tilly, *The Rebellious Century 1830–1930* (London: J. M. Dent & Sons, 1975).

Tracy, T., *Irishness and Womanhood in Nineteenth-Century British Writing* (Aldershot: Ashgate, 2009).

Trumpener, K., *Bardic Nationalism: The Romantic Novel and the British Empire* (Princeton: Princeton University Press, 1997).

Turnbull, M. T. R. B., *Monuments and Statues of Edinburgh* (Edinburgh: Chambers, 1989).

Tytler, P. F., *Lives of the Scottish Worthies* (London: John Murray, 1831).

Urry, J., *The Tourist Gaze: Leisure and Travel in Contemporary Societies* (London: Sage, 1990).

Walker, I. C., 'Barbour, Blind Harry, and Sir William Craigie', *Studies in Scottish Literature*, 1, 3 (1963–4).

Walker, J., 'Culture and politics: the work of R. B. Cunninghame Graham and Scottish nationalism', *Scottish Tradition*, 17 (1992).

Wallerstein, I., *The Modern World System* (New York: Academic Press, 1989).

Watson, F. J., 'Sir William Wallace: What We Do – and Don't – Know', in E. J. Cowan (ed.), *The Wallace Book* (Edinburgh: John Donald, 2007).

Watson, F. J., *Under the Hammer: Edward I and Scotland, 1286–1306* (East Linton: Tuckwell Press, 1998).

Watson, F. J. 'The Enigmatic Lion', in D. Broun, R. Finlay and M. Lynch (eds), *Image and Identity: The Making and Re-making of Scotland through the Ages* (Edinburgh: John Donald, 1998).

Watts, A. A., ed., *The Literary Souvenir* (London: Longman, Rees, Orme, Brown & Green, 1930).

Whatley, C. A., *The Scots and the Union* (Edinburgh: Edinburgh University Press, 2006).

White, I. M., 'A diary of Jane Porter', *Scottish Review*, 29 (1897).

Whyte, C. (ed.), *Gendering the Nation: Studies in Modern Scottish Literature* (Edinburgh: Edinburgh University Press, 1995).

Wilson, M., *These Were Muses* (London: Sidgwick & Jackson, 1924).

Winter, J., *Sites of Memory, Sites of Mourning. The Great War in European Cultural History* (Cambridge: Cambridge University Press, 1995).

Withers, C. W. J., 'Landscape, memory, history: gloomy Memories and the 19th-century Scottish Highlands', *Scottish Geographical Magazine*, 121, 1 (2005).

Withers, C. W. J., 'The Historical Creation of the Scottish Highlands', in I. Donnachie and C. Whatley (eds), *The Manufacture of Scottish History* (Edinburgh: Polygon, 1992).

Withers, C. W. J., 'The social nature of map making in the Scottish Enlightenment, c. 1682–c. 1832', *Imago Mundi*, 54 (2002).

Wood, W., *Yours Sincerely for Scotland: The Autobiography of a Patriot* (London: Arthur Barker, 1970).

Woolf, S. (ed), *Nationalism in Europe: 1815 to the Present* (London and New York: Routledge, 1996).

Wordsworth, W., *The Complete Poetic Works by William Wordsworth* (London: Macmillan & Co., 1888).

Wright, P., *On Living in an Old Country: The National Past in Contemporary Britain* (London: Verso, 1985).

Young, A., *Robert the Bruce's Rivals: The Comyns, 1212–1314* (East Linton: Tuckwell Press, 1997).

Young, D., *A Clear Voice. Douglas Young Poet and Polymath. A Selection from his writings with a Memoir* (Loanhead: Macdonald, c.1974).

Young, J. D., *The Very Bastards of Creation. Scottish-International Radicalism: A Biographical Study, 1707–1995* (Glasgow: Clydeside Press, c.1996).

Yuval-Davis, N. and F. Anthias (eds), *Women–Nation–State* (London: Sage, 1989).

Zumkhawala-Cook, R., *Scotland As We Know It: Representations of National Identity in Literature, Film and Popular Culture* (Jefferson, NC and London: McFarland & Co., 2008).

Index